Interplay

Interplay

The Process of Interpersonal Communication

Second Edition

Ronald B. Adler
Santa Barbara City College

Lawrence B. Rosenfeld
University of North Carolina at Chapel Hill

Neil Towne
Grossmont College

Holt, Rinehart and Winston

New York   Chicago   San Francisco   Philadelphia
Montreal   Toronto   London   Sydney
Tokyo   Mexico City   Rio de Janeiro   Madrid

**Library of Congress Cataloging
in Publication Data**

Adler, Ronald B., date.
  Interplay: the process of interpersonal
communication.

  Includes bibliographies and indexes.
  1. Interpersonal communication.   I. Rosenfeld,
Lawrence B.   II. Towne, Neil, date.   III. Title.
BF637.C45A33   1983   302.2   82–15781
ISBN   0-03-062083-X

CBS College Publishing
Holt, Rinehart and Winston
The Dryden Press
Saunders College Publishing

Photo Credits

page 53 From the MGM release *The Wizard of Oz* © 1939 Loew's Incorporated. Copyright renewed 1966 by Metro-Goldwyn-Mayer Inc.

page 56 From the MGM release *The Asphalt Jungle* © 1950 Loew's Incorporated. Copyright renewed 1977 by Metro-Goldwyn-Mayer Inc.

page 98 From the MGM release *Mutiny on the Bounty* © 1962 Metro-Goldwyn-Mayer Inc. and Arcola Pictures Corp.

page 158 From the MGM release *The Sunshine Boys* © 1975 Metro-Goldwyn-Mayer Inc.

page 241 Courtesy of Twentieth Century-Fox. Copyright © 1968 Twentieth Century-Fox Film Corp. All rights reserved.

page 249 From the MGM release *The Sunshine Boys* © 1975 Metro-Goldwyn-Mayer Inc.

Acknowledgments

page 8 Cartoon by Hamilton reprinted by permission of Chronicle Features, San Francisco.
page 10 Excerpt abridged from pp. 64, 66–67 in *Dancer from the Dance* by Andrew Holleran. Copyright © 1978 by William Morrow and Company, Inc. By permission of the publisher.
page 13 *Shoe* cartoon © 1981 by Jefferson Communications, Inc. Reprinted by permission of Tribune Company Syndicate, Inc.
page 16 Excerpt from page xix in *Working: People Talk About What They Do All Day and How They Feel About What They Do*, by Studs Terkel. © Pantheon Books, a Division of Random House, Inc. Reprinted by permission.
page 18 "Eek & Meek" cartoon by Schneider. Reprinted by permission. © 1978 NEA, Inc.

page 31 Cartoon by Handelsman. Used by permission The New Yorker Magazine, Inc. © 1982.
page 32 Cartoon by Chon Day. Used by permission of Chon Day and copyright © by *Saturday Review*.

(Acknowledgments continued on p. 307.)

Preface

Interpersonal communication is a hot topic. From a mere handful of college courses on the subject fifteen years ago, today virtually every campus has at least one offering in the area. Outside academia, interest is also high. The racks of bookstores and supermarkets abound with countless books and magazines describing the "how" and "why" of communication.

Despite the abundance of writing about interpersonal communication, many people still have difficulty finding material that suits their needs. Popular advice is usually simplistic, failing to offer more than superficial prescriptions that explain little and provide even less workable advice. Many textbooks swing to the opposite extreme. The amount of research in the field is staggering, and findings often seem contradictory. Ambitious professors and textbooks often leave their audiences impressed but mystified about how to incorporate the lessons of social science into their own lives.

Our goal in the second edition of *Interplay* has been to provide a useful survey for intelligent nonexperts taking their first close look at the subject of interpersonal communication. To achieve this end, we have tried to do four things.

First, we have tried to be thorough. The number of research reports and articles published even since the first edition of this book seems to have grown exponentially, and we have attempted to summarize the most important of these findings. Sometimes they support one another, pointing to solid conclusions; in other areas they provide contradictory information. In both cases we have tried to reflect the state of the art.

Our second target has been to provide this information in a clear, understandable manner. The three of us have suffered through enough dry, convoluted writing to make us aware of the worst sins of academic writing. Having paid our dues as students and professors, we vowed to share our message in the most straightforward, least pretentious way we knew.

Our third goal in writing this edition has been to demonstrate how the theories and research of scholars operate outside of textbooks and classrooms. To achieve this "real world" perspective we have included a variety of quotations, photographs, cartoons, and poetry that dramatically and entertainingly illustrates the book's main points.

Our final, and perhaps most important, goal has been to provide a tool for helping readers improve their own communication behavior. Between the covers of *Interplay* are more ideas for change than anybody can put in practice in a single term of study. For readers who want to gain systematic practice in developing these skills, Susan R. Glaser's skills manual *Toward Communication Competency* provides a valuable companion to this book.

Like most projects of any magnitude, whatever success *Interplay* enjoys is due to the contributions of many people. In addition to the impeccable talents of our designer, Janet Bollow, the guidance of Tom Gornick and Ellen Parlapiano during the editorial stages and the management of Karen Mugler, Lester A. Sheinis, and Nancy Myers during editorial-production have been a great help. We are also grateful for the comments of the following professors around the country whose perspectives have helped make the book responsive to the needs of instructors and students: Jack Bibee, Anoka Ramsey Community College; Dan Dogherty, Eastern Wyoming College; Jackson Huntley, University of Minnesota; J. Atman Hutchinson, Araphoe Community College; Katherine Konsky, Illinois State University; Dawn Ohlendorf, Golden West College; Richard Paulson, Fresno City College; Virginia Waln, Texas Tech University; Dan Walther, Brazosport College; Deborah Weider-Hatfield, University of Georgia.

As always, our thanks go to our spouses. More than anyone else, they appreciate the ironic fact that writing about communication has often made it difficult to practice what we preach. For their sakes, as well as ours and yours, we hope the product is worth the effort.

R.B.A.
L.B.R.
N.T.

Contents

Contents

Interplay

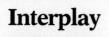

1

Interpersonal Process

■ *After studying the material in this chapter*

You should understand:

1. Three reasons for studying communication.

2. The needs that effective communication can satisfy.

3. Why people need to improve their communication.

4. The advantages and drawbacks of models.

5. The elements (italicized in the text) of one communication model.

6. The differences between linear, interactive, and transactive communication models.

7. Situational and developmental definitions of interpersonal communication.

8. The characteristics of effective interpersonal communicators.

You should be able to:

1. Identify the important needs you attempt to satisfy in your interpersonal communication.

2. Apply the elements of the communication models described in this chapter to your everyday interaction.

3. Identify the developmentally interpersonal relationships in which you are involved, as well as recognize those relationships that are only interpersonal in a situational sense.

4. Apply the list of effective characteristics of interpersonal communicators to yourself and others you know.

Everyone communicates. Students and professors, parents and children, employers and employees, friends, strangers, and enemies . . . all communicate. We have been communicating with others from the first weeks of life and will keep on doing so until we die.

Why study an activity you've done your entire life? There are two reasons. First, studying interpersonal communication will give you a new look at a familiar topic. For instance, in a few pages you will find that some people can go years—or even lifetimes—without communicating in a truly interpersonal manner. In this sense, exploring human communication is rather like studying anatomy or botany—everyday objects and processes take on new meaning.

A second reason for studying the subject has to do with the staggering amount of time we spend communicating. In research at the University of Cincinnati, Rudolph Verderber and his associates (1976) measured the amount of time a sample of college students spent on various activities. The researchers found that their subjects spent an average of over 61 percent of their waking time engaged in some form of communication. Whatever one's occupation, the results would not be too different.

There is a third, more compelling reason for studying interpersonal communication. To put it bluntly, none of us communicate as effectively as we could. Our friendships, jobs, and studies suffer because we fail to express ourselves well and understand others accurately. If you pause now and make a mental list of communication problems you have encountered you'll see that there is plenty of room for improvement in your everyday life. The information that follows will help you improve your communication skill with some of the people who matter most for you.

Why We Communicate

We can begin our study by examining the reasons we communicate.

Reduce uncertainty in the environment
Consider for a moment the world in which you live. It is a confusing and demanding place, bombarding you with an almost infinite number of pieces of information from the moment you open your eyes in the morning until you close them again at night. What should you wear? What toothpaste should you use? What route should you take to school? What notes should you copy into your book as the teacher's lecture drones on? What should you have for lunch? What friends need to be talked to, advised, sought out for counsel, discouraged, invited for dinner? The environment offers innumerable alternatives and vies for your attention in a thousand different ways. How can you make sense of all this? How can you function smoothly, assuredly, and with some confidence that you won't trip with the next step?

The world begins to make sense as we gain information that helps us make predictions about the people and things we encounter—as our uncertainty is reduced. We need to communicate with others to learn who and what "is out there" in order to determine the best ways to interact with them. Should you tell your date about the feelings of insecurity that plague you? Should you tell your boss the real reason you're late, or lie? Should you tell your neighbor how annoyed you are with his unkempt lawn, or let it slide? And we need to know what is out there to be able to make good decisions. Which is the best restaurant in town? What doctor is closest to the house? What courses are required, and which are electives?

3

Once the details of the environment are known, your understanding of them needs to be reinforced. For example, one of the details you might understand is that Sally is the kind of person with whom you can share your secrets. To reinforce your understanding you arrange to tell Sally a secret and see what she does. Does she run off to tell it to someone else? Does she laugh at you? Or does she listen with concern and respect for what you say? If she does the latter, your understanding of her is reinforced and you are more certain that Sally is someone with whom you can share your secrets. The world—at least the world including Sally—becomes more stable, more certain.

Once details of the environment are known and understood, we communicate to create a shared understanding of them. Do others see the world as you do? As others share the details and understanding they have of their environment, and as you communicate yours with them, a shared understanding develops. As you learn more about this other person, and as she learns more about you, you are both better able to predict each other's behavior. And the world becomes still more stable, more certain.

The circumstance that provides the greatest certainty, the greatest predictability, is when others not only comprehend the understanding you have of your environment, but have the *same* understanding. So we communicate to convince others that our "reality" is *the* "reality." Of course, if we all saw things the same way the world would be perfectly predictable—and boring; but we nonetheless strive for agreement.

Communicating satisfies most of our needs, one of which is our need to reduce uncertainty in the environment. We have other needs that communicating satisfies, providing more good reasons why we interact with others.

Physical needs In his landmark book *Motivation and Personality*, Abraham Maslow (1968) identifies five basic types of needs which each of us must satisfy if we are to live a safe and fulfilled life. Maslow argues that these needs are hierarchical; that is, we strive to satisfy the more basic ones before we move on to meeting others. Maslow states that the most fundamental category of needs is *physiological*. We must have sufficient food, air, water, and rest in order to live. Also, as a species, we must reproduce in order to survive. Unless we satisfy these basic physiological needs, we have no future.

The next category of needs involves *safety*. Once assured of nutrition and atmosphere, we have to find shelter and clothing to protect ourselves from the sometimes hostile elements. We must also ensure that we are safe from any forces that threaten our lives or health, including dangerous animals or people as well as life-threatening diseases.

It's obvious that the ability to communicate well plays a critical role in satisfying these basic needs. For most of us, earning the money that puts food on the table and clothes on our backs comes from holding a job, and both getting and carrying out that job requires an ability to express yourself and to understand others. Even if you chose to spend the rest of your life on welfare, you would have to convince an eligibility worker that you deserved public support, which would require communicative skills.

Communication also plays an important role in such basic needs as maintaining your health. Selecting a good physician and describing "where it hurts" requires you to speak clearly, and following the doctor's instructions calls for the ability to listen and to understand.

Social needs Once our basic physiological and safety needs are satisfied, the next most

Our Gang Comedy. (Culver Pictures, Inc.)

fundamental human concern, according to Maslow, is to establish and maintain social contact. Virtually all people have the desire to be accepted, appreciated, or loved by others. We become lonesome in the absence of human company, and thus tend to seek out others even when our physiological and safety needs do not require that we do so.

Psychologist William Schutz (1966) describes three social needs that we strive to satisfy by communicating. The need for *inclusion* involves building relationships that give us a sense of belonging, both to formal and informal alliances. *Control* needs involve the drive each of us has to influence others, so that we have some control over the important parts of our world. Schutz identifies *affection* as the third type of social need—a desire to care for others and know that they care for us. Like Maslow, Schutz argues that the desire to achieve inclusion, control, and affection aren't just desirable, but are *essential*. We interact with others because this is the only way to satisfy these basic needs. In other words, "people who need people" aren't the "luckiest people in the world," they're the *only* people in the world!

Ego needs As you'll read in Chapter 2, defining and confirming our personal identity provides the foundation for much of our behavior. Maslow recognizes this fact when he discusses the human need for *self-esteem*. We strive to respect ourselves and be re-

Groucho Marx in *Horsefeathers*, 1932. (Museum of Modern Art/Film Stills Archive)

spected by others, and much of our communication is devoted to these goals. We put in extra effort at school or on the job not so much for the pay increase or the high grade, but to be able to think "I've done well; I'm competent," and to hear others say this about us.

Another category of ego needs involves what Maslow describes as *self-actualization*—the need to maximize our potential, to become everything we are capable of being. Just as a mountaineer climbs a challenging peak "because it's there," we sometimes express ourselves because we feel some kind of drive to say what needs to be said for the simple purpose of creating a message. This need for self-actualization explains why many people write, paint, dance, and otherwise express themselves. After we're physically and socially secure, a need to reach out and create messages still exists—because the ideas and feelings are there.

The Need for Better Communication

The needs we've just discussed are obviously important. If most people were able to satisfy them on their own, there would be no reason to have written this book. The truth, however, is that few people communicate well enough to satisfy their physiological, social, and ego needs completely. Many fall desperately short of these goals. In the next few pages we'll look at three areas in which there is a need for better communication.

Life and health We've already seen that failure to satisfy our physiological needs may prove fatal. It would be an overstatement to say that there are many incidents where people communicate so poorly that they starve, or meet some similar fate. But consider the other types of needs we've discussed. What happens if we don't satisfy our desire for inclusion, control, or affection? Do we die in such cases? At first, the answer would seem to be "no"; but, in fact, there does seem to be a connection between social interaction and physical health—and even longevity.

In a nine-year study of 7,000 subjects, Lisa Berkman (1979, pp. 65–66), an epidemiologist for the California Department of Health, found that people with few or no strong social relationships died at a rate of from two to four and one-half times greater than more socially oriented people. The context in which social interaction occurred did not seem to matter: Some of the longer-lived subjects gained support from marriages, others had friendships, and still others were members of some organization. But people with no such affiliations apparently failed to meet a life-sustaining need.

Suicide figures are also indicative of people's inability to meet interpersonal needs. In the United States in 1975 there were 12.6 deaths by suicide for every 100,000 population. In 1965 there were 11.6 suicides per 100,000. This increase amounts to a bit more than 8 percent in ten years. In the last fifteen years there has been a 90 percent increase in suicides among young people between the ages of fifteen and twenty-one. In this age group suicide now ranks second to automobile accidents as the cause of death.

This depressing picture is based on officially reported figures. The number of suicides disguised as auto accidents, poisonings, and so on will never be known. Moreover, sociologists working in this area estimate that seven to eight times as many people attempt suicide as those who actually succeed in killing themselves. This statistic means that every year in the United States about 175,000 to 200,000 individuals evidently want to give up the struggle to live a satisfying life. Many suicides take their lives to escape from loneliness or unhappy relationships. Hence, an inability to communicate is again a problem.

Of course, not everyone who has trouble communicating dies prematurely. But even for the survivors, a life of ineffective communication can have its physical consequences. As you will see in Chapter 8, failure to express anger clearly and directly results in the stomach producing excessive amounts of acids and gastric juices, often leading to ulcers and other digestive ailments. In other cases, failure to express oneself assertively over time can lead to a constant state of physiological tension that damages the lungs, circulatory system, and muscle joints, and in addition lessens the body's ability to resist infections (McQuade and Aikman, 1974).

Better relationships "What about me?" you might ask. "I'm alive, I'm not suicidal, and I'm reasonably healthy. Why should I worry about communicating better?" We can answer this question by suggesting that while your life might not be terrible, it's probably not as good as it could be. One reason why you may be less than totally satisfied is that your important relationships are sometimes unrewarding. And one source of relationship problems can come from difficulties communicating effectively.

Family relationships certainly suffer when

> ■ *Man lives by affirmation even more than he lives by bread.*

Victor Hugo

members have trouble communicating effectively. This situation is probably most apparent in households with adolescents. Along with the physical changes that occur during the teenage years, the emotional stages of adolescents and other family members can lead to communication problems. For instance, while family relationships may be of prime importance to parents, to teenagers the associations with peers become the most critical. Teenagers need to break away from the family (usually to reestablish emotional ties later), while parents often want to hang on to their children. As this struggle develops, the family union loses its previous

stability, or homeostasis. Typical patterns of interaction are disrupted and the predictability which is often a prime benefit of family life is shattered. During this stressful period the friction between family members grows, often becoming intolerable.

While learning to communicate effectively certainly won't dissolve these generational differences, it can help family members cope with them in a way that doesn't threaten their relationships with each other. If families can use communication skills such as this book describes, their ability to share and adapt to each others' needs will provide a foundation which can survive the turbulence of stressful periods.

Husbands and wives often have as much trouble communicating with each other as with their children. In 1965 there was about one divorce for every four marriages. Ten years later, in 1975, there were 2.1 million

"If you want to talk, why don't you call up a radio talk-show?"

Gloria Swanson and Thomas Meighan in *Why Change Your Wife?* 1920. (Museum of Modern Art/Film Stills Archive)

marriages and one million divorces recorded annually. That works out to about one marriage dissolved for every two that started. The 1975 ratio of divorces to marriages in California was even higher, with about thirteen divorces for every sixteen marriages. The 1980 census showed that the number of divorced persons in the United States had doubled in only ten years, as well as revealing that more than twice as many people were living alone. Of course, marriage in itself doesn't guarantee social compatibility, increased self-esteem, or self-actualization. And divorce isn't always a sign of failure. It does seem fair to assume, however, that many marriages end because the partners

> ▬ *While his life was impeccable on the surface, he felt he was behind glass: moving through the world in a separate compartment, touching no one else. This was painful. . . . One night going home on the train to Connecticut he found himself in the air-conditioned car staring at a page of* The New Yorker *on his lap. His mind stopped. The page gleamed with a high, cold gloss in the fluorescent light: He stared at its shining surface, the pale gray pinstripe of his dark pants leg. Eventually his stop appeared. He got off in a somnambulistic daze. No one met him at the station. He felt he should call someone for help—but who?*
>
> Andrew Holleran
> DANCER FROM THE DANCE

---

are unable to communicate with each other successfully. Furthermore, partners incapable of meeting each others' needs in one relationship may have the same problem in subsequent ones.

Outside of the family, the inability to communicate keeps many people from having the amount and quality of friendships they desire. In a survey of students at Pennsylvania State University, Gerald Phillips and Nancy Metzger (1976) explored the relationship between communication and friendship. The responses of their subjects indicated a strong need for better communication skills. A majority of the people Phillips and Metzger questioned reported that their friendships needed improving. Of these, many expressed frustration over their efforts to explain their behavior to others, while another group had trouble explaining to others how they wanted them to behave. The three main sources of pain in friendship were all communication-related: failure of friends to live up to promises; betrayal of confidences; and the friends' use of confessed weaknesses to intimidate the subjects.

These results demonstrate a wider problem, and one that also stems at least partially from an inability to communicate well. In his book, *We, the Lonely People*, Ralph Keyes (1973) takes a careful look at contemporary society and concludes that the loss of community contributes greatly to the difficulty we have in meeting our needs:

> The problem of community, which sociologist Robert Nisbet calls "the single most impressive fact in the twentieth century in Western Society," is relatively modern. For most of man's history, group life was a given, and grew naturally out of the ways we were forced to be with each other—to live, work, wash clothes, and die.
>
> This is no longer true. We have less and less necessity to be together, and fewer ways of knowing each other, while our need for community remains constant. So we're forced back on the only immutable reason for joining hands: the human need for company. Without place, without cause, common work or religion most of us must make that humiliating admission: I can't live alone.
>
> . . . But to join that community, each one of us must take the hard, terrifying first step—saying—even to one other person—"I need you."

Keyes' message comes through loud and clear—we are doomed to disappointment if we can't reestablish community in some way to provide the kind of social intercourse necessary to meet our interpersonal needs.

Self-understanding So far, we've seen that communication problems can estrange parents and their children, contribute to failing marriages, threaten friendships, weaken communities, and even shorten our lives. There is one final reason for learning to communicate more skillfully. By relating clearly with others we can come to understand ourselves better.

The fact that many people seek self-understanding becomes apparent as soon as you survey the amount of written material currently available on that subject. Almost any bookstore (not to mention airport, supermarket, and drugstore) has a large number of books devoted to teaching you more about yourself, often through bettering your communication. Besides the obvious social benefits, these books promise—though they don't always deliver—other benefits of improved communication.

Communication can lead to better self-understanding in two ways. First, by becoming open to the way others view us we can learn more about ourselves. As you'll read in Chapter 2, the reflected appraisals of others serve as a kind of mirror in which we may view ourselves. The more we open ourselves up to such appraisals, the better idea we'll have of how we appear.

Secondly, besides learning about ourselves by listening to others, we can gain self-understanding from speaking. Virtually everyone has had the experience of understanding their own position better after having explained it to another. There are benefits in expressing our thoughts and feelings about almost any subject, from the process for factoring a quadratic equation to how to bake a cheesecake to why you are or aren't in love.

Probably the most dramatic validation of self-expression as a road to understanding is evidenced by the handsome living that many psychotherapists earn by primarily allowing their clients to talk themselves into better mental health. Of course, it would be an oversimplification to suggest that the only skill a therapist must possess is to keep quiet and let the patient rattle on, but few therapists would dispute the value of being a supportive, empathic listener.

We don't want to overstate our case and suggest that communicating better will solve every problem. Loneliness, illness, confusion about oneself, conflict, and other unsatisfying conditions often have causes that go far beyond communicative behaviors. It would be a mistake to think that simply reading this book will leave you with a completely trouble-free life. But as you'll see from reading on, research does suggest that personal functioning and social relationships improve as we become more effective communicators.

What Is Communication?

So far we've been talking about communication as if the actions described by this word were perfectly clear. We've found, however, that most people aren't aware of all that goes on whenever two or more people share ideas. Before going further we want to show you what does happen when one person expresses a thought or feeling to another. By doing so, we can introduce you to a common working vocabulary that will be useful as you read on, and at the same time preview some of the activities we'll cover in later chapters.

A communication model A model is a simplified representation of some process. For instance, consider what a model of the human digestive process might look like. At one end of a page we could draw a mouth with food going into it, followed by tubes running into and out of a baglike object representing the stomach. To represent the intestines we could draw a coiled hose trailing below the stomach.

While this figure might tell us something about digestion, it also says a great deal about the characteristics of all models:

1. Models can represent the relevant elements of a process. Even though our diagram is crude, it does provide a good introduction to the basic parts of the digestive tract.

2. Models organize the parts of a process and indicate how they are related to each other. For example, an uninformed viewer would learn from our drawing that the stomach is below the esophagus and above the intestines.

3. Most models make a complex event simple. This simplification helps promote understanding. It's certainly easier to an uninitiated learner to start exploring the digestion process with a simple model than by delving into the intricacies of an extremely complex event.

Charlie Chaplin in *His New Job,* 1915. (Museum of Modern Art/Film Stills Archive)

© Jefferson Communications, Inc., 1981

4. A model provides an opportunity to look at a familiar process in a new way. By doing so, models sometimes make us aware that we've been operating on misconceptions. For instance, by adding an explanation of what goes on in each part of our digestion model, it becomes clear how little digestion actually goes on in the stomach, contrary to the belief of many people.

While models have several advantages, they also suffer from a number of potential drawbacks. Most of their disadvantages stem from three characteristics. First, a model is always *symbolic:* It represents, but does not copy the phenomenon it describes. Along with this symbolism usually comes a degree of *oversimplification.* For instance, the stomach is not a collection of bags and hoses, and the communication process is not the assortment of boxes, lines, and arrows pictured in the following pages. This fact might seem obvious as you read it here, yet there is always a danger that the model will be taken too literally. For instance, someone not versed in physics might actually believe that an atom is similar to a group of marbles spinning around a grapefruit. It is also important to realize that models are *selective* and *arbitrary,* focusing on some parts of the process while ignoring others. Our digestion model, for example, does not consider the effects of different types of food on the digestive tract. There's nothing wrong with this selectivity as long as we recognize it: There is no "correct," comprehensive model that can completely describe a phenomenon. Models are built with specific purposes in mind, and they usually reflect the builder's purpose for developing them. One final danger is that a model can cause us to stop thinking about the process it represents and cause us to conclude that we know everything significant about the subject. This mistake is termed *premature closure,* and, of course, should be avoided.

Keeping the advantages and dangers of models in mind, we can begin to build a representation of what goes on in the process of communication. Since we need to begin somewhere, let's start with you wanting to express an idea. If you think about it for a moment, you'll realize that most ideas you have don't come to you already put into words. Rather, they're more like mental images, often consisting of unverbalized thoughts and feelings. We can represent your mental image like this:

Figure 1–1

Since people aren't mind readers, you have to translate this mental image into symbols (usually words) that others can understand. No doubt you can recall times when you actually shuffled through a mental list of words to pick exactly the right ones to explain an idea. This process, called *encoding,* goes on every time we speak.

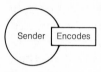

Figure 1–2

Once the idea is encoded, the next step is to send it. We call this step the *message* phase of our model. You have a number of ways by which you can send a message. For instance, you might consider expressing yourself in a letter, over the telephone, or face to face. In this sense, writing, talking on the phone, and speaking in person are three of the *channels* through which we send our messages. In addition to these channels we transfer our thoughts and feelings by touch, posture, gestures, distance, clothing, and many other ways. The important fact to realize now is that there are a number of such channels.

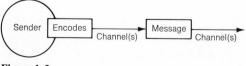

Figure 1–3

When your message reaches another person, much the same process we described earlier occurs in reverse. The receiver must make some sense out of the symbols you've sent by *decoding* them back into feelings, intentions, or thoughts that mean something to her (see Figure 1–4).

This model presents a *linear* view of communication. It characterizes communication as a one-way activity in which information flows from sender to receiver. In a linear model, communication seems like something that an active sender "does" to a passive receiver. A linear model suggests that messages exist in a sender, and that conveying meaning is the sender's role alone. As John Stewart and Gary D'Angelo (1980, p. 13) metaphorically suggest, a linear model implies that communication is like giving or getting an inoculation: Ideas and feelings are prepared in some form of message and then injected in a straight line into a receiver. While some types of messages (printed and broadcast media, for example) appear to flow in a one-way manner, a linear model is not a complete or accurate representation of any type of communication, especially the interpersonal variety. What's missing? The model we've just examined ignores the fact that receivers *react* to messages.

Consider, for instance, the significance of a friend's yawn as you describe your pet rock collection. Imagine the blush you might see as a listener's response to one of your raunchier jokes. Nonverbal behaviors like these show that most communication—especially in interpersonal situations—is two-way. The discernible response of a receiver to a sender's message is called *feedback.* Not all feedback is nonverbal, of course. Sometimes it is oral, as when you ask questions to clarify a speaker's remarks. In other cases it can be written, as when you demonstrate your knowledge of this material to your instructor on an examination.

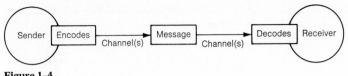

Figure 1–4

When we add the element of feedback to our model we have a description of communication as an *interactive* event. A sender formulates and transmits a message to a receiver who, in turn, formulates and sends a response (see Figure 1–4).

The model in Figure 1–5 suggests that after a period of interaction the mental images of the sender and receiver ought to match. If this happens, we can say that an act of successful communication has occurred. However, as you know from your own experience, things often go wrong somewhere between the sender and the receiver. For instance:

Your constructive suggestion is taken as criticism;

Your carefully phrased question is misunderstood;

Your friendly joke is taken as an insult;

or

Your hinted request is missed entirely.

And so it often goes. Why do such misunderstandings occur? To answer this question we need to add more detail to our model. We recognize that without several more crucial

elements our model would not represent the world.

First, it's important to recognize that communication always takes place in an *environment*. By this term we do not mean simply a physical location, but also the personal history that each person brings to a conversation. The problem here is that each of us has a different environment because of our differing backgrounds. While we certainly have some experiences in common, we also see each situation in a unique way. For instance, consider how two individuals' environments would differ if:

A was well rested and *B* was exhausted;

A was rich and *B* was poor;

A was rushed and *B* had nowhere special to go;

A had lived a long, eventful life and *B* was young and inexperienced; or

A was passionately concerned with the subject and *B* was indifferent to it.

Obviously this list could go on and on. The problem of differing environments is critical to effective communication. Even now,

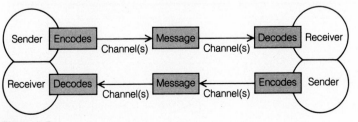

Figure 1–5

> The portable tape recorder . . . can be tiny and well-concealed, a means of blackmail, an instrument of the police state or, as is most often the case, a transmitter of the banal. Yet, a tape recorder, with microphone in hand, on the table or the arm of the chair or on the grass, can transform both the visitor and the host. On one occasion, during a play-back, my companion murmured in wonder, "I never realized I felt that way." And I was filled with wonder, too.
>
> Studs Terkel
> WORKING

though, you can see from just these few items that the world is a different place for sender and receiver. We can represent this idea on our model shown in Figure 1–6.

Notice that we've overlapped the environments of *A* and *B*. This overlapping represents those things that our communicators have in common. This point is important because it is through our shared knowledge and experiences that we are able to communicate. For example, you are able at least partially to understand the messages we are writing on these pages because we share the same language, however imprecise it often may be.

Different environments aren't the only cause of ineffective communication. Communicologists use the term *noise* to label other forces that interfere with the process,

and point out that it can occur in every stage (see Figure 1–6).

There are primarily two types of noise that can block communication—physical and psychological. Physical noise includes those obvious things that make it difficult to hear, as well as many other kinds of distractions. For instance, too much cigarette smoke in a crowded room might make it hard for you to pay attention to another person, and sitting in the rear of an auditorium might make a speaker's remarks unclear. Physical noise can disrupt communication almost anywhere in our model—in the sender, channel, message, or receiver.

Psychological noise refers to forces within the sender or receiver that make these people less able to express or understand the message clearly. For instance, an out-

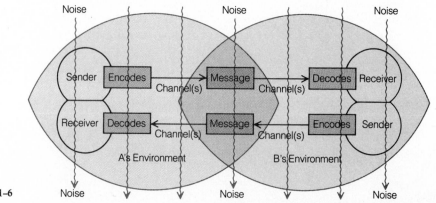

Figure 1–6

doorsman might exaggerate the size and number of fish caught in order to convince himself and others of his talents. In the same way, a student might become so upset upon learning that he failed a test that he would be unable (perhaps unwilling is a better word) to clearly understand where he went wrong. Psychological noise is so important a problem in communication that we have devoted much of Chapter 10 to investigating its most common form, defensiveness.

Even with the addition of these new elements our model isn't completely satisfactory. Notice that the preceding discussion portrays communication as a static activity. It suggests that there are discrete "acts" of communication that begin and end in identifiable places, and that a sender's message "causes" some "effect" in a receiver. Furthermore, it suggests that at any given moment a person is either sending or receiving.

In fact, none of these characterizations are valid for interpersonal communication. The activity of communicating is usually not interactive, but *transactive:* Communicators usually send and receive messages simultaneously, so that the two sender-receiver representations in Figure 1-6 should not be placed one under another, but rather superimposed. At a given moment we are capable of receiving, decoding, and responding to another person's behavior, while at the same time that other person is receiving and responding to us. Thus, it's difficult to isolate a single, discrete "act" of communication that can be separated from the events that precede and follow it. Communication is more like a motion picture film than a gallery of still photographs. Like a motion picture, communication is irreversible. Despite the warnings issued by judges in jury trials, it's impossible to "unreceive" a message. Words said and deeds done are irretrievable.

How can we represent this transactive nature of communication? Should we use the terms "sender/receiver" or "receiver/sender" to characterize each party? We could create a new word, such as "senreiver" or "recender," although such terms are awkward. A third alternative would be to return to the familiar term "communicator," but with the new knowledge that the word implies the simultaneous activities of sending and receiving. By making the arrows in our model which represent the transmission of messages point both ways we can show that messages flow back and forth between two communicators in an almost nonstop manner. While Figure 1–7 does a fair job picturing the phenomenon we call communication, an animated version in which the environments, communicators, and mes-

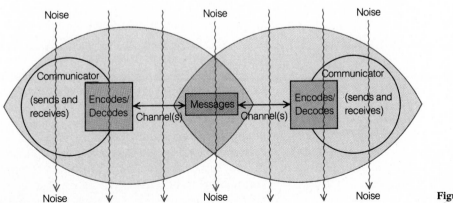

Figure 1–7

sages constantly change (perhaps by changing colors) would be an even better way of capturing the process.

Before moving on to examine the special nature of communication in interpersonal contexts, let's summarize our definition. Communication is a *continuous, irreversible, transactive process* involving *communicators* who occupy different but overlapping *environments* and are *simultaneously senders and receivers* of *messages*, many of which are distorted by physical and psychological *noise*.

Interpersonal communication defined Now that you have a clearer understanding of the overall process of communication, it's time to see what distinguishes interpersonal communication from other varieties.

A situational definition The most obvious distinction—although not the most useful—involves the context in which the interaction occurs. We can look at how many people are involved, whether they are close or far from each other, and how much access they have to each other (for example, how much of each other they can see, hear, and touch, and how easy it is to offer each other feedback). Interpersonal communication using this approach is defined as involving a "small number" of communicators who are "close" together and who have a "great deal" of access to each other.

Using a situational approach we can see that mass communication is easily distinguished from interpersonal communication because it involves more people with greater distances between them, and with very limited access to each other. In some cases, mass communication may involve feedback that takes months to process, as in the case of letters to TV stations about the most and least popular shows.

Public communication—usually consisting of a speech given before an audience—is also easily distinguished from interpersonal communication. Greater numbers of communicators at greater distances from each other are involved in public communication, and access—especially in the form of feedback—is relatively limited, although not so much as in the case of mass communication.

Matters become a little more confusing when we compare interpersonal and small group communication. However, clear differences between these modes do exist. For example, issues such as conformity, leadership, division of labor, and decision making are much more prominent in groups due to the greater number and complexity of interrelationships.

On the other hand, there are strong similarities in one-to-one and small group interaction. Both involve a small number of communicators who are physically close and who have great access to each other. And certainly there is a strong degree of "interpersonalness" in many group settings. Consider, for instance, a small work, study, or social group to which you've belonged. The relationships in such a group almost certainly involved elements you'll be studying in this interpersonal text: resolution of conflicts, issues of self-disclosure, the expression of feelings, changes in the emotional climate, and so on.

A developmental definition This fact suggests another way to define interpersonal communication—one which doesn't concern itself with the number of participants, but rather the *quality* of interaction between individuals, the way they deal with one another. Gerald Miller (1978) describes this second approach as "developmental." John Stewart and Gary D'Angelo (1980, p. 63) describe the qualitative difference between developmentally interpersonal and what we might call "impersonal" communication as the contrast between personifying and objectifying others. In impersonal communication we treat others as if they were objects, or things. Consider, for example, the typical way you might respond to a gas station attendant or checkout clerk at the supermarket. Most transactions of this sort are hardly personal: Except for a ritual smile and perhaps a perfunctory "How are you doing?" we might as well be interacting with a machine. This doesn't mean that such impersonal transactions are cruel, or that you need to establish a warm relationship with every person you meet. The important fact to recognize is that, if we take a developmental viewpoint, not all two-person interaction is interpersonal.

Several characteristics distinguish developmentally interpersonal relationships from impersonal ones. First, in less personal relationships we tend to classify the other person by using labels. We fit others into neat pigeonholes: "Anglo," "woman," "professor," "preppie," and so on. Such labels may be accurate as far as they go, but they hardly describe everything that is important about the other person. On the other hand, it's almost impossible to use one or two labels to describe someone you know well. "He's not *just* a policeman," you want to say. Or "Sure, she's against abortions, but there's more . . ."

A second element of "interpersonalness" in relationships is the degree to which communicators rely on standardized rules to guide their interactions. When we meet someone for the first time we know how to behave because of the established social rules we have been taught. We shake hands, speak politely, and rely on socially accepted subjects: "How are you?" "What do you do?" "Lousy weather we've been having." The rules governing our interaction have little to do with us or the people with whom we interact; we are not responding to each other as individuals.

As we continue to interact, however, we sometimes gain more information about each other, and use that information as the basis for our communicating. As we share experiences, the rules that govern our behavior will be less determined by cultural mores, and more determined by the unique features of our own relationship. This doesn't mean that we abandon rules altogether, but rather that we often create our *own* conventions, ones that are appropriate for us. For example, one pair of friends might develop a procedure for dealing with conflicts by expressing their disagreements as soon as they arise, while another could tacitly agree to withhold a series of gripes, then clear the air periodically. While we could digress here and speculate about which procedure is more productive, the important point to recognize is that in both cases the individuals created their own rules.

A third characteristic of interpersonal

19

qualities in a relationship involves the amount of information the communicators have about each other. When we meet people for the first time we have little information about them, usually no more than what we are told by others and the assumptions we make from observing what they wear and how they handle their bodies. As we talk, we gain more information in a variety of areas. The first topics we talk about are usually nonthreatening, nonintimate ones. If we continue talking, however, we may decide to discuss relatively few impersonal things. We may decide to increase the number of topics we talk about and choose to be more revealing of ourselves in doing so.

As we learn more about each other, and as our information becomes more intimate, the degree to which we share an interpersonal relationship increases. This new degree of intimacy and sharing can come almost immediately, or else may grow slowly over a long period of time. In either case, we can say that the relationship becomes more interpersonal as the amount of self-disclosure increases. We'll have a great deal to say about this subject in Chapter 7.

If we accept the characteristics of individual regard, creation of unique rules, and sharing of personal information as criteria for a developmentally interpersonal relationship, then several implications follow. First, many one-to-one relationships never reach an interpersonal state. This is not surprising in itself, since establishing a close relationship takes time and effort. In fact, such relationships are not always desirable or appropriate. Some people, however, fool themselves into thinking that they have close interpersonal friendships when in fact their associations are interpersonal only in a situational context.

Another implication that follows from looking at interpersonal communication in developmental terms is that the ability to communicate interpersonally is a skill that people possess in varying degrees. For example, some communicators are adept at recognizing nonverbal messages, listening effectively, acting supportively, and resolving conflicts in satisfying ways, while others have no ability or no idea how to do so. The skills you will learn by studying the material in *Interplay* can help you become a more skillful communicator.

Characteristics of Effective Communicators

Now that you have an idea of exactly what constitutes communication—both interpersonal and otherwise—it's time to see what distinguishes effective communicators from their less successful counterparts. In an attempt to discover the difference, Paul Feingold (1976) conducted an exhaustive review of research in the various disciplines concerned with communication: speech, psychology, guidance counseling, sociology, and human relations. After gathering and evaluating a large body of information, Feingold concluded that there are five general characteristics a person must exhibit in order to be perceived as an effective communicator. Let's take a brief look at these five characteristics.

Adeptness at creating messages There are several characteristics that constitute adeptness. The first is an ability to speak about the world in a way that *coincides with a receiver's perceptions*. In order to make a message intelligible and acceptable, the sender has to have some awareness of how the receiver perceives the world. This includes a knowledge of the receiver's sociological and cultural background as well as his or her present psychological state. To understand the importance of this ability, think about both effective and ineffective instructors you've known. Often the difference between helpful and obscure instructors involves their ability to put a concept in terms with which you're familiar—to imagine how the field of chemistry, philosophy, or electronics appears to you.

The second aspect of adeptness is the ability to express ideas *clearly*. Consider the following quotes taken from letters written by individuals to their welfare departments in application for support:

This is my eighth child. What are you going to do about it?

I cannot get sick pay. I have six children. Can you tell me why?

In accordance with your instructions, I have given birth to twins in the enclosed envelope.

Unless I get my husband's money pretty soon, I will be forced to lead an immortal life.

You have changed my little boy to a girl. Will this make a difference?

My husband had his project cut off two weeks ago and I haven't had any relief since.

Letters to school from parents explaining the absence of their child are no clearer:

My daughter was absent from school. She is totally exhausted. She spent the weekend maneuvering with the Marines.

John was late for class because he was home in bed with the doctor.

Mary was late for school because she had to run to the doctor with a swollen foot.

Although we can decipher the meaning of each of these, the conclusion we must draw is that the writer is not a clear communicator!

The man who lives by himself and for himself is apt to be corrupted by the company he keeps.

Charles H. Parkhurst

Feingold identifies *credibility* as a third component of adeptness, and it's certainly true that we only allow others to influence us when we view them as competent and trustworthy. Robert Young has established himself with millions of television viewers over the years as a warm, loving father *(Father Knows Best)* and a compassionate, dedicated physician *(Marcus Welby)*, and so people now follow his commercial advice and buy the brand of decaffeinated coffee he recommends. While this consumer behavior may not be logical, it certainly demonstrates the persuasive power of credibility.

The last aspect of the adeptness principle is one that is most obviously connected with our notion of "interpersonalness": A communicator we perceive as effective *reveals something personal about himself* in his messages. We've already seen that self-disclosure is one characteristic of close relationships, and it should be no surprise to find that most people judge communicators as most understandable and believable when they offer personal information to support their messages.

Similarity with the receiver Similarity can be demographic—including such factors as age, sex, and social class—or attitudinal, involving beliefs, likes, and dislikes. All we have to do is examine the current crop of television commercials to gain ample evidence of the principle. Advertisers know that one way to influence the public is to present people who are "average," people the viewers can identify as being like themselves.

21

███ *Instead of loving your enemies, treat your friends a little better.*

Edgar Watson Howe

One commercial for a product aimed at relieving heartburn and acid indigestion presents, in one short spot on television, a fat person, a thin person, an Anglo, an Hispanic-American, a Black, a teacher, a carpenter, an executive, and a secretary—all of varying ages, of course—to spell out their favorite product.

The more we perceive someone as similar to ourselves, the more we think we know about the person. This knowing extends beyond sociological and cultural data, and we get the feeling that we also share psychological characteristics. This assumption is often incorrect, but the feeling that we share an interpersonal relationship with the speaker persists.

Adaptability The third characteristic that causes us to identify communicators as effective involves their ability to adapt to the situation at hand. We perceive effective communicators as those able to meet the demands placed on them by varying circumstances. We probably appreciate this adaptability most when it allows others to meet our needs. For instance, think about how much you appreciate those people (probably few in number) who can recognize when you're having some personal problem and find a way to help you cope with it. Truly flexible helpers have a wide repertoire of behaviors available—offering advice, lending support, clarifying our feelings, and even simply listening quietly. Furthermore, effective communicators know when to use each style.

Adaptability extends into other areas as well. Some communicators seem able to get along well with a wide range of people from various ages, ethnic backgrounds, or educational levels. Others seem comfortable in diverse settings. In any case, we admire flexible, adaptable communicators.

Commitment to the receiver Not surprisingly, we view people who are responsive and interested in us as effective communicators. Commitment can be demonstrated in many ways. In a business setting it might be an obvious desire for the relationship to be mutually profitable. On a personal level commitment might appear as a genuine concern for our emotional welfare. Sometimes commitment can show up in small but significant ways: arriving on time for appointments, spending time with us when other demands beckon, remembering special occasions, or defending us from the attacks of others.

Adeptness at receiving messages The fifth characteristic of effective communicators changes our emphasis somewhat. So far we have focused on communicators primarily as senders, identifying the kind of messages they send to us. We also value those people who are skillful receivers. This ability actually ties in closely with the previous ones, for skillful listening requires adaptability, a certain amount of similarity with the speaker, and most certainly a commitment to us. As you'll see in Chapter 6, listening involves much more than simply sitting quietly and occasionally nodding your head.

So now we've taken a first look at the subject of communication. We've outlined a number of reasons why people communicate, demonstrated that we often need to do a better job, explained in some detail exactly what goes on in the communication process, distinguished interpersonal communication from other types, and talked about the qualities of effective communicators. In the remainder of this book we'll build on this foundation. By the time you're finished, you should not only understand the concepts of communication better, but should also be able to express yourself more effectively and understand others better as well.

Readings

Barnlund, Dean C. "A Transactional Model of Communication." In *Language Behavior: A Book of Readings in Communication*, Johnnye Akin, Alvin Goldberg, Gail Myers, and John Stewart, eds. The Hague: Mouton, 1970.

Berelson, Bernard, and Gary A. Steiner. *Human Behavior: An Inventory of Scientific Findings*. New York: Harcourt, Brace and World, 1964.

Berkman, Lisa. "Social Relationships and Longevity." In *Organizational Communication* (2nd Ed.), Gerald M. Goldhaber, ed. Dubuque, Iowa: Wm. C. Brown, 1979: 65–66.

Caplan, Gerald. *Support Systems and Community Mental Health*. New York: Behavioral Publications, 1974.

*Dance, Frank E.X. "The 'Concept' of Communication." *Journal of Communication* 20 (1970): 201–210.

Dance, Frank E.X. "Toward a Theory of Human Communication." In *Human Communication Theory: Original Essays,* Frank E.X. Dance, ed. New York: Holt, Rinehart and Winston, 1957.

Feingold, Paul. *Toward a Paradigm of Effective Communication: An Empirical Study of Perceived Communicative Effectiveness*. Doctoral dissertation, Purdue University, 1976.

*In the Readings section at the end of each chapter, items identified by an asterisk are recommended as especially useful follow-ups to the concepts presented in the text.

Gerbner, George. "Toward a General Model of Communication." *Audio-Visual Communication Review* 4 (1956): 173.

Haley, Jay. *Uncommon Therapy: The Psychiatric Techniques of Milton H. Erickson*. New York: W.W. Norton, 1973.

Herzberg, Frederick. "One More Time: How Do You Motivate Employees?" *Harvard Business Review* 46 (1968): 53–62.

*Holtzman, Paul D., and Donald Ecroyd. *Communication Concepts and Models*. Skokie, Ill.: National Textbook Co., 1976.

Katz, Elihu. "The Two-Step Flow of Communication: An Up-to-Date Report on an Hypothesis." *Public Opinion Quarterly* 21 (1957): 61–78.

Keyes, Ralph. *We, the Lonely People: Searching for Community*. New York: Harper and Row, 1973.

Luce, Gay G. *Biological Rhythms in Psychiatry and Medicine*. Washington, D.C.: National Institute of Mental Health, 1970.

Maslow, Abraham H. *Motivation and Personality* (Revised Ed.). New York: Harper, 1970.

Maslow, Abraham H. *Toward A Psychology of Being*. New York: Van Nostrand Reinhold, 1968.

McQuade, W., and A. Aikman. *Stress: What It Is and What It Does to You*. New York: E.P. Dutton, 1974.

*Miller, Gerald R. "On Defining Communication: Another Stab." *Journal of Communication* 16 (1966): 88–98.

*Miller, Gerald R. "The Current Status of Theory and Research in Interpersonal Communication." *Human Communication Research* 4 (Winter 1978): 164–178.

Phillips, Gerald, and Nancy Metzger. *Intimate Communication*. Boston: Allyn and Bacon, 1976.

Schutz, William. *The Interpersonal Underworld*. Palo Alto, Calif.: Science and Behavior Books, 1966.

Shannon, Claude E., and Warren Weaver. *The Mathematical Theory of Communication*. Urbana, Ill.: University of Illinois Press, 1949.

Stevens, S.S. "Introduction: A Definition of Communication." *Journal of the Acoustical Society of America* 22 (1950): 689.

*Stewart, John, and Gary D'Angelo. *Together: Communicating Interpersonally.* Reading, Mass.: Addison-Wesley, 1980.

Verderber, Rudolph, Ann Elder, and Ernest Weiler. "A Study of Communication Time Usage among College Students." Unpublished study, University of Cincinnati, 1976.

Wenburg, John, and William Wilmot. *The Personal Communication Process.* New York: Wiley, 1973.

2

Self-Concept

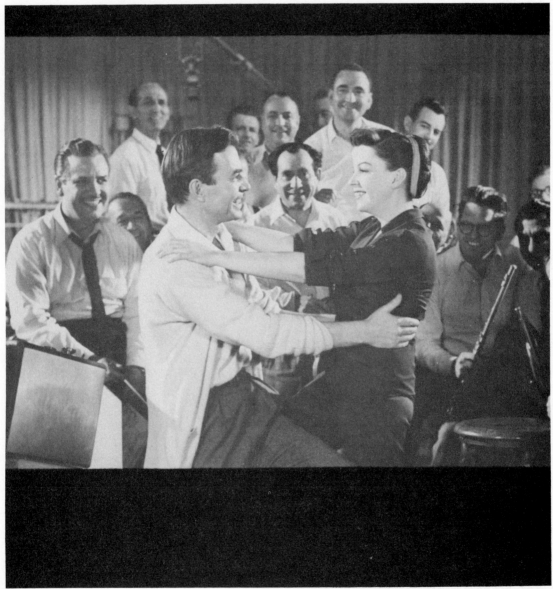

Judy Garland in *A Star Is Born*, 1954. (Culver Pictures)

■■■■ *After studying the material in this chapter*

You should understand:

1. How the self-concept is defined.

2. How the self-concept develops.

3. The multidimensional, subjective, resistant nature of the self-concept.

4. Some personality correlates of individuals with high and low self-concepts.

5. The role of self-fulfilling prophecies in shaping self-concept and influencing communication.

You should be able to identify:

1. The key elements of your own self-concept.

2. The most important forces that have shaped your self-concept.

3. The influence you have on shaping the self-concept of others.

4. The differences between your perceived, desired, and presenting selves.

5. The elements of your perceived self that may be inaccurately favorable or unfavorable.

6. Any self-fulfilling prophecies that you impose on yourself or on others, and that others impose on you.

Who are you?

Before reading on, take a few minutes to answer this question by trying the following simple exercise. First, make a list of the ten words or phrases that describe the most important features of who you are. Some of the items on your list might involve social roles: student, son or daughter, employee, and so on. Or you could define yourself through physical characteristics: fat, skinny, tall, short, beautiful, ugly. You might focus on your intellectual characteristics: smart, stupid, curious, inquisitive. Perhaps you can best define yourself in terms of moods, feelings, or attitudes: optimistic, critical, energetic. Or you could consider your social characteristics: outgoing, shy, defensive. You may see yourself in terms of belief systems: pacifist, Christian, vegetarian, libertarian. Finally, you could focus on particular skills (or lack of): swimmer, artist, carpenter. In any case, choose ten words or phrases that best describe you and write them down.

Now choose the one item from your list that is the most fundamental to who you are and copy it on another sheet of paper. Then pick the second most fundamental item and record it as number two on your new list. Continue ranking the ten items until you have reorganized them all.

Now comes the most interesting part of the experience. Find a place where you won't be disturbed and close your eyes. Take a few moments to relax and then create a mental image of yourself. Try to paint a picture that not only captures your physical characteristics, but that also reflects the attitudes, aptitudes, feelings, and/or beliefs included on your list. Take plenty of time to create this image.

Now recall (or peek at) your second list noting the item you ranked as number ten—the one least essential to your identity. Keeping your mental image in focus, imagine that this item suddenly disappeared from your personality or physical makeup. Try to visualize how you would be different without that tenth item. How would it affect the way you act? The way you feel? The way others behave toward you? Was it easy to give up that item? Do you like yourself more or less without it? Take a few minutes with your eyes closed to answer these questions.

Now, without regaining the item you've just given up, continue your fantasy by removing item number nine. What difference does its absence make for you?

Now slowly, at your own pace, continue the process by jettisoning one item at a time until you have given them all up. Notice what happens at each step of the process. After you've gone through your entire list, reclaim the items one by one until you are back to where you started.

How do you feel after trying this exercise? Most people find the experience a powerful one. They say that it clarifies how each of the items selected are fundamental to their identity. Many people say that they gain a clear picture of the parts of themselves they value and the parts with which they are unhappy.

What you've accomplished in developing this list is to partially describe your *self-concept*. There are many different ways of defining self-concept, but probably the clearest way to think of the term is as the image you hold of yourself. If you had a special mirror that not only reflected physical features, but also allowed you to view other aspects of yourself—emotional states, talents, likes, dislikes, values, roles, and so on—then the reflection in that mirror would be your self-concept.

You probably recognize that the self-concept list you recorded is only a partial one. To make the description of yourself complete, you'd have to keep adding items until your list ran into hundreds of words.

Take a moment now to uncover the many parts of your self-concept by simply responding to the question "Who am I?" over and over again. Add these responses to the list you have already started.

Of course, not every item on your self-concept list is equally important. For example, the most significant part of one person's self-concept might consist of social roles, whereas for another it might be physical appearance, health, friendships, accomplishments, or skills.

Now you have a clearer picture of your self-concept, but what does this have to do with the way you communicate? We can begin to answer this question by looking at how your present self-concept developed.

How the Self-Concept Develops

Researchers generally agree that the self-concept does not exist at birth (Fitts, 1971). An infant lying in a crib has no notion of self, no notion—even if verbal language were miraculously made available—of how to answer the question at the beginning of this chapter. Consider what it would be like to have no idea of your characteristic moods, physical appearance, social traits, talents, intellectual capacity, beliefs, or important roles. If you can imagine this experience—*blankness*—you can start to understand how the world appears to someone with no sense of self. Of course, you have to take one step further and *not know* you do not have any notion of self.

Soon after birth the infant begins to differentiate among the things in the environment: familiar and unfamiliar faces, the sounds that mean food, the noises that frighten, the cat who jumps in the crib, the sister who tickles—each becomes a separate part of the world. Recognition of distinctions in the environment probably precedes recognition of the self.

At about six or seven months the child begins to recognize "self" as distinct from surroundings. If you've ever watched children this age you've probably marveled at how they can stare with great fascination at a foot, hand, and other body parts which float into view, almost as if they were strange objects belonging to someone else. Then the connection is made, almost as if the child were realizing "The hand is *me*"; "The foot is *me*." These first revelations form the child's earliest concept of self. At this early stage, the self-concept is almost exclusively physical, involving the child's basic realization of existence and of possessing certain body parts over which some control is exerted. This self-concept is a rather limited one, and barely resembles more fully developed self-concepts held by older children.

What happens next? What are the next influences that help expand this rudimentary self-concept? There are two theories defining how a person's self-concept develops (Rosenberg, 1979): *reflected appraisal* and *social comparison*. These theories are complementary, each explaining a distinct way in which people come to an image of who they are.

Reflected appraisal   Before examining this view of self-concept development, try the following exercise. Either by yourself or aloud with a partner, recall someone you know or once knew who helped enhance your self-concept by acting in a way that made you feel accepted, worthwhile, important, appreciated, or loved. This person needn't have played a crucial role in your life, as long as the role was positive. Often one's self-concept is shaped by many tiny nudges as well as a few giant events. For instance, you might recall a childhood neighbor who took a special interest in you or a grandparent who never criticized or questioned your youthful foolishness.

After thinking about this supportive person, recall someone who acted in either a big or small way to diminish your self-esteem. Teachers, for instance, recall students who yawn in the middle of their classes. (The students may be tired, but it's difficult for teachers not to think that they are doing a poor, boring job.)

After thinking about these two types of people, you should begin to see that everyone's self-concept is shaped by those around them. To the extent that you have received supportive messages, you have learned to appreciate and value yourself. To the degree that you have received critical signals, you are likely to feel less valuable, lovable, and capable. In this sense it's possible to see that the self-concept you described in your list is a product of the messages you've received throughout your life.

The family is the first place we receive these sorts of messages. It provides us with our first feelings of adequacy (and inadequacy), acceptance (and rejection), and what constitutes an acceptable goal in life. Even before children can speak, people are making evaluations of them. The earliest months of life are full of messages—the ones that shape the self-concept. The amount of time parents allow their children to cry before attending to their needs communicates nonverbally to the children over a period of time just how important they are to the parents. The parental method of handling infants speaks volumes: Do they affectionately play with the child, joggling her gently and holding her close, or do they treat her like so much baggage, changing diapers or carrying out feeding and bathing in a brusque, businesslike manner? Does the tone of voice with which they speak to the child show love and enjoyment or disappointment and irritation?

■■■ Children Learn What They Live

If a child lives with criticism
  he learns to condemn.
If a child lives with hostility
  he learns to fight.
If a child lives with ridicule
  he learns to be shy.
If a child lives with shame
  he learns to feel guilty.
If a child lives with tolerance
  he learns to be patient.
If a child lives with encouragement
  he learns confidence.
If a child lives with praise
  he learns to appreciate.
If a child lives with fairness
  he learns justice.
If a child lives with security
  he learns to have faith.
If a child lives with approval
  he learns to like himself.
If a child lives with acceptance and
  friendship
  he learns to find love in the world.

Dorothy Law Nolte

Of course, most of these messages are not intentional ones. It is rare when a parent deliberately tries to tell a child he or she is not lovable; but whether the messages are intentional or not doesn't matter—nonverbal statements play a big role in shaping a youngster's feelings of being "OK" or "not OK."

As children learn to speak and understand language, verbal messages also contribute to their developing self-concept. Close your eyes for a moment and think about messages you heard when you were being raised.

███ *The unconscious parental feelings communicated through touch or lack of touch can lead to feelings of confusion and conflict in a child. Sometimes a "modern" parent will say all the right things but not want to touch his child very much. The child's confusion comes from the inconsistency of levels: if they really approve of me so much like they say they do, why won't they touch me?*

William Schutz
HERE COMES EVERYBODY

"What a beautiful child!"

"Can't you do anything right?"

"Come give me a hug."

"I don't know what to do with you!"

As you can clearly see, each of these messages implies some sort of appraisal. And because a child has no way of defining "self" other than through the eyes of surrounding adults, these evaluations have a profound influence on the developing self-concept.

In a review of self-concept literature, William Fitts (1971) summarizes parental influence on self-concept formation. Parents with healthy self-concepts tend to have children with healthy self-concepts, and parents with poor, negative, or deviant self-concepts tend to have children who view themselves in primarily negative ways. Interestingly, if one parent has a good self-concept and the other a poor self-concept the child is most likely to choose the more positive parent as a model. If neither parent has a strong self-concept, it is likely that the child will seek an adult outside the family with whom to identify.

In families where one parent has a strong, positive self-concept, the child is usually provided with a secure environment in the form of love and attention. A child brought up in such an environment is able to face the world as a secure, confident person. If both parents have strong, positive self-concepts, then the effect is even more pronounced.

Later in life the self-concept continues to be shaped by how others respond to us, especially when messages come from what sociologists term "significant others"—those people whose opinions we especially value. A look at the uppers and downers you described earlier (as well as others you can remember) will show that the evaluations of a few especially important people can have long-range effects. A teacher from long ago, a special friend or relative, or perhaps a barely known acquaintance whom you respected can all leave an influential imprint on how you view yourself. To see the importance of significant others, ask yourself how you arrived at your opinion of yourself as a student, as a person attractive to the opposite sex, as a competent worker, and you'll see that these self-evaluations were probably influenced by the way others regarded you.

What determines whether an appraisal is accepted or rejected? At least four requirements must be met for an appraisal to be regarded as important (Gergen, 1971):

1. First of all, the person who offers a particular appraisal must be someone we see as competent to offer it. Parents satisfy this requirement extremely well because as young children we perceive that our parents know so much about us—more than we know about ourselves sometimes—and thus are able to make any number of accurate evaluations of us.

2. The person who offers the evaluation must be perceived as being highly personal. The more the other person indicates that he or she knows a great deal about us and the more he or she adapts what is being said to accurately describe us, the more likely we are to accept judgments from this person.

3. The appraisal must be reasonable in light of what we believe about ourselves. If an appraisal is *similar* to one we give ourselves we will believe it; if it is *somewhat dissimilar* we will probably still accept it; but if it is *completely dissimilar* we will probably reject it.

4. Appraisals that are consistent and numerous are more persuasive than those that contradict usual appraisals or those that only occur once. As long as only a *few* students yawn in class, a teacher can safely disregard them as a reflection of teaching abil-

ity. In like manner, you could safely disregard the appraisal of the angry date who may have told you in no uncertain terms what kind of person behaves as you did. Of course, when you get a second or third similar appraisal in a short time, the evaluation becomes harder to ignore.

In addition to specific influential individuals, each of us also formulates a self-concept based on the influence of various reference groups to which we are exposed. A youngster who is interested in ballet and who lives in a setting where such preferences are regarded as weird will start to accept this label if there is no support from sig-

"You have to decide, Peter. Am I your significant other or am I your tootsie-wootsie?"

"Guess who Miss Price picked to play poison ivy in the class play."

nificant others. Adults who want to share their feelings but find themselves in a society that discourages such sharing might, after a while, think of themselves as oddballs, unless they can get some reassurance that such a desire is normal. Again, we encounter the idea of knowing ourselves through the "mirrors" of others. To a great degree, we judge ourselves by the way others see us.

You might argue that not every part of your self-concept is shaped by others, that there are certain objective facts recognizable by self-observation alone. After all, nobody needs to tell you whether you are taller than others, speak with an accent, have curly hair, and so on. These facts are obvious.

While it's true that some features of the self are immediately apparent, the *significance* we attach to them—that is, the rank we assign them in the hierarchy of our list and the interpretation we give them—depends greatly on the opinions of others. After all, there are many of your features that are readily observable, yet you don't find them important at all because nobody has regarded them as significant.

Recently we heard a woman in her eighties describing her youth. "When I was a girl," she declared, "we didn't worry about weight. Some people were skinny and others were plump, and we pretty much accepted the bodies God gave us." In those days it's unlikely that weight would have found its way onto the self-concept list you constructed, since it wasn't considered significant. Compare this attitude with what you find today: It's seldom that you pick up a popular magazine or visit a bookstore without reading about the latest diet fads, and TV ads are filled with scenes of slender, happy people. As a result you'll rarely find a person who doesn't complain about the need to "lose a few pounds."

Obviously the reason for such concern has a lot to do with the attention paid to slimness these days. Furthermore, the interpretation of characteristics such as weight depends on the way people important to us regard them. We generally see fat as undesirable because others tell us it is. In a society where obesity is the ideal (and there are such societies) a person regarded as extremely heavy would be admired. In the same way, the fact that one is single or married, solitary or sociable, aggressive or passive takes on meaning depending on the interpretation society attaches to those traits. Thus, the importance of a given characteristic in your self-concept has as much to do with the significance you and others attach to it as with the existence of the characteristic.

Social comparison Whereas it's true that each one of us is to a large extent a product of our environment, we are not totally passive recipients of environmental influence. Both consciously and unconsciously we each create our environment as well as respond to it.

In *The Concept of Self*, Kenneth Gergen (1971) describes the theory of social comparison and how it shapes our self-concept.

Gergen explains that people have a continuing need to establish the value and correctness of their beliefs, something that is often difficult to do since exact standards are hard to come by. Therefore, people often look at

Woody Allen and Diane Keaton in *Play It Again, Sam*, 1972. (Culver Pictures, Inc.)

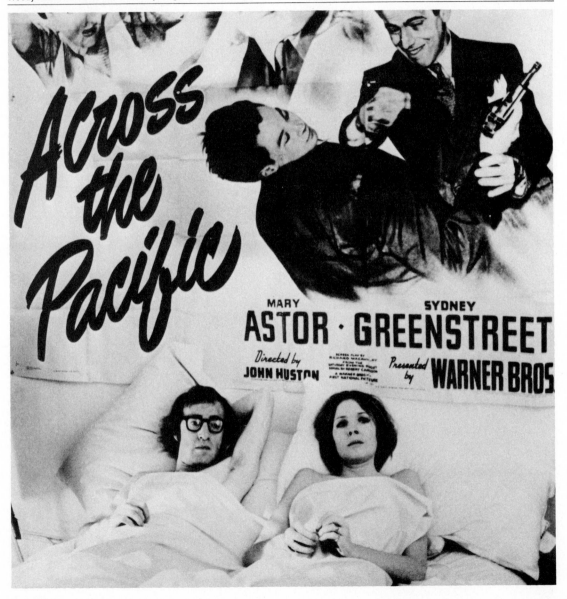

> ■ *Man wishes to be confirmed in his being by man, and wishes to have a presence in the being of the other . . . secretly and bashfully he watches for a Yes which allows him to be and which can come to him only from one human person to another.*
>
> Martin Buber

others as a way of judging themselves. They compare their beliefs, attitudes, and behaviors with those around them in order to establish the value of their own position. Just as we determine height or size by comparison (a five-foot, seven-inch warrior would be a giant in pygmy territory), we also determine other characteristics by comparison. For instance, if you see people all around you as being generally miserable, then you might view yourself as a happy, content person; whereas, in a different environment you could wind up looking unfulfilled by comparison with others.

At first glance, social comparison theory seems pretty deterministic. Besides being the product of how others see us, we are also shaped by how we measure up to others. At second glance, however, the concept of social comparison offers a way of reshaping an unsatisfying self-concept.

Since, to some degree, we're in control of who is available for comparison, it's possible to seek out people with whom we compare favorably. This technique may bring to mind a search for a community of idiots in which you could appear as a genius, but there are healthier ways of changing your standards for comparison. For instance, you might decide that it's foolish to constantly compare your athletic prowess with professionals or campus stars, your looks with movie idols, and your intelligence with only Phi Beta

Kappas. Once you place yourself alongside a truly representative sample, your self-concept may change.

Besides offering a chance for boosting an unnecessarily low self-concept, the social comparison theory allows for delusions of grandeur. For instance, suppose you wanted to think of yourself as a tremendously effective communicator (many people do), even though others disagreed with this image. You could achieve your goal by choosing those with whom to compare yourself. If you chose to be a big fish in a small pond you could hang around with extremely shy or aggressive or ignorant people, and thereby assure yourself of looking top-notch in comparison with them.

Another way of using comparison to (unrealistically) boost self-esteem would be to argue that those who don't approve of you have worthless opinions, whereas others who think as you do have excellent judgment. Also, you could set up standards that only you and a few other people meet and thereby argue that you are a rare individual indeed. Somewhat illogical, but when a self-concept is at stake, who worries about logic?

Evidence that we exercise a great deal of control over our self-concepts comes from investigations of changes in self-concepts over time. Fitts (1971) summarizes an investigation that found that the degree to which a self-concept is positive *increases with age*. Measurement of the self-concepts of people twenty, thirty, forty, fifty, sixty, and sixty-nine years old indicate that there is a steady increase in positive self-concept; generally, people feel better about themselves as they get older. Although the correlation is between self-concept and age, the real relationship is between self-concept and what happens as we get older. And one of the things that happens is we gain more and

Friday in Mrs. Gainey's sixth-grade class at P.S. 25 in New York City was the weekly day of reckoning for us. The mornings were spent taking tests which she graded during lunch period (who ate?). When we reassembled after recess, all thirty of us cleared out our belongings from the "old" desks and stood at attention around the perimeter of the classroom. We waited to discover for whom the bells would toll and for whom the chimes would ring out. On the basis of a combined average of the test scores, each child was ranked from one to thirty and seated accordingly. The best and brightest would be placed up front from left to right in the first row closest to the teacher's desk. There would always be a lot of tension between these ambitious little hotshots to determine if they would keep their exalted places or move even further toward Row 1, Seat 1. There was also the sex thing: would a boy beat out Joanie this week or would the girls continue their stranglehold on the top spot?

After the first ten names were sung out by the teacher and the pupils took their seats, the tension eased somewhat as the insignificant middle-level kids were put into their places. As Mrs. Gainey got down to the final ten kids already standing nervously at the back of the room, all forty eyes were riveted on them. Accompanying each name called was the math grade, spelling grade, history grade, and science grade. Smiles broke into snickers as these grades got lower and lower. Sometimes you'd have to bite the inside of your mouth not to laugh out loud as these unfortunates squirmed in agony. It didn't help to have the teacher remind us not to laugh at them because one day we might be in the same boat and then we'd be sorry. Unimaginable! As usual, "Baby" Gonzales brought up the rear. I was sure he did so on purpose as a status thing to hear the teacher say, "And last again this week, Mr. Gonzales." No one laughed or looked his way; "Baby" was the biggest kid in the class and did not "work and play well with others."

Philip Zimbardo

---

more control over our lives, we gain the opportunity to structure things to ensure that we'll have good feelings about ourselves.

With age we seek interpersonal relationships and work at tasks that reinforce our view of ourselves. For example, if you think of yourself as a "bad person" you might surround yourself with people who do not like you so that you can say, "Gee, I must really be a bad person because look at all the people who don't like me." And if you think of yourself as a "failure" you might continuously take on jobs that are too difficult so that you can fail and prove to yourself you really are a failure. Of course, given that the self-concept seems to improve with age, the opposite is probably happening: You tell yourself that you're a "good person" and surround yourself with people who like you, and that you're competent and take on jobs that are both important and within your capability of accomplishing. This principle makes sense when we realize that children have less control over their lives than adults, and so have less opportunity to structure positive events for themselves, all of which makes them more prone to believe evaluations presented by adults.

Dimensions of the Self-Concept

Now that you have a better idea of how your self-concept has developed, we can take a closer look at some of its characteristics.

The self-concept is multidimensional Just as the universe is composed of countless galaxies, each person's self-concept is a conglomeration of many beliefs. Various dimensions of the self-concept can be measured in an instrument called the Tennessee Self-Concept Scale, developed by William Fitts (1971). According to Fitts, our core, the internal self-concept, is made up of three different perceptions we have of ourselves: what we *do*, what we *are*, and how we *feel* about what we are.

The first perception Fitts labels the *Behavioral Self*. We see ourselves behave, and these perceptions form the basis for this aspect of our self-concept. For example, in the fantasy at the beginning of this chapter, you may have listed your talents. You might have indicated you like to work on your car, to do the minor repair work. The behaviors involved in that activity would form the behavioral part of your self-concept.

The second perception, what we *are*, Fitts labels the *Identity Self*. For example, al-

though you may like to do the minor repairs on your car, you may not think of yourself as a mechanic. What you *do* is differentiated from what you *are*. On the other hand, you may indeed see yourself as a mechanic—that may be a part of your identity—and so what you *do* is intimately connected with what you *are*. The labels and symbols you use to identify yourself, whether it's "mechanic," "student," "son," or "daughter," make up your Identity Self.

Fitts labels the third perception, how we *feel* about what we are, as the *Judging Self*. First we observe ourselves to see what we do, then we generalize these observations and label what we are, and finally we judge the product. You may like to do minor repairs on your car, may see yourself as a mechanic, and may also judge yourself as a good mechanic.

This third self-perception—the judgments we make—forms the basis for the most crucial aspect of our self-concept: *self-esteem.* (When the term self-concept is used without clarification, it's likely that what is being referred to is self-esteem, the generalization from the Judging Self.) If the bulk of evaluations made by the Judging Self are positive, the result is positive self-perception and high self-esteem; if most are negative, the result is low self-esteem.

If the core, or *internal* part of the self-concept is made up of these three self-perceptions, then the outside, or *external* part is made up of all the numerous "selves" we present to the world in the countless situations we encounter.

The Tennessee Self-Concept Scale measures five dimensions of the external self, each of which is composed of a Behavioral Self, an Identity Self, and a Judging Self. The first subself is the *physical self*, which includes our view of our bodies, state of health, skills, and sexuality. This subself, like the other four, can be analyzed in terms of the three internal selves. For example, the Behavioral Self: "I *play* racquetball"; the Identity Self: "I *am* a racquetball player"; the Judging Self: "I am a *mediocre* racquetball player."

The second subself, the *moral-ethical self,* describes our relationship to the supernatural and our feelings of being a "good" and "bad" person. The third subself, the *personal self,* reflects our sense of personal worth apart from the feelings we have about our bodies and the kinds of relationships we have with others. The fourth subself, the *family self,* reflects our feelings about ourselves as family members. The fifth and last subself, the *social self,* reflects our feelings of self-worth in interactions with other people in general.

Keep these categories in mind and take another look at the terms you used to describe yourself at the beginning of this chapter. Now, which dimensions of self seem to predominate in your self-concept: physical, moral-ethical, personal, family, or social? And how do you perceive yourself internally: in terms of your behaviors, your identity, or the value of your attributes?

We've already pointed out that each person's self-concept contains a multitude of elements, some of which are more important than others. The self-concept is multidimensional in another way as well. In fact, it is something of an oversimplification to talk about "the" self-concept as if each of us possesses only one. Morris Rosenberg (1979; Civikly, 1982) describes three ways to view this construct: (1) how we view ourselves; (2) how we would like to view ourselves; and (3) how we present ourselves to others.

The first view—we can call it the *perceived self*—is quite complex. It contains your view of your social status (including age, sex, socio-economic standing, and occupational position), social labels (such as "jock" or "parent"), past and present membership groups (religious, political, and ethnic), and "ego extensions" (material possessions with which you identify).

The second view of self, the *desired self,* also contains a variety of elements. First there is the idealized image, which you recognize as an unobtainable fantasy. Second is the committed image, the one which you actually make efforts to obtain: degree, job, partner, and so on. Finally there is the moral image, which consists of all the messages you send about how you ought to think and act.

The third view of self, the *presenting self,* involves the ways you actually behave with others. The presenting self sometimes matches the perceived self. For instance, you might confess to the belief that you behaved admirably or made a fool of yourself last Saturday night. In other cases we present ourselves publicly in ways that more closely match the desired self, as when you know you behaved poorly but try to pass your behavior off as justified, or even virtuous ("I didn't file an income tax return because I wanted to make a statement about the unconstitutional activities of the I.R.S.!"). There are also cases in which the image you present to others falls somewhere between the perceived and ideal selves, as when you say "Well, maybe I did act a *little* unfairly . . ."

Rosenberg notes that, while the presenting self is important throughout life, it undergoes the greatest changes during adolescence:

> . . . In a groping and tentative way, different selves may be rehearsed—the glamour girl, the caustic wit, the world-weary sophisticate, the dedicated revolutionary. Selves may be tried on or discarded like garments as adolescents attempt to convince others of their sophistication, cheerfulness, their allure, their in-

You've no idea what a poor opinion I have of myself, and how little I deserve it.

W.S. Gilbert

---

telligence. . . . When an adolescent—or anyone else—tries to achieve a certain goal, he does so not simply for the direct advantage it affords, but because it enables him to *prove* something about himself to himself. (pp. 48–49)

The self-concept is subjective The way you view yourself isn't always the same as the way others view you. Sometimes the image you hold of yourself might be more favorable than the way others regard you. You might, for instance, see yourself as a witty joketeller when others can barely tolerate your attempts at humor. You might view yourself as highly intelligent while one or more instructors would see your scholarship as substandard. Perhaps you consider yourself an excellent worker, in contrast to the employer who wants to fire you.

There are several reasons why some people have a self-concept that others would regard as being unrealistically favorable. First, a self-estimation might be based on obsolete information. Perhaps your jokes used to be well received, or your grades were high, or your work was superior, and now the facts have changed. As you'll soon read, people are reluctant to give up a familiar self-image. This principle makes especially good sense when it's possible to avoid the unpleasant truth of the present by staying in the more desirable past.

A self-concept might also be excessively favorable due to distorted feedback from others. A boss may think of himself as an excellent manager because his assistants lavish him with false praise in order to keep their jobs. A child's inflated ego may be based on the praise of doting parents.

A third reason for holding what appears to be an unrealistically high self-concept has to do with the expectations of a society that demands too much of its members. Much of the conditioning we receive in our early years implies that anything less than perfection is unsatisfactory, so that admitting one's mistakes is often seen as a sign of weakness. Instructors who fail to admit they don't know everything about a subject are afraid they will lose face with their colleagues and students. Couples whose relationships are beset by occasional problems don't want to admit that they have failed to achieve the "ideal" relationship they've seen portrayed in fiction. Parents who don't want to say, "I'm sorry, I made a mistake," to their children are afraid they'll lose the youngsters' respect.

Once you accept such an irrational idea—that to be less than perfect is a character defect—admitting your frailties becomes difficult. Such a confession becomes the equivalent of admitting one is a failure—and failure is not an element of most peoples' self-concept. Rather than label themselves failures, many people engage in self-deception, insisting to themselves and to others that their behavior is more admirable than the circumstances indicate. We'll have more to say about the reasons behind such behavior and its consequences when we discuss defense mechanisms in Chapter 10.

In contrast to the cases we've just described are times when we view ourselves *more* harshly than the objective facts suggest. You may have known people, for instance, who insist that they are unattractive or incompetent in spite of your honest insistence to the contrary. In fact, you have probably experienced feelings of excessively negative self-evaluation yourself. Recall a time when you woke up with a case of the "uglies," convinced that you looked terrible.

Remember how on such days you were unwilling to accept even the most sincere compliments from others, having already decided how wretched you appeared. Whereas many of us only fall into the trap of being overly critical occasionally, others constantly have an unrealistically low self-concept.

Sidney Simon (1977), in his delightful book *Vulture: A Modern Allegory on the Art of Putting Oneself Down*, describes how we diminish our self-worth. Vultures have gained their unsavory reputation for swooping down on their victims and plucking away at their flesh: not a pretty sight. The psychological vulture Simon describes is just as unappealing. It waits for a self-put-down and then uses this moment of weakness to peck away at the self-esteem of its weakened victim. These psychological vultures, of course, are subjective: They are the unnecessary creations of their own victims.

There are two types of vulture attacks, one more subtle than the other. The most obvious kind occurs whenever we engage in an overt act of self-criticism. For example, a colleague of ours has a habit of bumping into things, which is not unusual. However, her response to such events is to exaggerate and overgeneralize them by criticizing herself: "I'm such a klutz!"

The more subtle kind of vulture attack occurs when we set unrealistic limitations on ourselves. Any statement that limits your capability to think or act within the limits of your potential invites another nibble at your self-esteem. "I couldn't say that to her!" "I could never give a speech!" "They'd never hire me for that job!" As soon as it senses such thoughts the vulture swoops down, claws extended, and carries off another chunk of self-esteem.

Simon suggests that we set ourselves up for vulture attacks in six areas: *physical* ("I'm too fat, thin, short, tall, clumsy"); *sexual* ("I'm unattractive to the opposite sex," "Nobody would want to go out with me"); *creative* ("I have no imagination," "I can't draw"); *family* ("I'm a disappointment to my parents," "I don't spend enough time with them"); *intelligence* ("I'm just dumb, I guess," "I'm no good in math"); and *relationships* ("Nobody would want me for a friend," "I'm too shy").

What are the reasons for such excessively negative self-evaluations? As with unrealistically high self-esteem, one source for an overabundance of self-put-downs is obsolete information. A string of past failures in school or with social relations can linger to haunt a communicator long after they have occurred, even though such events don't predict failure in the future. Similarly, we've known slender students who still think of themselves as fat and clear-complexioned people who still behave as if they were acne-ridden.

Distorted feedback can also create a self-image that is worse than a more objective observer would see. Having grown up around overly critical parents is one of the most common causes of a negative self-image. In other cases the remarks of cruel friends, uncaring teachers, excessively demanding employers, or even memorable strangers can have a lasting effect. As you read earlier, the impact of significant others and reference groups in forming a self-concept can be great.

A third cause for a strongly negative self-concept is again the myth of perfection, which is common in our society. From the time most of us learn to understand language we are exposed to models who appear to be perfect at whatever they do. This myth is most clear when we examine the stories commonly told to children. In these stories the hero is wise, brave, talented, and victorious, whereas the villain is totally evil and doomed to failure. This kind of model is easy for a child to understand, but it hardly paints a realistic picture of the world. Unfortunately, many parents perpetuate the myth of perfection by refusing to admit that they are ever mistaken or unfair. Children, of course, accept this perfectionist facade for a long time, not being in any position to dispute the wisdom of such powerful beings. And from the behavior of the adults around them comes the clear message: "A well-adjusted, successful person has no faults."

Thus children learn that in order to gain acceptance, it's necessary to pretend to "have it all together," even though they know this isn't the case. Given this naive belief that everyone else is perfect and the knowledge that you aren't, it's easy to see how one's self-concept would suffer. We'll have a great deal to say about perfection and other irrational ideas, both in this chapter and in Chapter 8. In the meantime, don't get the mistaken impression that we're suggesting it's wrong to aim at perfection as an *ideal*. We're only suggesting that achieving this state is usually not possible, and to expect that you should do so is a sure ticket to an inaccurate and unnecessarily low self-concept.

A final reason people often sell themselves short is also connected to social expectations. Curiously, the perfectionistic society to which we belong rewards those people who downplay the strengths we demand they possess (or pretend to possess). We term these people "modest" and find their behavior agreeable. On the other hand, we consider those who honestly appreciate their own strengths to be "braggarts" or "egotists," confusing them with the people who boast about accomplishments they do not possess. This convention leads most of us to talk freely about our shortcomings while downplaying our accomplishments. It's all

right to proclaim that you're miserable if you have failed to do well on a project, whereas it's considered boastful to express your pride at a job well done. It's fine to remark that you feel unattractive, but egocentric to say that you think you look good.

After a while we begin to believe the types of statements we repeatedly make. The self-put-downs are viewed as modesty and become part of our self-concept, whereas the strengths and accomplishments go unmentioned and are thus forgotten. And in the end we see ourselves as much worse than we are.

A healthy self-concept is flexible People change. From moment to moment we aren't the same. We wake up in the morning in a jovial mood and turn grumpy before lunch. We find ourselves fascinated by a conversational topic one moment, then suddenly lose interest. One moment's anger often gives way to forgiveness the next. Health turns to illness and back to health. Alertness becomes fatigue, hunger becomes satiation, and confusion becomes clarity.

We also change from situation to situation. You might be a relaxed conversationalist with people you know but at a loss for words with strangers. You might be patient when explaining things on the job but have no tolerance for such explanations at home. You might be a wizard at solving mathematical problems but have a terribly difficult time putting your thoughts into words. We change over long stretches of time. We grow older, learn new facts, adopt new attitudes and philosophies, set and reach new goals, and find that others change their way of thinking and acting toward us.

Since we change in these and many other ways, our self-concept must also change in order to keep a realistic picture of ourselves. Thus an accurate self-portrait of the type described would probably not be exactly the same as it would have been a year ago or a few months ago or even the way it would have been yesterday. This doesn't mean that you will change radically from day to day. There are fundamental characteristics of your personality that will stay the same for years, perhaps for a lifetime. It is likely, however, that in other important ways you are changing—physically, intellectually, emotionally, and spiritually.

The self-concept resists change In spite of the fact that we change and that a realistic self-concept should reflect this change, the tendency to resist revision of our self-perception is strong. When confronted with facts that contradict the mental picture we hold of ourselves, we tend to dispute the facts and cling to the outmoded self-perception.

It's understandable why we're reluctant to revise a previously favorable self-concept. Some professional athletes, for instance, doggedly insist that they can be of value to the team when they are clearly past their prime. It must be tremendously difficult to give up the life of excitement, recognition, and financial rewards that comes with such a talent. Faced with such a tremendous loss,

Fredric March in *Dr. Jekyl and Mr. Hyde*, 1932. (Culver Pictures)

███ *Most people cling to pretensions of self as a drowning man grasps at a straw.*

Karen Horney

---

it's easy to see why the athlete would try to play one more season, insisting that the old skills are still there.

In the same way a student who did well in earlier years but now has failed to study might be unwilling to admit that the label "good scholar" no longer applies. Or a previously industrious worker, citing past commendations in a personnel file, might insist on being considered a top-notch employee despite a supervisor's report of increased absences and low productivity. (Remember that the people in these and other examples aren't *lying* when they insist that they're doing well in spite of the facts to the contrary; they honestly believe that the old truths still hold precisely because their self-concepts have been so resistant to change.)

Curiously, the tendency to cling to an outmoded self-perception also holds when the new image would be more favorable than the old one. We recall a former student who almost anyone would have regarded as being beautiful, with physical features attractive enough to appear in any glamour magazine. In spite of her appearance, this woman characterized herself as "ordinary" and "unattractive" in a class exercise. When questioned by her classmates, she described how as a child her teeth were extremely crooked, and how she had worn braces for several years in her teens to correct this problem. During this time she was often kidded by her friends, who never let her forget her "metal mouth," as she put it. Even though the braces had been off for two years, our student reported that she still saw herself as

ugly, and brushed aside our compliments by insisting that we were just saying these things to be nice—she knew how she *really* looked.

Examples such as this illustrate one problem that occurs when we resist changing an inaccurate self-concept. Our student denied herself a much happier life by clinging to an obsolete picture of herself. In the same way some communicators insist that they are less talented or worthy of friendship than others would suggest, thus creating their own miserable world when it needn't exist. These unfortunate souls probably resist changing because they aren't willing to go through the disorientation that comes from redefining themselves, correctly anticipating that it *is* an effort to think of one's self in a new way. Whatever their reasons, it's sad to see people in such an unnecessary state of mind.

A second problem that comes from trying to perpetuate an inaccurate self-concept involves self-delusion and lack of growth. If you hold an unrealistically favorable picture of yourself, you won't see the real need for change that may exist. Instead of learning new talents, working to change a relationship, or improving your physical condition, you'll stay with the familiar and comfortable delusion that everything is all right. As times goes by this delusion becomes more and more difficult to maintain, leading to a third problem.

To understand this third problem you need to remember that communicators who are presented with information that contradicts their self-perception have two choices: They can either accept the new data and change their perception accordingly, or they can keep their original viewpoint and in some way refute the new information. Since most communicators are reluctant to downgrade a favorable image of themselves, their tendency is to opt for refutation, either by discounting the information and rationalizing it away or by counterattacking the person who holds it.

Personality Correlates of Self-Concept

People with high or low self-concepts behave in significantly different ways. Research in this area recently reviewed by Mary Ann Sheirer and Robert Draut (1979) shows that there is a strong correlation between the type of self-concept a person has and the patterns of thought and actions that person displays. It is unclear whether the self-concept causes these behaviors, whether the behaviors shape the self-concept, or whether the relationship is reciprocal. In any case, the link between a positive self-concept and personal adjustment is a strong one.

One element of a positive self-concept is *security*, a firm belief in the correctness of one's actions and values—a belief that is relatively immune to the judgments of others. For example, a person with a strong positive self-concept would not be terribly bothered by criticisms that career plans or personal relationships were flawed, whereas a less secure person would find such evaluations upsetting.

Along with security, the characteristic of *self-acceptance* goes hand in hand with a positive self-concept. People who accept themselves possess a number of valuable assets: the ability to change their opinions, to utilize new ideas, to more easily accept the opinions and feelings of others, to be sensitive to others, and to comfortably engage in appropriate self-disclosure.

A third aspect of a positive self-concept is *high self-esteem*. People with high self-esteem have all the benefits that accompany self-acceptance, plus the following: popularity, little nervousness or defensiveness, few if any feelings of inferiority, and strong feelings of security. People having high self-esteem usually do well in school, are generally happy with their lives, tend to reach out more to others, make others feel welcome and less alienated. They are more involved with high self-concept people than those with low self-concepts, and more able to "hook into" people with whom they share an interpersonal relationship.

In addition to all of the characteristics just mentioned, high self-concept people enjoy a proportionately greater share of the benefits that come with their richer vocabularies, their ability to give and take criticism comfortably, their more confident tone of voice, and their optimistic attitude toward competition.

A dramatic illustration of the effect of self-concept on communication comes from a comparison between kindergarten children with high and low self-concepts. Children with high self-concepts generally exhibit the following characteristics:

1. They are unafraid of new situations;
2. They make friends easily;
3. They experiment with new materials without much hesitation;
4. They trust their teacher, even though the teacher is a stranger;
5. They are cooperative and can follow rules;
6. They are largely responsible for controlling their own behavior;
7. They are creative, imaginative, and have ideas of their own;
8. They talk freely and are eager to share their own experiences;
9. They are independent and need only a minimal amount of direction;
10. They are happy.

Typical kindergarten children with low self-concepts demonstrate the following characteristics:

1. They rarely show initiative;
2. They rely on others for direction;
3. They ask permission to do most everything;
4. They seldom show spontaneity;
5. They seldom enter new activities;
6. They isolate themselves;
7. They talk very little;
8. They are possessive of objects;
9. They make excessive demands;
10. They either withdraw or aggress;
11. They act frustrated.

Although these behaviors refer to children about six years old, research with older children and adults indicates that this is a good list of the general characteristics of both high and low self-concept people regardless of age.

Though it would be simplistic to divide the world into people having high self-concepts and those having low ones, the picture here is rather clear. The more positively we feel about ourselves, the more easily we will form and maintain interpersonal relationships, and the more rewarding those relationships will be.

The Self-Fulfilling Prophecy and Communication

The self-concept is such a powerful force on the personality that it not only determines how you see yourself in the present, but can actually influence your future behavior and that of others. Such occurrences come about through a phenomenon called the self-fulfilling prophecy.

A self-fulfilling prophecy occurs when a person's expectation of an event makes the outcome more likely to happen than would otherwise have been true. Self-fulfilling prophecies occur all the time, although you might never have given them that label. For example:

1. You expected to become nervous and botch a job interview and later did so;
2. You anticipated having a good (or terrible) time at a social affair and found your expectations being met;
3. A teacher or boss explained a new task to you, saying that you probably wouldn't do well at first; you did not do well;
4. A friend described someone you were about to meet, saying that you wouldn't like the person, which turned out to be correct—you didn't like the new acquaintance.

In each of these cases there is a good chance that the event happened because it was predicted. You needn't have botched the interview, the party might have been boring only because you helped make it so, you might have done better on the job if your boss hadn't spoken up, and you might have liked the new acquaintance if your friend hadn't given you preconceptions. In other words, what helped make each event take place as it did was the expectation that it would happen exactly that way.

There are two types of self-fulfilling prophecies. The first occurs when the expectations of one person govern another's actions. The classic example was demonstrated by Robert Rosenthal and Lenore Jacobson in a study they described in their book, *Pygmalion in the Classroom* (1968):

Twenty percent of the children in a certain elementary school were reported to their teachers as showing unusual potential for intellectual growth. The names of these 20 percent were drawn by means of a table of random numbers, which is to say that the names were drawn out of a hat. Eight months later

Audrey Hepburn in *My Fair Lady*, 1964. (Culver Pictures, Inc.)

these unusual or "magic" children showed significantly greater gains in IQ than did the remaining children who had not been singled out for the teachers' attention. The change in the teachers' expectations regarding the intellectual performance of these allegedly "special" children had led to an actual change in the intellectual performance of these randomly selected children.

In other words, some children may do better in school, not because they are more intelligent than their classmates, but because they learn that their teacher—a significant other—believes they can achieve.

Teachers usually convey their expectations in indirect, subtle ways. Rosenthal (1979) summarizes the research in this area by describing four kinds of messages that label students as "special": *climate* (teachers are more supportive and confirming for certain students); *feedback* ("special" students get more positive and negative reactions than their classmates); *input* (the "special" students get more material and material of a different nature than other children); and *output* (teachers give some students more opportunities and more time to respond). The overall effect is clear: Students who are

45

██ *There is an old joke about a man who was asked if he could play a violin and answered, "I don't know. I've never tried." This is psychologically a very wise reply. Those who have never tried to play a violin really do not know whether they can or not. Those who say too early in life and too firmly, "No, I'm not at all musical," shut themselves off prematurely from whole areas of life that might have proved rewarding. In each of us there are unknown possibilities, undiscovered potentialities—and one big advantage of having an open self-concept rather than a rigid one is that we shall continue to expose ourselves to new experiences and therefore we shall continue to discover more and more about ourselves as we grow older.*

S.I. Hayakawa

treated in a special way respond to their teacher's expectations.

To put this phenomenon in context with the self-concept, we can say that when a teacher communicates to a child the message, "I think you're bright," the child accepts that evaluation and changes self-concept to include that evaluation. Unfortunately, the same principle holds for students whose teachers send the message, "I think you're stupid."

This type of self-fulfilling prophecy has been shown to be a powerful force for shaping the self-concept and thus the behavior of people in a wide range of settings outside the schools. Medical patients who unknowingly use placebos—substances such as injections of sterile water or doses of sugar pills that have no curative value—often respond just as favorably to treatment as people who actually receive an active drug. The patients believe they have taken a substance that will help them feel better, and this belief actually brings about a "cure." In psychotherapy Rosenthal and Jacobson describe several studies suggesting that patients who believe they will benefit from treatment do so, regardless of the type of treatment they re-

ceive. In the same vein, when a doctor believes a patient will improve, the patient may do so precisely because of this expectation, whereas another person for whom the physician has little hope often fails to recover. Apparently the patient's self-concept as being sick or well—as shaped by the doctor—plays an important role in determining the actual state of health.

In business the power of the self-fulfilling prophecy was proved as early as 1890. A new tabulating machine had just been installed at the U.S. Census Bureau in Washington, D.C. In order to use the machine the bureau's staff had to learn a new set of skills that the machine's inventor believed to be quite difficult. He told the clerks that after some practice they could expect to punch about 550 cards per day; to process any more would jeopardize their psychological well-being. Sure enough, after two weeks the clerks were processing the anticipated number of cards, and reported feelings of stress if they attempted to move any faster.

Sometime later an additional group of clerks was hired to operate the same machines. These workers knew nothing of the devices, and no one had told them about the upper limit of production. After only three days the new employees were each punching over 2,000 cards per day with no ill effects. Again, the self-fulfilling prophecy seemed to be in operation. The original workers believed themselves capable of punching only 550 cards and so behaved accordingly, whereas the new clerks had no limiting expectations as part of their self-concepts and so behaved more productively.

The self-fulfilling prophecy operates in families as well. If parents tell children long enough that they can't do anything right, each child's self-concept will soon incorporate this idea, and each will fail at many or most of the tasks attempted. On the other hand, if children are told that they are capable or lovable or kind, there is a much greater chance of their behaving accordingly.

Our beliefs are so important to us that we will do anything to keep them intact. One way we do this is by claiming that an exception to our belief is "the exception that proves the rule." For example, in our organizational consulting work, we have heard

male executives argue that "women don't make good managers." When presented with evidence that sex is not a determinant of good managerial behavior, the usual response is, "Oh, sure, but those women behaved like men!"

The prophecies that others impose contribute to a person's self-concept. The statement "You'll never understand algebra" leads to the belief "I'm a mathematical idiot," and the message "We asked you to do the job because we know it will be outstanding" helps shape the belief, "I'm a talented and competent person."

Once established, a person's self-concept leads to a second type of self-fulfilling prophecy; one in which the expectations we hold about ourselves influence our own behavior. Like the botched job interview and the unpleasant party mentioned at the beginning of this section, there are many times when an event that needn't have occurred does happen because you expected it to. In sports you've probably psyched yourself into playing either better or worse than usual, so that the only explanation for your unusual

▆▆▆ *Once upon a time there was a very sad bear who was kept in a very small cage in the town zoo. When the sad bear wasn't eating, or sleeping, he occupied his time pacing . . . eight paces forward, and eight paces back again. Again and again he paced the parameters of his very small cage.*

One day the zookeeper said, "It's sad to see this bear pacing back and forth in his confining cage. I shall build him a great, open, and elegant space so that he may romp with great freedom and abandon." And so he did.

As the space was completed, great waves of excitement charged through the town, and finally the magic day came to move the bear to his new headquarters. The town Mayor delivered an arousing invocation to the disdain of the screaming hordes of harried children.

The municipal marching brass band manifested a brassy bravado of sound that reached a crescendo at the glorious moment that the sad bear was ushered into his elegant new quarters. Whispers of curious expectation rose from the crowd as they watched the great beast frozen in the uncertainty of the moment. Then the sad bear looked to his left, and to his right, and then began to move . . . one step, two, five, eight paces forward, and eight back again . . . again and again. To the shocked amazement of the crowd, he paced the parameters of his old very small cage.

Harry Emerson Fosdick, retold by Bill Higginbotham
THE JOURNAL OF CREATIVE BEHAVIOR

---

performance was your attitude that you'd behave differently. Similarly, you've probably faced an audience at one time or another with a fearful attitude and forgotten your remarks, not because you were unprepared, but because you said to yourself, "I know I'll blow it."

Certainly you've had the experience of waking up in a cross mood and saying to yourself, "This will be a bad day." Once you have decided this, you may have acted in ways that made it come true. If you approached a class expecting to be bored, you most probably did lose interest, due partly to a lack of attention on your part. If you avoided the company of others because you expected that they had nothing to offer, your suspicions would have been confirmed—

nothing exciting or new did happen to you. On the other hand, if you approached the same day with the idea that it had the potential of being a good one, this expectation probably would also have been met. Smile at people, and they'll probably smile back. Enter a class determined to learn something, and you probably will—even if it's how not to instruct students! Approach many people with the idea that some of them will be good to know, and you'll most likely make some new friends. In these cases and similar ones your attitude has a great deal to do with how you see yourself and how others will see you.

The self-fulfilling prophecy is an important force in interpersonal communication, but we don't want to suggest that it explains *all* behavior. There are certainly times when the expectation of an event's outcome won't bring about that occurrence. Believing you'll do well in a job interview when you're clearly not qualified for the position is unrealistic. In the same way, there will probably be people and situations you won't enjoy no matter what your expectations. Thus, to connect the self-fulfilling prophecy with the "power of positive thinking" is an oversimplification.

In other cases your expectations will be borne out because you're a good predictor, and not because of the self-fulfilling prophecy. For example, children are not equally well equipped to do well in school. In such cases it would be wrong to say that the child's performance was shaped by a parent or teacher, even though the behavior did match that which was expected. In the same way, some workers excel and others fail, some patients recover and others don't, all according to our predictions but not *because* of them.

Keeping these qualifications in mind, it's important to recognize the tremendous influence that self-fulfilling prophecies play in our lives. To a great extent we are what we believe we are. In this sense we and those around us constantly create our self-concepts and thus our "selves."

Changing Your Self-Concept

After reading this far, you've probably begun to realize that it is possible to change an unsatisfying self-concept. In the next sections we'll discuss some methods for accomplishing such a change.

Have realistic expectations It's extremely important to realize that some of your dissatisfaction might come from expecting too

To love oneself is the beginning of a lifelong romance.

Oscar Wilde

much of yourself. If you demand that you handle every act of communication perfectly, you're bound to be disappointed. Nobody is able to handle every conflict productively, to be totally relaxed and skillful in conversations, to always ask perceptive questions, or to be 100 percent helpful when others have problems. Expecting yourself to reach such unrealistic goals is to doom yourself to unhappiness at the start.

Sometimes it's easy to be hard on yourself because everyone around you seems to be handling themselves so much better than you. It's important to realize that much of what seems like confidence and skill in others is a front to hide uncertainty. They may be suffering from the same self-imposed demands of perfection that you place on yourself.

Even in cases where others definitely seem more competent than you, it's important to judge yourself in terms of your own growth, and not against the behavior of others. Rather than feeling miserable because you're not as talented as an expert, realize that you probably are a better, wiser, or more skillful person than you used to be and that this is a legitimate source of satisfaction. Perfection is fine as an ideal, but you're being unfair to yourself if you actually expect to reach that state.

Have a realistic perception of yourself One source of a poor self-concept is inaccurate self-perception. As you've already read, such unrealistic pictures sometimes come from being overly harsh on yourself,

49

PEANUTS

PERHAPS YOU CAN GIVE ME AN ANSWER, LINUS...

WHAT WOULD YOU DO IF YOU FELT THAT NO ONE LIKED YOU?

I'D TRY TO LOOK AT MYSELF OBJECTIVELY, AND SEE WHAT I COULD DO TO IMPROVE... THAT'S MY ANSWER, CHARLIE BROWN

I HATE THAT ANSWER!

© 1967 United Feature Syndicate, Inc.

believing that you're worse than the facts indicate. Of course it would be foolish to deny that you could be a better person than you are, but it's also important to recognize your strengths. A periodic session of "bragging"—of acknowledging the parts of yourself with which you're pleased and the ways you've grown—is often a good way to put your strengths and shortcomings into perspective.

An unrealistically poor self-concept can also come from the inaccurate feedback of others. Perhaps you are in an environment where you receive an excessive number of downer messages, many of which are undeserved, and a minimum of upper messages. We've known many housewives, for example, who have returned to college after many years spent in homemaking where they received virtually no recognition for their intellectual strengths. It's amazing that these women have the courage to come to college at all, their self-concepts are so low; but come they do, and most are thrilled to find that they are much brighter and more competent intellectually than they suspected. In the same way, workers with overly critical supervisors, children with cruel "friends," and students with unsupportive teachers are all prone to suffering from low self-concepts due to excessively negative feedback.

If you fall into this category, it's important to put the unrealistic evaluations you receive into perspective, and then to seek out more supportive people who will acknowledge your assets as well as point out your shortcomings. Doing so is often a quick and sure boost to the self-concept.

Have the will to change Often we say we want to change, but aren't willing to do the necessary work. In such cases it's clear that the responsibility for growing rests squarely on your shoulders. Often, we maintain an unrealistic self-concept by claiming that we "can't" be the person we'd like to be, when in fact we're simply not willing to do what's required. You *can* change in many ways, if only you are willing to put out the effort.

Have the skill to change Often trying isn't enough. There are some cases where you would change if you knew of a way to do so.

First, you can seek advice—from books such as this one, the references listed at the end of each chapter, and other printed sources. You can also get advice from instructors, counselors, and other experts, as well as from friends. Of course, not all the advice you receive will be useful, but if you read widely and talk to enough people, you have a good chance of learning the things you want to know.

A second method of learning how to change is to observe models—people who handle themselves in the ways you would like to master. It's often been said that people learn more from models than in any other way, and by taking advantage of this principle you will find that the world is full of teachers who can show you how to communicate more successfully. Become a careful observer. Watch what people you admire do and say, not so that you can copy them, but so that you can adapt their behavior to fit your own personal style.

At this point you might be overwhelmed at the difficulty of changing the way you think about yourself and the way you act. Remember, we never said that this process would be an easy one (although it sometimes is). But even when change is difficult, you know that it's possible if you are serious. You don't need to be perfect, but you *can* improve your self-concept—*if you choose to.*

Readings

Briggs, Dorothy C. *Your Child's Self-Esteem.* Garden City, N.Y.: Doubleday, 1975.

Campbell, Colin. "Our Many Versions of the Self: An Interview with M. Brewster Smith." *Psychology Today* 9 (February 1976): 74–79.

Civikly, Jean M. "Self-Concept, Significant Others and Classroom Communication." In *Communication in the Classroom,* Larry Barker, ed. Urbana: University of Illinois Press, 1982.

*Fitts, William H. *The Self Concept and Self-Actualization.* Nashville, Tenn.: Counselor Recordings and Tests, 1971.

*Gergen, Kenneth J. *The Concept of Self.* New York: Holt, Rinehart and Winston, 1971.

Gergen, Kenneth J. "The Healthy, Happy Human Being Wears Many Masks." *Psychology Today* 5 (May 1972): 31–35, 64–66.

Insel, Paul M., and Lenore Jacobson. *What Do You Expect? An Inquiry Into Self-Fulfilling Prophecies.* Menlo Park, Calif.: Cummings Publishing Co., 1975.

*Rosenberg, Morris. *Conceiving the Self.* New York: Basic Books, 1979.

Rosenfeld, Lawrence B. "Self-Concept and Role Behavior." In *Now That We're All Here . . . Relations in Small Groups.* Columbus, Ohio: Charles E. Merrill Publishing Co., 1976.

Rosenthal, Robert. "The Pygmalion Effect Lives." *Psychology Today* 7 (1973): 56–63.

*Rosenthal, Robert, and Bella M. DePaulo. "Expectancies, Discrepancies, and Courtesies in Nonverbal Communication." *Western Journal of Speech Communication* 43 (1979): 76–95.

Rosenthal, Robert, and Lenore Jacobson. *Pygmalion in the Classroom.* New York: Holt, Rinehart and Winston, 1968.

Samuels, Shirley C. *Enhancing Self-Concept in Early Childhood: Theory and Practice.* New York: Human Sciences Press, 1977.

Scheirer, Mary Ann, and Robert E. Kraut. "Increasing Educational Achievement Via Self-Concept Change." *Review of Educational Research* 49 (Winter 1979): 131–150.

Simon, Sidney B. *Vulture: A Modern Allegory on the Art of Putting Oneself Down.* Niles, Ill.: Argus Communications, 1977.

Snyder, Mark, E.D. Tanke, and Ellen Bersheid. "Social Perception and Interpersonal Behavior: On the Self-Fulfilling Nature of Social Stereotypes." *Journal of Personality and Social Psychology* 35 (1977): 656–666.

Survant, A. "Building Positive Self-Concepts." *Instructor* 81 (1972): 94–95.

3

Perception

■■■■ *After studying the material in this chapter*

You should understand:

1. How the processes of selection, organization, and interpretation operate in human perception.

2. The physiological factors that influence interpersonal perception.

3. How social roles influence interpersonal perception.

4. How occupational roles influence interpersonal perception.

5. How cultural factors influence interpersonal perception.

You should be able to:

1. Identify the physiological, social, occupational, and cultural influences that shape your perception of important people and events.

2. Describe an interpersonal conflict from the different points of view of each disputant, showing how and why the parties view that event so differently.

"Look at it my way . . . "

"Put yourself in my shoes . . . "

"If you really knew how I felt . . . "

"YOU DON'T UNDERSTAND ME!"

Statements like these reflect one of the most common barriers to effective, satisfying communication. We talk to (or at) one another until we're hoarse and exhausted, yet we still don't understand each other . . . not really. We're left feeling isolated and alone, despairing that our words don't seem able to convey the depth and complexity of what we think and feel. Something more seems necessary.

We've often fantasized about what that "something more" might be. Sometimes our image of the ideal understanding-promoter takes the shape of a device with two chairs. The users would seat themselves and place electrically connected metallic caps on their heads. When the switch was thrown, each person would instantly experience the other's world. Each would see through the other's eyes, possess the other's memories, and in all other ways know what it felt to be the other person.

You can imagine how misunderstandings would disappear and tolerance would increase once everyone had used our invention. It's hard to dislike someone once you've been inside his or her skin.

Since our miracle chair doesn't exist, this chapter will have to attempt the same goal. In the following pages, we'll try to show you the many ways in which each of us experiences the world differently and, in so doing, hope to show you how to experience the world as others do. In our survey we'll explore several areas: the physiological factors that shape our perceptions; the role culture plays in creating our world views; and, finally, how our personal needs, interests, and biases cause us to see things differently.

The Perception Process

Before we begin looking at the specific factors that shape our beliefs, we need to take a look at how the perception process operates. The first point to realize is that we do not take notice of every stimulus that is available to us. William James made this point poetically when he said "to the infant the world is just a big blooming, buzzing confusion." Newborn children certainly are overwhelmed with an overload of new sensations, and the first years of life are spent learning which stimuli are meaningful and important.

Even as adults we are faced with more stimuli than we can manage. It would be impossible to focus on every word, noise, sight, or other sensation, and so we find ways of screening out stimuli that seem unimportant. The perception process occurs in three steps.

Selection Since we are exposed to more input than we can possibly manage, the first step in perceiving is to select what data we will attend to. There are several factors that cause us to notice some messages and ignore others.

Stimuli that are *intense* often attract our attention. Something (or someone) that is louder, larger, or brighter stands out. This explains why—other things being equal—we're more likely to remember extremely tall or short people, and why someone who laughs or talks loudly attracts more attention (not always favorable) than do more quiet people.

Stimuli that are *repetitious* also attract attention. Just as a quiet but steadily dripping faucet can dominate your awareness, messages we hear again and again become noticeable.

Attention also is related to *contrast* or *change* in stimulation. Unchanging things or

The Asphalt Jungle, 1953.

people become less and less noteworthy, until some change reminds us of them. This principle explains why we sometimes come to take wonderful people for granted, and why we only appreciate them when they stop being so wonderful or go away.

A final factor that influences selection involves *motives*. Just as a hungry person looks for a restaurant or a tardy one glances at clocks, someone looking for romance might notice potential partners while another person with a product to sell might scan the same group looking for prospective customers.

Organization Along with selecting information from the environment, we must arrange those data in some meaningful way. Many messages are ambiguous and can be organized in more than one manner. For instance, consider the picture of the boxes in Figure 3–1. How many ways can you view the figures? Most people have a hard time finding more than one perspective. (There are four.) If you can't find all of them, turn to Figure 3–2 for some help.

We can see the principle of alternative organizing patterns in human interaction. Young children usually don't classify people according to their skin color. They are just as likely to identify a black person, for example, as being tall, wearing glasses, or being a certain age. As they become more socialized, however, they learn that one common organizing principle in today's society is race, and their perceptions of others change. Do you organize according to age, education, occupation, physical attractiveness, or some other scheme? Imagine how different your relationships would be if you used different criteria for organizing.

Interpretation There are many ways to interpret an event. Is the person who smiles at you across a crowded room interested in romance or simply being polite? Is a friend's kidding a sign of affection or an indication of irritation? Should you take an invitation to "drop by any time" literally or not?

There are several factors that cause us to interpret an event in one way or another:

1. Past experience. What meanings have similar events held? If, for instance, you've been gouged by landlords in the past, you might be skeptical about an apartment man-

> *For the most part we do not see first and then define; we define first and then see.*

Walter Lippmann

---

ager's assurances that careful housekeeping will assure the refund of your cleaning deposit.

2. Assumptions about human behavior. "People do as little work as possible." "In spite of their mistakes, people generally do the best they can." Beliefs like these shape the way you interpret another's actions.

3. Expectations. Anticipation shapes interpretation. If you imagine your boss is unhappy with you you'll probably feel threatened by a request to "see me in my office Monday morning." On the other hand, if you imagine that your work will be rewarded, your weekend will be filled with pleasant anticipation of a reward from the boss.

4. Knowledge. If you know a friend has just been jilted by a lover or fired from a job, you'll interpret his aloof behavior differently than if you were unaware of what happened. If you know an instructor is rude to all students, then you won't be likely to take such remarks personally.

5. Personal moods. When you're feeling insecure the world is a different place than when you're confident. The same goes for happiness and sadness or any other opposing emotions. The way we feel determines how we'll interpret events.

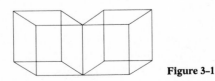

Figure 3–1

The self-concept and perception Sometimes the way we select, organize, and interpret data causes interpersonal conflict. Such cases usually revolve around an individual's desire to maintain a self-concept that has been threatened. Recall that in Chapter 2 we described the tendency people have to behave in ways that support the image they hold of themselves. If I see myself as a good student or musician, then an instructor who gives me a poor grade or a critic who doesn't appreciate my music *must* be wrong, and I'll find evidence to show it. If I've committed myself to support the government in what I believe is a moral cause, and someone tells me about illegal or immoral acts, I'll find a way to prove that no such event happened. If I want to think of myself as a good sport, and someone shows me that the athletic team I've identified with all season plays dirty, I'll do everything I can to contradict this evidence.

As you can imagine, this tendency to protect our self-concept sometimes leads us to distort the facts. You only need scan the long list of defense mechanisms in Chapter 10 to see how inventive people can be when a threatened self-concept is at stake. And needless to say, when two or more people perceive the same event differently, communication between them suffers.

A classic illustration of selective perception in action began on a fall Saturday afternoon in 1951, when the Dartmouth and Princeton football teams met in the final game of the season (Hastrof and Cantril, 1954). The game was important for both teams. Princeton was defending an unbeaten season, and Dartmouth hoped to beat their traditional rival. The game was rough. In the second quarter Princeton's star player left the field with a broken nose. Later a Dartmouth player suffered a broken leg. Dartmouth was penalized seventy yards, while Princeton (the home team) was penalized twenty-five yards. After the game (which Princeton won) the hostilities continued. The newspapers of both schools accused the other of dirty football and poor sportsmanship. Psychologists Albert Hastrof from Dartmouth and Hadley Cantril of Princeton decided that the contest offered a perfect chance to study selective perception. The researchers recruited students from both schools who knew the rules of football, had no personal friends on either team, and who were otherwise educationally, culturally, and economically similar. Equal numbers of both groups had attended the game or had seen films of it. The psychologists asked a series of questions designed to check the students' perception of the game.

Although predictable, the results were still dramatic. Nearly all the Princeton students

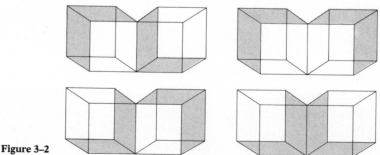

Figure 3–2

James Cagney and Anita Louise in *A Midsummer Night's Dream,* 1935. (Culver Pictures, Inc.)

(whose star player was sidelined by injuries) saw the game as "rough and dirty," and not a single one thought it was "clean and fair." By contrast, only 42 percent of the Dartmouth students agreed with the "rough and dirty" evaluation.

Princeton students saw the Dartmouth players make over twice as many infractions as their own team, whereas the Dartmouth students saw the number of infractions as about equal. Additionally, Dartmouth stu-

dents saw their own team make only half the number of violations that the Princeton students saw them make.

Looking at these results, the researchers concluded that

. . . there is no such "thing" as a "game" existing "out there" in its own right, which people merely "observe." Out of all the occurrences going on in the environment, a person selects those that have some significance for him from his own egocentric position. . . .

▬ *I strive automatically to bring the world into harmony with my own nature.*

George Bernard Shaw

From this point of view it is inaccurate and misleading to say that different people have different "attitudes" concerning the same "thing." For the "thing" simply is *not* the same for different people whether the "thing" is a football game, a presidential candidate, Communism, or spinach.

As Hastrof and Cantril suggest, this kind of selective perception isn't limited to football. The same principle operates in other areas: criminal trials, where supposedly impartial eyewitness accounts can be distorted by the attitude of the witness toward the defendant; religious discussions, where each person chooses evidence to support one side and ignores information that argues against it; and, perhaps most commonly, in our personal evaluations of others. If, for instance, you describe an acquaintance of yours whom you'll soon be introducing to me by claiming that she is a terrific person, my expectations and my subsequent impression of her will probably be different than if you described the same person as an obnoxious fool.

Physiological Influences

Visit a large camera store and you'll be confronted by an impressive array of equipment: everything from cheap pocket models to sophisticated systems including lenses, filters, tripods, and timers. Some cameras can photograph miniature items at close range and others can capture distant objects clearly. With the right film, it's even possible to take pictures of objects invisible to the

unaided eye. There's only one world "out there," but different equipment allows us to see different parts of it. In the same way, each person's perceptual equipment gives a different image of the world. And sometimes these pictures are so unalike that it seems as if we're not talking about the same events at all.

Taste The sense of taste depends on a chemical reaction for its information (Alpern, Lawrence, and Wolsk, 1967). Taste receptors *(buds)* located in pores in the mouth respond to food which enters each pore by sending a message to the brain. Although we may *think* there are an infinite variety of tastes (recall the last good meal you had), only four basic tastes exist: sweet, sour, salty, and bitter. Each part of the tongue is sensitive to only one of these tastes.

The degree to which each of us possesses the four different types of taste buds determines how foods taste. Not everyone tastes the same food in the same way. Older people, for example, taste a wide variety of things as predominantly bitter. This phenomenon happens because the taste buds for sweet, salty, and sour die off and are not as readily replaced, leaving the taste buds for bitter as the primary sources of taste information.

Differences are not merely a function of age; heredity also plays a role. You can test this fact by trying the following experiment. From your biology department or a chemical supply house, obtain strips of litmus paper treated with the chemical phenyl-thiocarbamide (PTC). (This litmus paper is quite inexpensive.) Give one strip to each member of your group, and have everyone taste their paper at the same time. Now immediately conduct a survey: "How many people found the paper salty? How many found it sweet? How many found it bitter? How many found no taste at all? Did anyone find a different taste?

Chances are that the paper tasted bitter to some people, while to others it was sweet, sour, or salty. Somewhat less than half your group probably didn't taste anything at all. If you've inherited a dominant "taster" gene from someone in your family, you'll get one taste or another. Otherwise, the treated paper won't seem any different from the untreated type.

The fact that the paper has different tastes for different people is interesting in itself, but it also has important implications for communication. At one time or another you have probably accused a companion of being "crazy" for not liking a food you find enjoyable. We argue as if the food either tastes good or terrible, as if one person must be wrong and the other right. This sort of remark is likely to generate a defensive response, probably resulting in a spoiled meal for everyone. Keeping the PTC experiment in mind might help you remember at times like these that things may simply taste *different*.

Smell   Located in the nostrils, the receptors for smell are also "triggered" by a chemical

reaction (Alpern, Lawrence, and Wolsk, 1967). The sense of smell is extremely sensitive in that it takes little stimulus to activate the receptors and send a message to the brain (although if inundated with a particular smell, the receptors eventually "shut off").

Just as the ability to taste varies among people, so does the ability to smell. Some people are better at detecting odors than others, and the difference, as with most differences in taste, are inherited. The ability to smell is related to the yellow and brown pigments in the smell receptors—the darker the colors, the more sensitive the receptors. (Albino individuals have virtually no sense of smell.)

The ability to detect smells affects our interpersonal interactions. For example, R.A. Schneider (1971) reports that women are more sensitive to smells in the morning, whereas men are more sensitive to smells in the evening, and women are more sensitive to smells than men generally. To complicate the situation, male and female extroverts are more sensitive to smells than male and female introverts.

Putting all this information together may account for someone saying, "She's so sensi-

tive" about a female extrovert in the morning who mentions a perfume she finds particularly offensive—a smell many others may not even detect to any significant degree. A great many differences in the ability to detect odors and in preferences for odors exist. However, most people can easily agree about what odors they like least (burnt rubber or vomit, for example), and to a lesser degree, the ones they especially like (deep rose, fresh strawberries, honeysuckle), but there's no real consistency about whether most smells are "good" or "bad" (Moncrieff, 1966). For example, in one study people ranked their preferences among 132 different odors. Bay leaf (a spice commonly used in cooking) ranged from 9th to 98th; peppermint from 1st to 76th; and raw onion from 5th to 110th. Age and sex seem to play some part in people's odor preferences. Children and men generally like sweeter fruit odors, whereas women prefer odors less sweet; men ranked musky-smelling perfumes higher than women did; and children tolerate unpleasant odors such as those from feces more than adults do.

Differences such as these demonstrate that smells or tastes pleasing to one person can be repulsive to somebody else. So whether it's your perfume, ladies, or your aftershave lotion, gentlemen, that provokes the comment, "What stinks?" don't be upset—the other person may only be perceiving the odor differently than you do.

Touch   Sense organs located in the skin depend on physical contact for information about the environment (Alpern, Lawrence, and Wolsk, 1967). The amount of surface area that contains receptors amounts to about a million sensory fibers entering the spinal cord. And the amount of space taken up in the brain for processing tactile infor-

mation is large (areas devoted to the lips, index finger, and thumb take up a disproportionately large portion of space in the brain). In light of these facts, the importance of environmental information received from our skin is clear.

Sensitivity to temperature is part of our sense of touch. Interestingly, we are sensitive to changes and contrasts in temperature, and not actual temperatures. We are able to detect changes as small as 1/100th of a degree every second! To test this sensitivity, try the following: Place your left hand in hot water, and your right hand in cold water, then place both hands in lukewarm water. To your right hand the lukewarm water most likely seemed hot, and to your left hand it seemed cold. It was the *change* that mattered, and not the temperature itself.

Like the other senses, sensitivity to temperature varies from person to person; forgetting this fact can block communication. For example, think of the times you've called someone "chicken" who thought the water was too cold for swimming or gotten angry at someone for turning the heat up or down when you were comfortable.

Again, the root of the problem may be biological. People's sensitivity to temperature varies greatly. Thus, if you're less sensitive to cold, it might be that 65° F. to you feels like 55° F. to somebody else. If people could keep this in mind, they'd have less reason to disagree over who's right about the temperature. Rather than fighting, they could figure out alternative behaviors that would suit everyone involved. (That's why electric blankets with dual controls are so popular.)

Hearing   Let's continue our study of the senses by examining hearing. We'll try to give you some feeling for how the world sounds to people who hear differently than

▆▆▆ Why Communications Falter

I receive many letters from wistful and well-intentioned correspondents who want to know "why people can't communicate better with one another." Whenever I hear this complaint, it reminds me of the pertinent fact that William James pointed out a half-century ago in one of his psychological texts.

James said that in any dialog between two persons there are six participants; it is not merely a dialog between Jones and Smith, which would be simple, but between three aspects of each personality.

First of all, there is Jones as he appears to himself, Jones as he appears to Smith, and Jones as he really is; the complementary triad, of course, is Smith as he appears to himself, Smith as he appears to Jones, and Smith as he really is.

It is within this multiplicity of identities that the communication gets lost. It is not merely that Jones says one thing and Smith thinks he means another thing. It is that Jones himself is divided into the man as he appears to himself, and the man he really is. Even before the listener is involved, the communicator himself may be confused, or contradictory, or self-delusive.

We can see the difficulty most clearly in domestic disputes of the sort that happen every day. A wife complains about a certain attitude or activity of her husband—but she is really complaining about something else. Only neither of them is aware of the nature of the true complaint.

Thus, an argument begins on a false basis, and can have no good or final ending. The wife, as she appears to herself, is saying one thing; as she appears to her husband, she is saying another; and as she really is, she is expressing some different and deeper grievance locked within her unconscious and allowed to trickle out only in this distorted form.

Likewise, the generally poor communication between parents and growing children is largely based on differing self-conceptions. The parent, as he appears to himself, is asking only "what is for the child's good." But the child sees it differently; to him the parent is serving his own private needs.

If persons cannot genuinely communicate, how can societies, communities, governments communicate with one another? The answer is that they cannot, except on a formal, superficial level; and even such a communication breaks down in a crisis. Mankind has not even begun to tackle seriously the prime problem of sending, receiving, and decoding messages.

Sydney J. Harris

you do (a normal person can distinguish 340,000 tones), and then we'll examine the implications this has for communication.

Suppose you have normal hearing. You can represent this visually by holding your book at arm's length and reading what's written below:

LOUDNESS

You should have no trouble reading this comfortably, just as the person with normal hearing has no difficulty understanding others in a conversation. However, it's possible to have a hearing loss without ever knowing it; in fact, it's likely that you know someone who does have a hearing loss. These people would have difficulty understanding the same sounds you hear so easily. You can represent how a person with the most common type of loss might hear a word by again holding your book at arm's length and reading this word:

LOUDNESS

You probably had to magnify these letters or move closer and also mentally fill in the blanks to understand the word. Likewise, hard-of-hearing people try to understand sounds by magnifying the volume (often with a hearing aid) or by getting closer to the source; they utilize clues in the situation and context to "fill in" sounds they can't hear or are unable to read on a speaker's lips.

The increased noise level of our civilization has caused permanent damage to the ears of many people, especially those who spend much of their time in noisy environments—factories, war zones, rock concerts, and so on. These people with hearing losses are usually the ones who may have to turn up the TV or radio to a volume that's uncomfortable for the rest of us.

Forgetting the difference between people's sensitivity to sound can lead to sad con-

sequences. Audiologists and physicians report many cases of children being held back in school for being "slow learners" and punished at home for "not paying attention," when the real problem was that they simply couldn't hear what was going on. Whispering "sweet nothings" in your lover's ear may indeed turn out to be nothing!

Sight We are a visual society. Rarely do you hear someone say, "Touch you later," "Hear you later," "Smell you later," or "Taste you later," even though any one of these may be as accurate a description as the everyday "See you later." Other common expressions show the importance of vision:

"Seeing is believing."

"You're a sight for sore eyes."

"I see what you mean."

"Look me up when you're in town."

"We don't see eye to eye."

It's logical that our language should stress visual images. Information received via sight is probably the most important information we receive, with sound—what we hear—second most important. The other three senses usually serve to "tone" and "integrate" the data we receive from our eyes and ears, as opposed to providing unique information on their own.

The normal eye can differentiate 7.5 million color shades, and make up 1 million discriminations each second (Alpern, Lawrence, and Wolsk, 1967). Most of this information is lost because the brain can only process it in limited amounts.

The part of the eye called the retina is crucial for gathering this sense data. The retina contains rods, which detect weak amounts of light, and cones, which detect high levels of illumination, distinguish points in space, discriminate fine details, and determine

▊▊▊▊ *During the preoperational stage, the child is also quite* egocentric, *meaning he is unable to take the viewpoint of other people. His ego seems to stand at the center of his world. To illustrate, show the child a two-sided mirror and then hold it between the two of you so the child can see himself in it. If you ask him what he thinks* you *can see, he imagines that you see* his *reflected image instead of your own . . . The concept of egocentrism helps us to understand why children can seem exasperatingly selfish or uncooperative at times. A child who blocks your view by standing in front of a television set assumes that you can see if he can. If you ask him to move so you can see, he may move so that he can see better!*

Dennis Coon
INTRODUCTION TO PSYCHOLOGY

---

color. The cones contain three pigments, a red-sensitive one, a green-sensitive one, and a blue-sensitive one. Individuals vary in the degree to which they have sufficient amounts of each of the pigments, giving rise to the general term "color-blindness." A person labeled "color-blind" may be deficient in (or missing) one or two of the pigments, or, on rare occasions, all three (in which case the person can only see black and white). A common form of color-blindness is an absence (as opposed to a deficiency) of either the red-sensitive or blue-sensitive pigment. This problem, found in twice as many males as females, results in seeing reds and greens as yellows.

Consider selling color-blind people something to wear, or talking to them about a particular piece of art, or what color to paint the house. The number of problems in communication that may arise from color-blindness are numerous.

More common than color-blindness are visual defects such as nearsightedness and farsightedness. It's obvious that people with uncorrected visual problems see differently than the rest of us, and that sometimes the corrections may not solve all the problems. Sherri Adler, Ron's wife, explains:

I started wearing glasses when I was eight years old, and my eyesight continued to deteriorate until I was about seventeen. So practically all my life I've had to account for communication difficulties because of my very poor vision. (In my last eye test I couldn't even read the big "E" at the top of the chart without my contact lenses!)

When I was young I went through the embarrassment of having "four eyes" and would only put my glasses on to sneak a look at the blackboard. Asking the teacher if I could sit closer to the front would have solved part of the problem, but also would have singled me out again as a glasses-wearer. I stayed quiet, and my grades declined.

Since I've known Ron we've had some experiences that have caused communication problems because of our differences in vision: He has perfect eyesight, and even when I'm wearing contacts, he can see better than I. I have to sit in the front half of a movie theater to be able to see well. Ron has adjusted to this, but he says he always sat in the back before he met me.

Sex So far we've taken a look at how your five senses can make the world seem a different place to you and to other people. Now let's talk about another physiological factor that causes us to perceive things differently and show you how it can affect communication.

Men and women go through recognizable mood cycles, even though they aren't always marked by obvious physical changes (Ramey, 1972). Although they may not be aware of it, many people seem to go through biologically regulated periods of good spirits followed by equally predictable times of depression. The average length of this cycle is about five weeks, although in some cases it's as short as sixteen days or as long as two months. However long it may be, this cycle of ups and downs is quite regular.

If you were to ask most people why they were feeling so bad during the low part of their mood cycle, you'd get plenty of reasons: troubles with the family, troubles at work, the state of the economy, the "cussedness" of politicians, or other explanations. However reasonable these woes may sound, they're often not the real cause of the problem. Although extremely good or bad events can alter feelings, more often they're governed by the internal biological clock everyone carries around inside (Rosenfeld and Civikly, 1976).

Although neither men or women can change these emotional cycles, simply learning to expect them can be a big help in improving communication. When you understand that the cause of a bad mood is predictable and caused by physiological factors, you can plan for it. You'll know that every few weeks your patience will be shorter, and you'll be less likely to blame your bad moods on innocent bystanders. The people around you can also learn to expect your periodic lows and attribute them to biology instead of getting angry at you.

Other physiological factors So far we've only looked at the most obvious physical differences that influence our perception. Even a casual second look shows many other ways in which the state of our bodies determines how we perceive the world, and thus shapes the way we communicate.

Health Recall the last time you came down with a cold, flu, or some other ailment. Do you remember how different you felt? You probably had much less energy. It's likely that you felt less sociable, and that your thinking was probably a bit slower than usual. It's easy to see that these kinds of changes have a strong impact on how you relate to others. Obvious as this seems, it's easy to forget that someone else may be behaving differently due to illness. In the same way, it's important to let others know when you feel poorly so they can give you the understanding you need.

Fatigue Just as being ill can affect your relationships, so too can being overly tired. Again we don't want to belabor an obvious point, but it's important to recognize the fact that you or someone else may behave differently when you're fatigued, and that trying to deal with important issues at such a time can get you into trouble.

Age One reason older people view the world differently than younger ones is because of their generally greater scope and number of experiences. But there are also age-related physical differences that shape perceptions. Although none of the authors are exactly old geezers, each of us has had a share of troubles with our kids due to age. If you've been around children, you know that their energy level is quite high, to put it mildly. To us it often seems as if our children are superactive—"little maniacs," we sometimes call them. To the children, of course, adults must often seem like old bores. After all, what's wrong with someone who doesn't want to wrestle or play hide and seek five hours a day?

Height To understand the role height plays in perception, imagine two people attending a parade—one six feet three inches tall and the other five feet two inches tall. Clearly what would be an enjoyable spectacle for the first person would probably be a frustrating jumble for the shorter companion. Countless other activities are affected by height, such as dancing, visiting the theater, and playing many sports. What does all this have to do with interpersonal communication? It's easy to see how failing to recognize the different worlds in which shorter and taller people live can lead to unnecessary frustration. Think, for instance, of the troubles children encounter in a world designed for people twice their size. Drinking from a fountain, climbing onto a chair, or even going to the bathroom can be chores. Parents

would be wise to remember these difficulties before blaming kids for not being quick or tidy.

Hunger This factor is an obvious one, at least once you consider it. People often get grumpy when they haven't eaten and sleepy after stuffing themselves. Yet how often do we forget these simple facts and try to conduct important business at times when our stomachs are running our lives?

Daily cycles Are you a "morning person" or a "night person"? Most of us can answer this question pretty easily, and there's a good physiological reason behind our answer. Each of us is in a daily cycle in which all sorts of changes constantly occur: body temperature, sexual drive, alertness, tolerance to stress, and mood (Luce, 1971). Most of these changes are due to hormonal cycles. For instance, adrenal hormones, which affect feel-

"This is nothing. When I was your age the snow was so deep it came up to my chin!"

ings of stress, are secreted at higher rates during some hours. In the same manner, the male and female sex hormones enter our systems at variable rates. We often aren't conscious of these changes, but they surely govern the way we relate toward each other. Once we're aware that our own cycles and those of others govern our feelings and behavior, it becomes possible to run our lives so that we deal with important issues at the most effective times.

Social Influences

So far you've seen how everyone's physiological makeup varies, and how these variations can block communication if people are not careful. But besides our physical makeup there's another set of perceptual factors that can lead to communication breakdowns. From almost the time we're born, each of us is indirectly taught a whole set of roles we're expected to play. In one sense this collection of prescribed parts is necessary because it enables a society to function smoothly and provides the security that comes from knowing what's expected of you. But in another way having roles defined in advance can lead to wide gaps in understanding. When roles become unquestioned and rigid, people tend to see the world from their own viewpoint, having no experiences to show them how other people view it. Naturally, in such a situation communication suffers.

Sex roles In every society one of the most important factors in determining roles is sex. How should a woman act? What kinds of behavior define being a man? Until recently most of us never questioned the answers our society gave to these questions. Boys are made of "snips and snails and puppy-dog

tails" and grow up to be the breadwinners of families; little girls are "sugar and spice and everything nice," and their mothers are irrational, intuitive, and temperamental. Not everyone fits into these patterns, but in the past the patterns became well established and were mainly unquestioned by most people.

Research on male and female behavior in small group settings supports some of these stereotypes. As a group males appear more confident, dominant, achievement-oriented, and task-oriented than females, and females are more accommodating and social-oriented than males. In an analysis of male and female democratic leaders, Rosenfeld and Fowler (1976) found that the personality variables that characterize democratic male leaders include the following: forcefulness, superior intellectual ability, being analytical of self and others, and being utilitarian. Democratic females were characterized as open-minded, helpful, affectionate, accepting of blame, and desirous of stability and unity.

In a follow-up study, Fowler and Rosenfeld (1979) observed the behavior of male and female democratic leaders. They found the communicative behavior of female democratic leaders to be predominantly socioemotional, expressing more friendly acts and agreement than male democratic leaders. The communicative behavior of male democratic leaders was concentrated in the task areas. For example, the male leaders offered more suggestions than female leaders, disagreed more, and performed more unfriendly acts.

These findings support the stereotyped sex-roles ascribed to males and females in our society. Males often behave in independent, aggressive, competitive, risk-taking, and task-oriented ways, whereas females tend to be more noncompetitive, dependent, empathic, passive, fragile, interpersonally oriented, expressive, and cooperative.

These stereotyped sex-role descriptions are also supported by research in the area of nonverbal communication, summarized by Rosenthal and DePaulo (1979) and LaFrance and Mayo (1979). Compared to men, for example, women are more supportive in conversations, laugh more at others' jokes, argue less, interrupt less, smile more, are visually more attentive, look more pleasant, and intrude less on others' personal space. The general conclusion that Rosenthal and DePaulo arrived at based on these findings was that "women are more polite in the nonverbal aspects of their social interactions than are men. They are more guarded in reading those cues that senders may be trying to hide but more open in the expression of their own affective states. . . . Perhaps women in our culture have been taught that there may be social hazards to knowing too much about others' feelings" (p. 95).

What accounts for these differences? In an earlier time most people would have automatically assumed that physical differences between men and women cause them to think and act in distinct ways. More recently, however, social scientists and lay people have recognized that human behavior—male and female—is also influenced by *psychological* differences, brought about by the social environment in which each of us lives. One needn't be a social scientist to realize that the ways in which boys and girls are socialized differ in many ways. Boys are discouraged from behaving in "feminine" ways: playing with dolls, dressing up (except for a brief stint as Spiderman or the Incredible Hulk on Halloween). They're reinforced for playing in competitive sports. Girls, on the other hand, find that adults are more willing to accept cuddles, tears, and other overt emotional expressions from them.

Mae West (Culver Pictures)

They don't receive much approval for assertive or aggressive acts.

J.M. Bardwick and E. Douvan (1971) point out another way in which the two sexes are socialized differently. They explain that male role behavior is more narrowly defined than female role behavior (young girls may behave in a moderately masculine way as well as acting feminine, whereas young boys are firmly discouraged from behaving any way but extremely masculine), creating a situation in which males receive more punishment than females. Because early relationships for girls are rewarding, they tend toward being people- or relationship-oriented when they get older, and because early relationships for boys are generally punishing, they tend to seek satisfaction outside relationships with other people, and so become object-oriented as opposed to people-oriented.

69

The combination of social expectations, physiological differences, and personal characteristics led Sandra Bem (1974), one of the first researchers in the area of sociosexual behavior, to expand the traditional male-female dichotomy to two separate dimensions. She reasoned that masculinity and femininity are not opposite poles of a single continuum, but rather two separate sets of behavior. With this view, an individual can be masculine, feminine, or exhibit both types of characteristics. The male-female dichotomy, then, is replaced with four psychological sex-types, including masculine, feminine, androgynous (masculine and feminine), and undifferentiated (neither masculine nor feminine). Combining the four psychological sex-types with the traditional physiological sex-types, we arrive at the following eight categories:

1. **Masculine males**—males who rate high on stereotypically masculine traits and low on stereotypically feminine traits;
2. **Feminine males**—males who rate high on feminine traits and low on masculine traits;
3. **Androgynous males**—males who rate high on both masculine and feminine traits;
4. **Undifferentiated males**—males who rate low on both masculine and feminine traits;
5. **Feminine females**—females who rate high on feminine traits and low on masculine traits;
6. **Masculine females**—females who rate high on masculine traits and low on feminine traits;
7. **Androgynous females**—females who rate high on both masculine and feminine traits;
8. **Undifferentiated females**—females who rate low on both masculine and feminine traits.

In a series of studies designed to test whether psychological sex was a better predictor of behavior than anatomical sex, Bem (1974, 1975, 1976; Bem and Lenny, 1976) observed the responses of psychological sex types to a variety of situations that called for independence, nurturance, and performance on sex-typed and nonsex-typed tasks. She found that only androgynous subjects (those who rate high on both masculine and feminine traits) display a high level of masculine independence as well as a high level of feminine nurturance. In general, research by Bem and others supports the conclusion that androgynous individuals are less restricted in their behaviors and are better able to adapt to situations that require characteristics presumed of men *or* women. This flexibility, this sex-role transcendence, may be the hallmark of mental health.

Masculine males and feminine females, the sex-typed individuals who most likely come to mind when we think of the words "male" and "female," experience more personality development problems, more marital problems, and more problem-solving difficulties than do androgynous males and females. Traditional sex-role stereotypes describe masculine males and feminine females fairly well.

What does this discussion of sexual stereotypes and attitudes have to do with perception and communication? A great deal. Each one of the eight psychological sex types, including the stereotyped masculine males and feminine females perceives the world differently. Given the traits describing each group, it's logical to assume that members of each group view interpersonal relationships differently. For example, masculine males probably see their interpersonal relationships as opportunities for competitive interaction, as opportunities to win something. Feminine females probably see their interpersonal relationships as opportunities to be nurturing, to express their feelings and emotions. Androgynous males and

■ *I have noticed*
that men
somewhere around forty
tend to come in from the field
with a sigh
and removing their coat in the hall
call into the kitchen
        you were right
        grace
        it ain't out there
        just like you've always said

and she
with the children gone at last
breathless
puts her hat on her head
        the hell it ain't

coming and going
they pass
in the doorway

Ric Masten

---

females, on the other hand, probably differ little in their perceptions of their interpersonal relationships.

Androgynous individuals probably see their relationships as opportunities to behave in a variety of ways, depending on the nature of the relationships themselves, the context in which a particular relationship takes place, and the myriad other variables affecting what might constitute appropriate behavior. These variables are usually ignored by the sex-typed masculine males and feminine females who have a smaller repertoire of behavior than the androgynous individuals.

Occupational roles The kind of work we do often governs our view of the world. Imagine five people taking a walk through the park. One, a botanist, is fascinated by the variety of trees and plants. The zoologist is on the lookout for interesting animals. The third, a meteorologist, keeps an eye on the sky, noticing changes in the weather. The fourth, a psychologist, is totally unaware of the goings-on of nature, concentrating instead on the interaction among the people in the park. The fifth, being a pickpocket, quickly takes advantage of the others' absorption to add to his collection of pocketbooks. There are two lessons in this little story. The first, of course, is to watch your wallet carefully. The second is that our occupational roles frequently govern our perceptions.

Even within the same occupational setting, the different roles of participants can affect their experience. Consider a typical

███ *Washing and ironing and cooking meals for me (yum yum)*
Cleaning and sewing, she's busy as a bee (buzz buzz)
I want to help her in every single way
Because I love my mommy every day.

Working, he's working, he works so hard for us (work work)
Though he is tired he never makes a fuss (nay nay)
I want to help him in every single way
Because I love my daddy every day.

Preschool Song
(overheard in 1979)

---

college classroom, for example: the experiences of the instructor and students are often quite dissimilar. Having dedicated a large part of their lives to their work, most professors see their subject matter—whether French literature, physics, or speech communication—as vitally important. Students who are taking the course to satisfy a general education requirement may view the subject quite differently; maybe as one of many obstacles standing between them and a degree, or as a chance to meet new people.

Another difference centers on the amount of knowledge possessed by the people. To an instructor who has taught the course many times, the material probably seems extremely simple; but to students encountering it for the first time it may seem strange and confusing. Toward the end of a semester or quarter the instructor might be pressing onward hurriedly to cover all the course material while the students are fatigued from their studies and ready to move more slowly. We don't need to spell out the interpersonal strains and stresses that come from such differing perceptions.

Even within occupational roles the different interests and personalities of each person can lead to differing perceptions. Some students, for instance, see the class as an ex-

tension of their home, a place to listen to "mom or dad" and do little thinking. Anxious-dependent students probably see the class as a place to look foolish, to lose part of their self-esteem. Independent students probably see it as a place to do well, to achieve important things. Attention-seekers see the class as a place to have some fun. Silent students find class a frustrating place, one in which they are torn between the desire to be accepted and the fear of being rejected.

The attitudes of instructors also govern their picture of a classroom. A teacher who takes on the role of expert probably sees the classroom as a place to display wisdom, to show off. Formal authorities most likely see the classroom as a place to play judge and jury, to represent the authority of the school, to wield power. Socializing agents see their students as children and see themselves as helpful fathers and mothers. Facilitators may see the classroom as a place to support egos, to help. Teachers who enact the role of ego ideal probably see the classroom as a place to obtain self-glorification, to be loved and admired. Other instructors see themselves as partners with their students in the learning process, cooperatively working with students whom they respect in the process of sharing new material. How would you characterize your instructors? Yourself as a student?

Perhaps the most dramatic illustration of how occupational roles shape perception occurred in 1971. Stanford psychologist Philip Zimbardo (1971) recruited a group of middle-class, well-educated young men, all white except for one Oriental. He randomly chose eleven to serve as "guards" in a mock prison set up in the basement of Stanford's psychology building. He issued the guards uniforms, handcuffs, whistles, and billy clubs. The remaining ten subjects became "prisoners" and were placed in rooms with metal bars, bucket toilets, and cots.

Zimbardo let the guards establish their own rules for the experiment. The rules were tough: No talking during meals, rest periods, and after lights out. Head counts at 2:30 A.M. Troublemakers received short rations.

Faced with these conditions, the prisoners began to resist. Some barricaded their doors with beds. Others went on hunger strikes. Several ripped off their identifying number tags. The guards reacted to the rebellion by clamping down hard on protesters. Some turned sadistic, physically and verbally abusing the prisoners. They threw prisoners into solitary confinement. Others forced prisoners to call each other names and clean out toilets with their bare hands.

Within a short time the experiment had become reality for both prisoners and guards. Several inmates experienced stomach cramps and lapsed into uncontrollable weeping. Others suffered from headaches, and one broke out in a head-to-toe rash after his request for early "parole" was denied by the guards.

The experiment was scheduled to go on for two weeks, but after six days Zimbardo realized that what had started as a simulation had become too intense. "I knew by then that they were thinking like prisoners and not like people," he said. "If we were able to demonstrate that pathological behavior could be produced in so short a time, think of what damage is being done in 'real' prisons . . ."

This dramatic exercise in which twenty-one well-educated, middle-class citizens turned almost overnight into sadistic bullies and demoralized victoms tells us that how we think is a function of our roles in society. It seems that *what* we are is determined largely by the society's designation of *who* we are.

Cultural Factors

In addition to physiology and social roles, there's another kind of perceptual gap that often blocks communication—the gap between people from different backgrounds (Condon and Yousef, 1975). Every culture has its own view, its own way of looking at the world, which is unique. When we remember these differing cultural perspectives, they can be a great way of learning more about both ourselves and others. But at times it's easy to forget that people everywhere don't see "reality" the way we do. For example, whereas most North Americans view spitting as a sign of disrespect or poor manners, to the Masai tribe of East Africa it symbolizes affection and blessing. And when done by an American Indian medicine man, spitting is a means of healing.

In Athens, a pinch on the behind of a woman is an almost expected, if unappreciated behavior. In America, the same pinch is much more of an assault, likely to be met with a slap, a mean look, or even a call for a police officer.

One of our students provided us with the following example of cultural differences.

West Side Story, 1961. (Culver Pictures)

He was visiting Lagos, Nigeria, and while walking down the street one afternoon he came upon two men, one a Nigerian and the other an American. The men were fighting wildly and cursing at each other, each in his own language. The police had come and seemed to be ready to take both fighters away when an English-speaking taxi driver saved the day.

After talking to both men, he explained the story: It seems that the American was hitchhiking through town, signaling for a ride the only way he knew—standing at the roadside with his thumb sticking out where the drivers could easily see it. Unfortunately for him, in Nigeria this gesture doesn't mean the same thing as in the United States. In fact, its closest equivalent in our terms is what we call "the finger." So, although the American meant to politely ask for a ride, instead he had insulted the Nigerian's honor.

Thanks to the taxi driver (who ought to be working for the U.N.), the last time our student saw the two former enemies they were heading arm in arm into a bar. They'd learned by experience that to members of different cultures even little differences can have big consequences when you're not aware of them.

After looking at these examples, you can see that different cultures have customs that can cause trouble for the unaware foreigner. But you don't have to go this far from home to come across people with differing cultural perspectives. Within the United States there are many cultures, and the members of each one have backgrounds that cause them to see things in unique ways.

Probably the clearest example of these differing perceptions is the gap between white and black people in America. Even to people of goodwill it seems that there's a barrier that makes understanding difficult; there just seem to be too many different experiences that separate us.

John Howard Griffin (1959) found one way to bridge the gulf that separates whites and blacks. Realizing the impossibility of truly understanding the black experience by reading and talking about it he went one step further: Through a series of treatments that included doses of skin-darkening drugs, he transformed himself into a black man—or at least a man with black skin. And he traveled through the southern United States to get in touch with what it truly meant to be black in America. He was treated like a black, and eventually, to his own surprise, came to find himself responding to white people's demands as if he were one. The insults, the prejudice, sickened him.

This experiment took place in the Deep South of 1959, and times have certainly changed since then. But to what extent is the world still a different place to contemporary whites and blacks? How about other groups—Hispanics, Orientals, Native Americans, old people, longhairs, military men and women. Do you ever find yourself prejudging or being prejudged before getting acquainted with someone from a different sector of society?

Perhaps by sharing the personal experiences of others in your group you can gain a more personal insight into how people from different subcultures view life in your community, not only in terms of discrimination, but also in terms of values, behavioral norms, and political and economic issues. How would life be different if you were of a different race or religion, social or economic class? See if you can imagine.

But talking can enable us to understand another person's viewpoint only to a certain degree. To comprehend what it's truly like to be someone else you have to almost become that person the way Griffin did. Have you ever read Mark Twain's famous novelette *The Prince and the Pauper*? If you have, you'll remember what an education the young prince had when he was mistaken for a young peasant and treated accordingly. In the same way, think of the huge growth in tolerance that would result if the rich could become poor for a bit, if teachers could recall their student days, if whites could become black.

Total role reversals aren't likely to happen, but it's possible to create experiences that give a good picture of another's perspective. The story of one Iowa schoolteacher and her class illustrates the point. Shortly after Martin Luther King's assassination in 1968, Mrs. Jane Elliott wanted to make sure her third graders never became prone to the sickness that caused such events. But how could she do this? Everyone in the small town of Riceville was white, and most of her eight-year-olds had never really known blacks. How could she bring home to them the nature of prejudice?

Her solution was to divide the class into two groups, one containing all the children with blue eyes, and the other made up of the brown-eyed students. Then for the next few days she treated the brown-eyes as better people. They all sat in the front of the room, had second helpings at lunch, got five extra minutes of recess, and received extra praise for their work from Mrs. Elliott. At the same time the blue-eyes were the butt of both subtle and obvious discrimination. Besides the back-row seats, skimpy meals, and other such practices, the blue-eyes never received praise for their schoolwork from Mrs. Elliott, who seemed to find something wrong with everything they did. "What can you expect from a blue-eyed person?" was her attitude. The level of the blue-eyed children's schoolwork dropped almost immediately.

At first the children treated the experiment as a game. But shortly they changed from cooperative, thoughtful people into small but very prejudiced bigots. Classmates who had always been best friends stopped playing with each other and even quit walking to school together.

After the level of intolerance had grown painfully high, Mrs. Elliott changed the rules. Now the blue-eyed people were on top, and the brown-eyes were inferior. And soon the tables were turned, with children who had only days before been the object of discrimination now being bigots themselves.

Finally Mrs. Elliott ended the experiment. When she asked the children if they wanted to go back to the old days, where everyone was the same, the class answered with a resounding "Yes!" Now they really knew what discrimination was, and they didn't like it.

Seeing things from the other person's point of view was all that was needed for the students to recognize what was happening. Selecting, organizing, and interpreting things from one perspective, adopting one particular role, limited the information available. The result was conflict. The perception process requires an understanding of how perception affects all the participants' behavior and not simply your own.

Readings

*Alpern, Mathew, Merle Lawrence, and David Wolsk. *Sensory Processes*. Belmont, Calif.: Brooks/Cole, 1967.

Alsbrook, Larry. "Marital Communication and Sexism." *Social Casework* 57 (1976): 517–522.

*Baird, John E., Jr. "Sex Differences in Group Communication: A Review of Relevant Research."*Quarterly Journal of Speech* 62 (1976): 179–192.

Bardwick, J.M., and E. Douvan. "Ambivalence: The Socialization of Women." In *Women in Sexist Society*, V. Gornick and B. Moran, eds. New York: Basic Books, 1971.

Bem, Sandra L. "Sex Role Adaptability: One Consequence of Psychological Androgyny." *Journal of Personality and Social Psychology* 31 (1975): 634–643.

*Bem, Sandra L. "Probing the Promise of Androgyny." In *Beyond Sex-Role Stereotypes: Readings Toward a Psychology of Androgyny*, A.G. Kaplan and J.P. Bean, eds. Boston: Little, Brown, 1976.

Bem, Sandra L. "The Measurement of Psychological Androgyny." *Journal of Consulting and Clinical Psychology* 42 (1974): 155–162.

Bem, Sandra L., and E. Lenney. "Sex-Typing and the Avoidance of Cross-Sex Behavior." *Journal of Personality and Social Psychology* 33 (1976): 48–54.

Benz, Carolyn R., Isobel Pfeiffer, and Isadore Newman. "Sex Role Expectations of Classroom Teachers, Grades 1-12." *American Educational Research Journal* 18 (1981): 289–302.

Bohannon, Laura. "Shakespeare in the Bush." *Natural History* 75 (Aug.-Sept., 1966): 28–33.

Braga, Joseph L. "Teacher Role Perception." *Journal of Teacher Education* 23 (1972): 53–57.

Buckhout, Robert. "Eyewitness Testimony." *Scientific American* 231 (December, 1974): 6.

Burke, Kenneth. *Permanence and Change*. Indianapolis: Bobbs-Merrill, 1965.

Cline, M. "The Influence of Social Context on the Perception of Faces." *Journal of Personality* 25 (1956): 142–158.

*Condon, John C., and F.S. Yousef. *Introduction to Intercultural Communication*. Indianapolis: Bobbs-Merrill, 1975.

Craig, Robert T. "Role-Taking in Descriptions of Self and Others in the Twenty Statements Test." Paper presented at the International Communication Association Convention, Minneapolis, May 1981.

Cushman, Donald P., and Robert T. Craig. "Communication Systems: Interpersonal Implications." In *Explorations in Interpersonal Communication*. G.R. Miller, ed. Beverly Hills, Calif.: Sage, 1976.

Dearborn, DeWitt C., and Herbert A. Simons. "Selective Perception: The Departmental Identifications of Executives." *Sociometry* 21 (1958): 140–144.

Fowler, Gene D., and Lawrence B. Rosenfeld. "Sex Differences and Democratic Leadership Behavior." *Southern Speech Communication Journal* 45 (1979): 69–78.

Gorman, Alfred H. *Teachers and Learners*, 2nd Ed. Boston: Allyn and Bacon, 1974.

Greenblatt, Lynda, James E. Hasenauer, and Vicki S. Freimuth. "Psychological Sex Type and Androgyny in the Study of Communication Variables: Self-Disclosure and Communication Apprehension." *Human Communication Research* 6 (1981): 117–129.

*Griffin, John Howard. *Black Like Me*. Boston: Houghton Mifflin, 1959.

Hastrof, Albert H., and Hadley Cantrill. "They Saw a Game: A Case Study." *Journal of Abnormal and Social Psychology* 49 (1954): 129–134.

Hix, C. "Smelling Swell." *Gentlemen's Quarterly* 44 (1974): 82.

Hoyle, Eric. *The Role of the Teacher*. New York: Humanities Press, 1969.

Ittelson, W.H., and F.P. Kilpatrick. "Experiments in Perception." *Scientific American* (August 1951).

*LaFrance, Marianne, and Clara Mayo. "A Review of Nonverbal Behaviors of Women and Men." *Western Journal of Speech Communication* 43 (1979): 96–107.

Leathers, Dale G. "The Tactile and Olfactory Communication Systems." In *Nonverbal Communication Systems*. Boston: Allyn and Bacon, 1976.

Luce, Gay Gaer. *Body Time*. New York: Pantheon Books, 1971.

Moncrieff, R.W. *Odour Preferences*. New York: Wiley, 1966.

Montgomery, Charles L., and Michael Burgoon. "An Experimental Study of the Interactive Effects of Sex and Androgyny on Attitude Change." *Communication Monographs* 44 (1977): 130–135.

*Ramey, Estelle. "Men's Cycles." *Ms.* (Spring 1972): 10–14.

Ringwald, Barbara, Richard D. Mann, Robert Rosenwein, and Wilbert J. McKeachie. "Conflict and Style in the College Classroom." *Psychology Today* 4 (1971): 45–47, 76, 78–79.

*Rosenfeld, Lawrence B., Jean M. Civikly, and Jane R. Herron. "Anatomical Sex, Psychological Sex, and Self-Disclosure." In *Self-Disclosure*, Gordon J. Chelune, ed. San Francisco: Jossey-Bass, 1979.

Rosenfeld, Lawrence B., and Jean M. Civikly. "Senses." In *With Words Unspoken: The Nonverbal Experience*. New York: Holt, Rinehart and Winston, 1976.

Rosenfeld, Lawrence B., and Gene D. Fowler. "Personality, Sex, and Leadership Style." *Communication Monographs* 43 (1976): 320–324.

*Rosenthal, Robert, and Bella M. DePaulo. "Expectancies, Discrepancies, and Courtesies in Nonverbal Communication." *Western Journal of Speech Communication* 43 (1979): 76–95.

*Schneider, David J., Albert H. Hastrof, and Phoebe C. Ellsworth. *Person Perception*, 2nd Ed. Reading, Mass.: Addison-Wesley, 1979.

Schneider, R.A. "The Sense of Smell and Human Sexuality." *Medical Aspects of Human Sexuality* 5 (1971): 156–168.

Segall, M.H., D.T. Campbell, and M.J. Herskovits.

The Influence of Culture on Visual Perception. Indianapolis: Bobbs-Merrill, 1966.

Trenholm, Sarah, and Toby Rose. "The Compliant Communicator: Teacher Perceptions of Appropriate Classroom Behavior." *Western Journal of Speech Communication* 45 (1981): 13–26.

Tyler, Leona. *The Psychology of Human Differences.* New York: Appleton-Century-Crofts, 1965.

Wilentz, Joan S. *The Senses of Man.* New York: Thomas Y. Crowell, 1968.

Zimbardo, Philip G. *The Psychological Power and Pathology of Imprisonment.* Statement prepared for the U.S. House of Representatives Committee on the Judiciary, Subcommittee No. 3, Robert Kastemeyer, Chairman. Unpublished manuscript, Stanford University, 1971.

4

Language

Audrey Hepburn and Rex Harrison in *My Fair Lady*, 1964. (Culver Pictures)

■ *After studying the material in this chapter*

You should understand:

1. The symbolic nature of language.

2. That language is rule-governed.

3. That meanings are in people, not words.

4. That language describes events at various levels of abstraction.

5. The problems that come from using overly abstract language.

6. The various types of troublesome language described in this chapter.

7. The Sapir-Whorf hypothesis.

8. How the use of metaphors shape our perceptions.

9. The ways that sexist and racist language shape the self-concept of the persons it describes.

10. The manner in which a speaker's language can reflect liking and responsibility.

11. The ways in which language use is perceived in sexually stereotypical ways.

You should be able to:

1. Recognize cases in which you have misunderstood others by failing to realize that meanings are in people, and not in words.

2. Express your personal problems, goals, appreciative messages, and requests in lower-level abstractions.

3. Identify from your personal experience each type of troublesome language described in this chapter and suggest a less troublesome alternative.

4. Identify the metaphor(s) that best characterize your definition of and approach to love.

5. Identify at least two other metaphors that reflect your approach to other important communication-related activities—for example, work, friendship, and conflict.

6. Identify ways in which your language and the language of others you know reflects degrees of liking and responsibility.

7. Identify the sex-type language you use and reflect on whether it adequately reflects your attitudes and the way you wish to be perceived by others.

Sometimes it seems as if none of us speak the same language. How often have you felt that nobody understood what you were saying? You knew what you meant, but people just didn't seem to understand you. And how often have the tables been turned—you couldn't understand someone else's ideas?

In this chapter we'll examine these problems by taking a quick look at the relationship between words and things. We'll try to show you some of the ways language can trip us up and some things you can do to make it work better. We'll also talk about how language not only describes how we see the world, but also shapes our view of it.

The Nature of Language

Let's begin our study by looking at some characteristics of language. Because we use words almost constantly, we often assume that they are ideally suited to convey meaning. Actually, there are several points to keep in mind if your verbal messages are going to be accurate and successful.

Language is symbolic As we said in Chapter 1, words are symbols that represent things—ideas, events, objects, etc.* Whatever they refer to, words are not the things themselves. For instance, it's obvious that the word "coat" is not the same as the piece of clothing it describes. You would be a fool to expect the letters c-o-a-t to keep you warm in a snowstorm. This point seems so obvious as to hardly be worth mentioning, yet people often forget the nature of language and con-

*Some of these "things," or referents, do not exist as uniquely identifiable objects in the physical world. For instance, some referents are mythical (such as unicorns), some are no longer tangible (such as the deceased Mr. Smith), and others are abstract ideas (such as "love").

fuse symbols with their referents. For example, some students will cram facts into their heads just long enough to regurgitate them into a blue book in order to earn a high grade, forgetting that letters like A or B are only symbols, and that a few lines of ink on paper don't necessarily represent true learning. In the same way, simply saying the words "I care about you" isn't necessarily a reflection of the truth, although many disappointed lovers have learned this lesson the hard way.

So far we have been using the terms "language" and "symbol" interchangeably, which isn't quite correct. Languages consist of collections of symbols, which possess certain properties. First, a language must contain *elements*. In English, these elements consist of the letters of our alphabet, along with punctuation marks such as commas and periods. In the language of mathematics the elements are the integers zero through nine, and other symbols such as plus and minus signs. Morse code has only two elements—dots and dashes.

Language is rule-governed The elements of any language have no meaning by themselves. And in many combinations, they are also meaningless. For example, the letters "flme oo usi oysk" are pure gibberish. But when rearranged into a more recognizable pattern they become understandable: "Kiss me, you fool!" This example illustrates the second characteristic of language, which is the existence of a body of *rules* that dictate the way in which symbols can be used.

Languages contain two types of rules. *Syntactic* rules govern the ways in which symbols can be arranged. For example, in English, syntactic rules require every word to contain at least one vowel, and prohibit sentences such as "Have you the cookies brought?" which would be perfectly acceptable if translated into a language such as German. While most of us aren't able to describe the syntactic rules which govern our language, it's easy to recognize the existence of such rules by noting how odd a statement that violates them appears.

Semantic rules also govern our use of the language. But where syntax deals with structure, semantics governs meaning. Semantic rules reflect the ways in which speakers of a language respond to a particular symbol. Semantic rules are what make it possible for us to agree that "bikes" are for riding and "books" are for reading; and they help us

know who we will and won't encounter when we use rooms marked "men" or "women." Without semantic rules, communication would be impossible, since each of us would use symbols in unique ways, unintelligible to one another.

Meanings are in people, not in words   After reading the last sentence you might object, thinking about the many cases when people don't follow the same semantic rules. Of course you would be correct, for there are many times when a single word has different meanings for different people. This is pos-

Deborah Kerr in *The King and I.* (Culver Pictures, Inc.)

The black speaker is apparently using a different grammar, which disregards is *in the Standard* He's working *and instead chooses to emphasize the auxiliary verb* be. He be workin' *means that the person referred to has been working continuously for a long time; but* He workin', *without the* be, *means that the person is working now, at this very moment. A speaker of Black English would no more say* He be workin' *right now (that is, use the habitual* be *to tell about something happening only at this moment) than a speaker of Standard English would say* He is sleeping tomorrow *(that is, ignore the tense of the verb). The use and non-use of the auxiliary* be *is clearly seen in the Black English sentence.* You makin' *sense, but you don't be makin' sense—which in Standard English means "You just said something smart, but you don't habitually say anything smart." The speaker of Black English, therefore, is obliged by his language to mark certain kinds of verbs as describing either momentary action or habitual action. In contrast, the speaker of Standard English is not obliged to make this distinction—although he must make others which speakers of Black English ignore, such as the tense of the verb.*

The wonder is that it took people so long to realize that Black English is neither a mispronunciation of Standard English nor an accumulation of random errors made in the grammar of Standard. Utterances in Black English are grammatically consistent and they are generated by rules in the same way that utterances in Standard English are generated by rules. Miss Fidditch may not regard utterances in Black English to be "good English"— but that is beside the point, because Black English is using a different set of rules than those of Standard English.

Peter Farb
WORD PLAY

---

sible because words, being symbols, have no meaning in themselves. Ogden and Richards (1923) illustrated this point graphically in their well-known "triangle of meaning." This model shows that there is only an indirect relationship—indicated by a broken line— between a word and the thing it claims to represent. Problems arise when people mistakenly believe that words automatically represent things—as when two people argue about "feminism" without realizing they are refering to different things.

It might seem as if one remedy to misunderstandings like this would be to have more respect for the dictionary meanings of words. After all, you might think, there would be few problems if people would just consult a dictionary whenever they send or receive a potentially confusing message.

This approach has three shortcomings.

> Each one of us is alone in the world. He is shut in a tower of brass and can communicate with his fellows only by signs, and the signs have no common value, so that their sense is vague and uncertain. We seek pitifully to convey to others the treasures of our heart, but they have not the power to accept them, and so we go lonely, side by side but not together, unable to know our fellows and unknown by them. We are like people living in a country whose language they know so little that with all manner of beautiful and profound things to say, they are condemned to the banalities of the conversation manual. Their brain is seething with ideas and they can only tell you that the umbrella of the gardener's aunt is in the house.

W. Somerset Maugham
THE MOON AND SIXPENCE

First, dictionaries indicate that many words have multiple definitions, and it isn't always clear which one applies in a given situation. The 500 words most commonly used in everyday communication have over 14,000 dictionary definitions, which should give you an idea of the limitations of this approach.

A second problem is that people often use words in ways you'd never be able to look up. Sometimes the misuse of a word is due to a lack of knowledge, as when you might ask your auto parts dealer for a new gener-ator when you really need an alternator. In other cases it's due to carelessness.

The third shortcoming of dictionaries is that they define most words in terms of *other* words, and this process often won't tell you any more about a term than you already know. For example, if somebody asks you for a little more "respect" and your diction-ary defines the term as "worthy of esteem," you probably won't have a much clearer idea of how the complainer wants to be treated.

Language is abstract We began this chap-ter by stating that language represents things, rather than being the things them-selves. This leads to the critically important fact that language can describe those things on many different levels, some of which are more abstract that others.

To understand the concept of abstraction, consider the object you're reading now. What would you call it? Probably a book. But you could narrow your description by calling it a "communication book," or more specifically, *Interplay*. You could be even more precise if you wanted: You could say you're reading Chapter 4 of *Interplay*, or

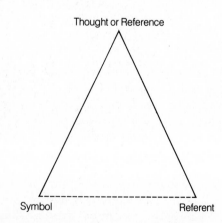

Figure 4–1 Ogden and Richards' triangle of meaning

Thought or Reference

Symbol   Referent

"I don't know what you mean by 'glory,' " Alice said.

Humpty Dumpty smiled contemptuously. "Of course you don't—till I tell you. I meant 'there's a nice knock-down argument for you!' "

"But 'glory' doesn't mean 'a nice knock-down argument,' " Alice objected.

"When I use a word," Humpty Dumpty said, in a rather scornful tone, "it means just what I choose it to mean—neither more nor less."

"The question is," said Alice, "whether you can make words mean so many different things."

"The question is," said Humpty Dumpty, "which is to be master—that's all."

Lewis Carroll
THROUGH THE LOOKING GLASS

---

even page 85 of Chapter 4 of *Interplay*. Instead of being more specific, you could go the other way and describe the book as educational literature, nonfiction writing, or printed material, each description being less and less specific.

Semanticist S. I. Hayakawa (1964) created an "abstraction ladder" to describe this process. This ladder consists of a number of descriptions of the same person, object, or event. The lowest description on the ladder describes the phenomenon at its most basic level: atoms and molecules interacting, nerve synapses operating, and so on. Moving still higher up the ladder, we come to increasingly general descriptions. The sample abstraction ladder illustrated in Figure 4–2 is an example of the many levels on which a phenomenon can be described.

Abstract Language and Interpersonal Communication

All language operates on some level of abstraction. But *which* level we use can make a tremendous difference in the quality of communication. We'll now take a look at some problems that come from operating on the

wrong level of abstraction, and then suggest some remedies.

Problems with abstractions Higher-level abstractions are convenient ways of general-

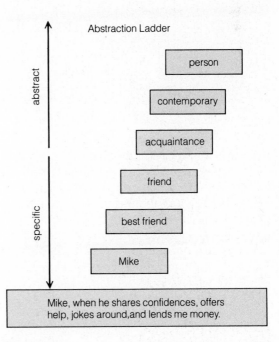

Figure 4–2

Groucho Marx, E. J. Le Saint, and E. H. Calvert in *Horsefeathers*, 1932. (Culver Pictures, Inc.)

izing about similarities between several objects, people, or events. For instance, rather than saying "Thanks for washing the dishes," "Thanks for vacuuming the rug," and "Thanks for making the bed," it's easier to move up the abstraction ladder and say "Thanks for cleaning up." But many interpersonal problems come from speaking too generally. Overly abstract language causes trouble in four ways.

Stereotyping Imagine someone who has had a bad experience while traveling abroad and as a result blames an entire country. "Yeah, those damn Hottentots are a bunch of thieves. If you're not careful, they'll steal you blind. I know, because one of 'em stole my camera last year." You can see here how lumping people into highly abstract categories ignores the fact that for every thieving Hottentot there are probably 100 honest ones. It's this kind of thinking that leads to mistaken assumptions that keep people apart: "None of those kids are any damn good!"; "You can't trust anybody in business"; "Those cops are all a bunch of goons." Each of these statements ignores the very important fact that sometimes our descriptions are too general, that they say more than we really mean.

When you think about examples like these, you begin to see how thinking in abstract terms can lead to ignoring individual differences, which can be as important as similarities. People in the habit of using highly abstract language begin to *think* in generalities, ignoring uniqueness. And as we discussed in Chapter 2, expecting people to be a certain way can become a self-fulfilling prophecy. If I think all policemen are brutal, I'm more likely to react in a defensive, hostile way toward them, which in turn increases the chance that they'll react to me as a threat. If I think that no teachers care about their classes, then my defensive indifference is likely to make a potentially helpful instructor into someone who truly doesn't care.

Failing to recognize abstractions for what they are can lead to a great deal of unnecessary grief. We know parents who were convinced that their child was abnormal because she hadn't learned to talk by the age of two. When we tried to tell them that some children begin talking later than others and that there was nothing to worry about, the parents wouldn't accept our help. "But something must be wrong with Sally," they said, pointing to a book on child development. "It says right here that children should be talking by one year, and Sally only makes funny noises." What the parent had failed to do was read the first chapters of the book, in which the authors stressed that the term *child* is an abstraction—that there's no such thing as the "typical" child because each one is an individual.

Confusing others Have you ever been disappointed with the way a haircut turned out? In spite of your instructions—"not too short," for example—you got up from the chair with a style unlike anything you wanted. Although the problem might have come from choosing a stylist who should have become a butcher, it's more likely that your instructions weren't clear enough. Terms like "not too short" or "more casual" are just too abstract to paint a clear picture of what you had in mind.

Of course, overly abstract explanations can cause problems of a more serious nature. Imagine the lack of understanding that could come from vague complaints such as:

A: *We never do anything that's fun anymore.*
B: *What do you mean?*
A: *We used to do lots of unusual things, but now it's the same old stuff, over and over.*
B: *But last week we went on that camping trip, and tomorrow we're going to that party where we'll meet all sorts of new people. Those are new things.*
A: *That's not what I mean. I'm talking about* really *unusual stuff.*
B: (becoming confused and a little impatient) *Like what? Taking hard drugs or going over Niagara Falls in a barrel?*
A: *Don't be stupid. All I'm saying is that we're in a rut. We should be living more exciting lives.*
B: *Well, I don't know what you want.*

Overly abstract language also leads to confusing directions:

Teacher: *I hope you'll do a thorough job on this paper.*
Student: *When you say thorough, how long should it be?*
T: *Long enough to cover the topic thoroughly.*
S: *How many sources should I look at when I'm researching it?*

T: *You should use several—enough to show me that you've really explored the subject.*
S: *And what style should I use to write it?*
T: *One that's scholarly but not too formal.*
S: *Arrgh!!!*

Along with unclear complaints and vague instructions, even appreciations can suffer from being expressed in overly abstract terms. Psychologists have established that behaviors that are reinforced will recur with increased frequency. This means that your statements of appreciation will encourage others to keep acting in ways you like. But if they don't know just what it is that you appreciate, the chances of that behavior being repeated are lessened. There's a big difference between "I appreciate your being so nice" and "I appreciate the way you spent that time talking to me when I was upset."

Bypassing   Bypassing occurs when people unintentionally use the same word to mean different things or use different words to represent the same thing. Have you ever gotten angry at a friend who calls to say, "I'll be a little late for our date," and then keeps you waiting an hour? This mix-up about the relative term *little* typifies bypassing. So does the argument we once heard between two students, one black and one white, who were talking about a particular model of car. The black student insisted the car was "bad," while the white claimed it was "great." After a few minutes they finally realized that they both liked the auto, but that the terms they chose to express themselves suggested a disagreement. Problems of bypassing such as these are much more likely to occur when we use abstract language since there's less possibility of checking terms against observable events.

Confusing yourself   Overly abstract language can even leave you unclear about your own thoughts. At one time or another we've all felt dissatisfied with ourselves and others. Often these dissatisfactions show up as thoughts such as "I've got to get better organized" or "She's been acting strangely lately." Sometimes abstract statements such as these are shorthand for specific behaviors that we can easily identify; but in other cases we'd have a hard time clearly explaining what we'd have to do to get organized or what the strange behavior is. And without clear ideas of these concepts it's hard to begin changing matters. Instead, the tendency is to go around in mental circles, feeling vaguely dissatisfied without knowing exactly what is wrong or how to improve matters.

Avoiding overly abstract thinking and language   If abstract language is often a problem, what can you do to reduce its inappropriate use in your life? Probably the best answer is to pay attention to your everyday conversations and thoughts. Every so often—especially when your emotions are strong—ask yourself whether you can translate your language down the abstraction ladder to less vague terms.

You can do this by learning to make *behavioral descriptions* of your problems, goals, appreciations, complaints, and requests. We use the word *behavioral* because descriptions of this sort move down the abstraction ladder to describe the specific, observable objects and actions about which we're thinking.

It's hard to overestimate the value of specific, behavioral language, for speaking in this way vastly increases the chance not only of you thinking clearly about what's on your mind, but also of others understanding you. A behavioral description should include three elements.

Who is involved?   At first the answer to this question might seem simple. If you're thinking about a personal problem or goal, you might reply "I am"; if you're expressing appreciation, complaining, or making a request of another person, then he or she would be the one who is involved. Although the question of involvement may be easy, it often calls for more detail. Ask yourself whether the problem or goal you're thinking about involves an entire category of people (women, salespeople, strangers), a subclass of the group (attractive women, rude salespeople, strangers you'd like to meet), or a specific person (Jane Doe, the salesclerk at a particular store, a new person in your neighborhood). If you're talking to another person, consider whether your appreciation, complaint, or request is directed solely at him or her or whether it also involves others.

In what circumstances does the behavior occur? You can identify the circumstances by answering several questions. In what places does the behavior occur? Does it occur at any particular times? When you are discussing particular subjects? Is there anything special about you when it occurs: are you tired, embarrassed, busy? Do you feel good or bad about your physical appearance? Is there any common trait shared by the other person or people involved? Are you friendly or hostile, straightforward or manipulative, nervous or confident? In other words, if the behavior you're describing doesn't occur all the time (and few do), you need to pin down what circumstances set this situation apart from other ones.

What behaviors are involved? While terms such as "more cooperative" and "helpful" might sound like concrete descriptions of behavior, they are usually too vague to do a clear job of explaining what's on your mind. Behaviors must be *observable*, ideally both to you and to others. For instance, moving down the abstraction ladder from the rela-

tively vague term "helpful," you might come to behaviors such as "does the dishes every other day," "volunteers to help me with my studies," or "fixes dinner once or twice a week without being asked." It's easy to see that terms like these are easier for both you and others to understand than are more vague abstractions.

There is one exception to the rule that behaviors should be observable, and that involves the internal processes of thoughts and emotions. For instance, in describing what happens to you when a friend has kept you waiting for a long time, you might say "My stomach felt like it was in knots—I was really worried. I kept thinking that you had forgotten and that I wasn't important enough to you for you to remember our date." What you're doing when offering such a description is to make unobservable events clear.

You can get a clearer idea of the value of behavioral descriptions by looking at the examples we've provided. Notice how much more clearly they explain the speaker's thought than do the vague terms.

One valuable type of behavioral description is the *operational definition*. Instead of defining a word with more words, an operational definition points, as it were, to the behaviors, actions, or properties that a word signifies.

We use operational definitions all the time: "The student union is that building with all the bikes in front"; "What I'd like more than anything is thirty acres of land on the Columbia River"; "My idea of a good time is eating a triple-decker, three-flavor, chocolate-dipped ice cream cone." Each of these statements is relatively clear; rather than using vague, more abstract language they tell in observable terms just what the speaker is talking about. Hayakawa points out that the best examples of operational definitions in our everyday lives are found in

	Abstract Description	Behavioral Description			Remarks
		Who Is Involved	*In What Circumstances*	*Specific Behaviors*	
Problem	I'm no good at meeting strangers.	People I'd like to date	When I meet them at parties or at school	Think to myself, "They'd never want to date me." Also, I don't originate conversations.	Behavioral description more clearly identifies thoughts and behaviors to change.
Goal	I'd like to be more assertive.	Telephone and door-to-door solicitors	When I don't want the product or can't afford it	Instead of apologizing or explaining, say "I'm not interested" and keep repeating this until they go away.	Behavioral description clearly outlines how to act; abstract description doesn't.
Appreciation	"You've been a great boss."	(no clarification necessary)	When I've needed to change my schedule because of school exams or assignments	"You've rearranged my hours cheerfully."	Give both abstract and behavioral descriptions for best results.
Complaint	"I don't like some of the instructors around here."	Professors A and B	In class when students ask questions the professors think are stupid	Either answer in a sarcastic voice (you might demonstrate), or accuse us of not studying hard enough	If talking to A or B, use only behavioral description. With others, use both abstract and behavioral descriptions.
Request	"Quit bothering me!"	You and your friends, X and Y	When I'm studying for exams	Instead of asking me over and over to party with you, I wish you'd accept my comment that I need to study and leave me to do it.	Behavioral description will reduce defensiveness and make it clear that you don't *always* want to be left alone.

cookbooks. They describe a dish by telling you what ingredients are combined in what amounts by what operations. ("To make a pizza, begin with the crust. Mix ¼ cup water with 2 cups flour . . . ")

But as we've already seen, some definitions aren't operational. They never point down the ladder of abstraction to more clearly understandable operations; instead, they only explain words with more words. A non-operational, highly abstract cookbook might define a pizza as "a delectable, flavorful treat that is both hearty and subtle."

This example illustrates both the advantages and limitations of operational definitions. On one hand, they paint a very clear picture of what you're talking about, leaving very little to the listener's imagination. This is important when you remember our discussion in Chapter 1 of how easy it is for others to misinterpret our words. On the other hand, operational definitions leave out some qualities that lend an emotional element to communication. While the recipe for pizza might tell you *how* to make one, it's not likely to make you *want* to eat it. Figurative language is appropriate at times. You're much more likely to win your true love's affection by reciting poetry than by talking about how your blood pressure changes whenever you're together. The trick, then, isn't to use just abstract or only specific language, but rather to use each when it will best suit your needs.

Troublesome Language

So far we have been talking about general characteristics of language. Certain types of words are especially likely to create problems, and thus deserve special attention. We'll examine them now.

Polarization Some language fosters a strong tendency to polarize objects, to see matters as "black" or "white," as either one thing or the other. Most objects, however, can only be categorized between the two extremes. How does language polarize the world? It provides a vocabulary with few midpoints and a great many opposites.

Try the following short exercise. First, write down the opposite of each of the following words:

tall _____

heavy _____

happy _____

strong _____

legal _____

This exercise probably took you no more than a few seconds. Now, write down the word that represents the *midpoint* between the two opposites. Did you find the second task easy? Probably not. In fact, you might have been unable to provide meaningful midpoints at all.

What's the midpoint between "tall" and "short"? *Average?* That's not very descriptive. In fact, most of the midpoint adjectives that could be used in this exercise are non-specific and vague.

Fact-inference confusion We can make statements about things we observe as well as about things we do not observe. The problem is that the grammar of our language does not distinguish between the two. "She is driving an MG sports-car" is *grammatically* equivalent to "She is seething with rage," yet the first sentence is a matter of fact while the second is inferential. While we can directly observe the car and her driving it, we cannot directly observe her seething rage. Any statement we make about rage is based on a few

The problems crop up when we start talking about other types of deviant behavior. We say of a person who drinks too much that he "is" an alcoholic, and we say of people who think bizarre thoughts that they "are" schizophrenic. This person is a drug addict and that person is a homosexual. Others are sadomasochists, pedophiliacs, juvenile delinquents. The English language is constructed in such a way that we speak of people being (certain things) when all we know is that they do certain things . . .

That kind of identity is a myth. Admittedly, if a person believes the myth, the chances rise that he will assume the appropriate, narrowly defined role. Believing that one is an addict, an alocholic, a schizophrenic, or a homosexual can result in relinquishing the search for change and becoming imprisoned in the role.

Edward Sagarian

observations and conclusions drawn from those observations.

There's nothing wrong with making inferences as long as we identify them as such. The danger comes when we confuse them with facts, which are (in fact) quite different. Facts are based on observations, whereas inferential statements may not be; factual statements can only be made by the observer, whereas anyone can make an inferential statement; facts are certain, whereas inferences are only probable; and facts are directly verifiable, whereas inferences are not.

Allness No one can say everything about anything; yet our language, especially the word "is," makes this statement seem true. "John is a poor student." Is that all John is?

Could John also be a father, a son, a mechanic, a taxpayer, a movie-goer, or a friend? The statement that John is a poor student implies two erroneous ideas: (1) a poor student is *all* John is, and (2) this information is all people need to know about John to understand him *completely*.

Static evaluation When people form a statement about a person, event, or thing, they tend to hold the opinion for a long period of time, and to avoid changing it, even though what it refers to may change a great deal. "John is a poor student" may suggest that John was, and will always be a poor student. One may reasonably ask *when* was John a poor student, and in *what* classes?

The confusing nature of language often leads people to cling to a label even after it is no longer accurate. Saying that "John is handsome, boring, or immature," isn't as correct as saying, "The John I encountered yesterday seemed to be . . . " There's a big difference between saying, "Beth is a phony" and "Beth seemed phony the other night." The second statement describes the way someone behaved at one point in time, and the first categorizes Beth as if she had always been a phony. This kind of verbal generalizing may cause teachers to think of students as "slow learners" or "troublemakers" because of past test scores or reports.

Edward Sagarian (1976) writes about an unconscious language habit that imposes a static view of others. Why is it, he asks, that we say "he *has* a cold," but say "he *is* a convict" or homosexual, slow learner, or any other set of behaviors that are also not necessarily permanent? Sagarian argues that such linguistic labeling leads us to typecast others, and in some cases force them to perpetuate behaviors that could be changed.

Describing John as "boring" (you can substitute "friendly," "immature," or many other adjectives) is less correct than saying, "The John I encountered yesterday seemed to me to be . . . " The second type of statement describes the way someone behaved at one point and the first categorizes him as if he had always been that way.

Albert Korzybski (1933) suggested the linguistic device of dating to reduce static evaluation. He suggested adding a subscript whenever appropriate to show the transitory nature of many objects and behaviors. For example, a teacher might write as an evaluation of a student: "Susan$_{May\ 12}$ had difficulty cooperating with her classmates." While the actual device of subscripting is awkward in writing and impractical in conversation, the idea it represents can still be used. Instead of saying "You are self-centered!," a more accurate statement might be "You've certainly been self-centered for the last few weeks." (Even the amended statement has its problems, some of which we'll discuss in this chapter and some of which will be covered in Chapter 10.)

Equivocal words Some statements, termed *equivocal*, are prone to more than one interpretation. Misunderstandings from equivocal words happen almost every day, usually when we least expect them. Not long ago we ordered dinner in a Mexican restaurant and noticed that the menu described each item as coming with rice or beans. We asked the waitress for a "tostada with beans." But when the order arrived, we were surprised to find that instead of a beef tostada with beans on the side, the waitress has brought a tostada *filled* with beans. At first we were angry at her for botching a simple order, but then we realized that it was as much our fault for not making the order clear as it was hers for not checking.

Often equivocal word problems are more serious. A nurse gave one of his patients a real scare when he told him that he "wouldn't be needing" his robe, books, and shaving materials any more. After that statement, the patient became quiet and moody for no apparent reason. When the nurse finally asked the patient why, he discovered that his statement led the poor man to think he was going to die soon although he had really meant that he'd be going home soon.

Many words can be interpreted in a number of ways. A good rule to remember for avoiding such misunderstandings is: If a word can be interpreted in more than one way, it probably will be.

Relative words Relative words gain their meaning by comparison. For example, do you attend a large or small school? This depends on what you compare it to. Alongside a campus such as the University of Michigan, with over 30,000 students, your school may look small; but compared with a smaller institution, it might seen quite large. Relative words such as "fast" and "slow," "smart" and "stupid," "short" and "long" are clearly defined only through comparison.

Using relative terms without explaining them can lead to communication problems. Have you ever responded to someone's question about the weather by saying it was warm, only to find out the person thought it was cold? Have you followed a friend's advice and gone to a "cheap" restaurant only to find that it was twice as expensive as you expected? Or have you at one time learned that classes you heard were "easy" turned out to be hard? The problem in each case resulted from failing to link the relative word to a more measurable term.

Emotive words Emotive words seem to describe something but really announce the speaker's attitude toward it. Do you like that old picture frame? If you do, you'd probably call it an "antique," but if you think it's ugly, you'd likely describe it as "a piece of junk." Whether the picture frame belongs on the mantle or in the garbage can is not a matter of fact but of opinion, although it's easy to forget this when you use emotive words.

Here's a list of emotive words:

If you approve, say	If you disapprove, say
thrifty	cheap
traditional	old-fashioned
extrovert	loudmouth
cautious	coward
progressive	radical
information	propaganda
strategic withdrawal	retreat
military victory	massacre
eccentric	crazy

Newspaper columnist Jim Murray (1979) described how sports fans and writers apply emotive language, using value-laden language in a way that distorts apparently neutral descriptions of contests. Following the pattern described above, he offers several examples:

If you approve, say	If you disapprove, say
The team was hard-hitting	The players were cheap-shot artists
The team was opportunistic	The team was lucky
The team fought hard	The team played dirty
The coach is a wizard	The coach had "all the horses"

Murray finishes with a supporter's view of the press: If the favorite team is rated number one the polls are "authoritative"; if not, they're "hollow" and "viewed with skepticism by knowledgeable people."

Bertrand Russell, the philosopher, provided a good method for seeing how emotive words work: "conjugating irregular verbs." First, examine an action or personality trait, and then show how it can be viewed either favorably or unfavorably, according to the label people give it. For example:

> I'm casual.
> You're a little careless.
> He's a slob.

Or try this one:

> I read love stories.
> You read erotic literature.
> She reads pornography.

Or:

> I'm thrifty.
> You're money conscious.
> He's a tightwad.

Now perform a few conjugations with the following statements:

> I'm tactful.
> I'm conservative.
> I'm quiet.
> I'm relaxed.
> My child is high spirited.
> I have a lot of self-pride.

Fiction words Semanticists use the label "fiction word" to describe terms such as freedom, truth, democracy, and justice. Fiction words make communication difficult because for many people the terms elicit strong emotional reactions that have little to do with dictionary meanings. The danger of such words comes from assuming their

■■■■ Is it any wonder that in such surreal circumstances, status rather than the work itself becomes important? Thus the prevalence of euphemisms in work as well as in war. The janitor is a building engineer; the garbage man, the gravedigger, a caretaker. They are not themselves ashamed of their work, but society, they feel, looks upon them as a lesser species. So they call upon a promiscuously used language to match the "respectability" of others, whose jobs may have less social worth than their own.

Studs Terkel
WORKING

meaning is clear. For example, candidates for office declare that they favor "peace," and many people automatically vote for them, assuming these candidates' election will initiate a new era of international friendship. Later, voters learn that their candidates' ideas of peace involved bombing into submission any country with different governmental policies.

Consider the following statement: "In many cases revolutions are justifiable ways of getting rid of repressive governments." How would people respond to such a statement? Statements such as these are vague—they mean different things to different people. Is this referring to a violent or nonviolent revolution? Or are all revolutions alike? If people defend one revolution, will they necessarily defend them all? And what

■■■■ He can compress the most words into the smallest ideas of any man I ever met.

Abraham Lincoln

about "repressive governments"? Does everybody share the same idea about this term? Probably not, yet few take much time trying to find a common definition. In discussions with statements such as the one above, people speak languages that only seem to be alike.

Euphemisms So far we've discussed cases where people use overly vague abstractions unintentionally. But other instances occur when people use abstractions to deliberately obscure others' intentions. Euphemisms (from the Greek word meaning "to use words of good omen") are pleasant terms substituted for blunt ones. Euphemisms soften the impact of information that might be unpleasant. Unfortunately, this pulling of linguistic punches often obscures the accuracy of a message.

Advertisers provide numerous examples of euphemisms. "Rinsing" and "tinting" hair creates a better impression than dyeing, and "dentures" seem less unattractive than false teeth! "Preowned" cars sound in better condition than second-hand ones, just as "credibility gap" skirts the issue of calling a politician a liar.

The war in Vietnam produced a great many euphemisms, perhaps more than any other event in current history. For instance, "pacification of the enemy infrastructure" meant blasting the Viet Cong out of a village, and "redeployment of troops" and "Vietnamization" both referred to American withdrawal of fighting personnel.

Although more people are developing a healthy skepticism toward euphemisms, there's still the danger that a few high-level abstractions will slip through. Therefore, it's necessary to keep on guard—to ask what those fine-sounding words refer to, and what they mean in specific, operational terms to the person who spoke them.

■■■ STRAIGHT, *strāt, adj.* direct, unbent, even; adjusted; honest, candid, forthright, true, reliable, veracious; clear, accurate, trustworthy; heterosexual. (From the *Thesaurus of Synonyms and Antonyms,* and *Webster's New Collegiate Dictionary*)

We are constantly being compared and contrasted; gay sensibilities versus straight sensibilities; gay lifestyles versus straight lifestyles; gay audiences versus straight audiences; gay press versus straight press; and here at the Greater Gotham Business Council, gay businesses versus straight businesses.

If they *are* straight, *then what, really, are* we?

The Thesaurus of Synonyms and Antonyms *lists the following as antonyms for the word* straight: *crooked, curved, unreliable, confused, false, ambitious, evasive. It lists the following as synonyms for the word* crooked: *twisted, dishonest, distorted, deformed, warped, corrupt.*

If they *are* straight, *are* we, *therefore, all of the above?*

I've considered using the word heterosexuals *when referring to* them, *but I find it too long and too clinical.* Heteros *or* hets *is short and easy to say, but opens us up to being called* homos.

The ad for the Oscar Wilde Memorial Bookstore in New York City says, "Think Straight, Be Gay," a sentiment with which I am in full agreement. But if we think, *and therefore we* are, *what does that make them? Queers?*

Breeders *gets right to the point, and of course we can always use the Yiddish word my grandfather used when he referred to non-Jews:* yenim, *"the others." This, however, can get confusing: sexual preferences and religious beliefs get mixed.*

May I suggest, then, when the subject comes up that we refer to those with different sexual preferences in a term that does not *reflect negatively on us. Instead of calling them* straights, *I propose that we call them* nongays.

Edward Sherman

Language Shapes Our World

In addition to clarifying and obscuring meaning, language actually structures our perceptions. Sometimes the entire structure of the language a people speak shapes their world view, and in other cases the particular grammar or vocabulary they use is the determining factor. We'll look at several of these influences now.

Language and culture: the Sapir-Whorf hypothesis Anthropologists have long known that the culture people live in shapes their

Trevor Howard in *Mutiny on the Bounty*.

perceptions of reality. Some social scientists believe that one's cultural perspective is at least partially shaped by the language the members of that culture speak. Benjamin Lee Whorf and Edward Sapir (Whorf, 1956) asserted this idea in their writings.

After spending several years with various North American Indian cultures, Whorf found that their patterns of thinking were shaped by the language they spoke. For example, Nootka, a language spoken on Vancouver Island, contains no distinction between nouns and verbs. The Indians who speak Nootka view the entire world as being constantly in process. While English speakers see something as fixed or constant (noun), Nootka speakers view it as constantly changing. Thus, the Nootka speaker might label a "fire" as a "burning," or a house as a "house-ing." In this sense our language operates much like a snapshot camera, whereas Nootka works more like a moving-picture camera.

What does this have to do with communication? Because of the static, unchanging nature of our grammar, we often regard people and things as never changing. Someone who spoke a more process-oriented language would view people quite differently, perhaps recognizing their changeable nature. Some cultures, for example, allow their members to change names whenever they wish. We can speculate that this practice might make it easier to see that others change over time, and in the same way it might make it easier for individuals to escape the inhibiting effects of an obsolete self-concept.

The Sapir-Whorf hypothesis has never been conclusively proved or disproved. In spite of its intellectual appeal, some critics point out that it is possible to conceive of flux even in static languages like English. Supporters of the hypothesis respond that while it is *possible* to conceptualize an idea in different languages, some languages make it easier to follow a certain thought pattern than others.

Metaphor: a framework for thought   Within our own language, certain terms shape our perceptions, and hence our behavior. One of the most pervasive examples of this kind of structuring involves the influence of metaphors, figures of speech in which a word or phrase is applied to an object or idea it does

■■■ *Learn a new language and get a new soul.*

Czech Proverb

---

not literally denote, suggesting a likeness between the two. Most of us learned about metaphors when studying literature. We saw that metaphorical language was one way to make descriptions picturesque: We read about babbling brooks, electric emotions, and icy stares.

But beyond their literary usefulness, metaphors are a powerful way of shaping thought and behavior. As Harvard biologist Robert Cook (1981) writes, "Metaphors do more than affect how we understand our perceptions: They actively shape the kinds of questions with which we approach our ignorance." Philosopher Robert Solomon (1981) suggests that the metaphor we use when thinking about love shapes the kind of relationship we seek and the way we behave with a partner. Solomon outlines a number of metaphors for love and describes the consequences of using each.

Love as a game   We often hear people talking about love as if it were a contest in which one person emerges as the winner. The term itself is a common one: the "game" of love. People "play the field," often trying to "score." Strategies—including lying and flattery—that lead to domination are common: after all, "All's fair . . . " "Playing hard to get" is another common tactic. For most game players, relationships are short-lived.

Love as a fair exchange   This view of love is based on the economic model of receiving fair value for one's goods and services. People who adopt this metaphor talk about their relationship being "a good arrange-

A proposal is put forward by a feminist group, the purpose of which is to get husbands and wives to share equally in household chores. The proposal involves having each partner sign a contract which specifies who would do what and on which days. The question is, Can the language of law solve a problem of this sort? It is true enough that marriage itself is a legal contract, but its stipulations are invoked only at the point where the marriage is in the process of being dissolved. Can anyone plausibly imagine an overburdened wife, having failed to persuade her husband that she needs his help, pulling out a contract from the bureau drawer and insisting he live up to its terms, on pain of legal sanctions? This is not marriage; it is the end of marriage. The language of the law is a great and useful instrument, but it is designed for the use of strangers, not lovers.

Neil Postman
CRAZY TALK, STUPID TALK

---

ment," and say they are getting "a good (or lousy) deal" from their partners. When things go wrong the complaint is "It isn't worth it any more." As these metaphors suggest, the overriding question for these love-traders is "What am *I* getting out of this?" The value of the relationship is measured by whether the return on one's investment (of time, energy, money, goodwill, and so on) is worth the effort. We will have more to say about the economic metaphor when we discuss social exchange theory in Chapter 9.

Love as communication Some people (including a few students in communication courses, we fear) measure love in terms of how well the lovers send and receive messages. For them, Solomon suggests, the essential moment is the "heavy conversation." "We really get through to each other," they say proudly. Their "feedback" is good, and "openness" is the ultimate goal—regardless of whether the messages are supportive or hostile. In other words, in the communication model, *expression* of feelings is

more important than the content of those emotions. The result of this attitude is interaction that is all form and little substance: *making* love as opposed to *loving*.

Communication is important in a loving relationship, of course, but as a *means,* and not an end in itself. When expression of feelings becomes more important than the content of those feelings, something is wrong.

Love as work Some people view love as an important job, and their language reflects this attitude. They "work on," "work out," or "work at" the relationship. There's nothing wrong with having fun, but the primary objective is to build a successful relationship in the face of life's inevitable obstacles. Solomon points out that some devotees of the work model pick the most inept or inappropriate partners "rather like buying a run-down shack—for the challenge" (p. 87). They feel somehow superior to couples who are merely happy together, and admire those who have survived years of fights and other pain for "making it work."

Love as a flame Solomon states that "red-hot" lovers act as if they were Mr. Coffee machines, " . . . bubbling over, occasionally overflowing, getting too hot to handle, and occasionally bursting from too much pressure" (p. 94). Partners who expect this sort of emotional fire can become disappointed when things "cool down," and may look for ways to "spice up their relationship." Unfortunately, the likelihood of those flames of love burning brightly for a long period is slim; and rather than settling for mere warmth, these romantic pyromaniacs frequently find themselves looking for a new flame.

Love as banal Banal lovers stand in almost direct opposition to their red-hot counterparts. While few lovers would intentionally seek a relationship based on blandness, this approach is a common one. Bland, unexcited lovers use bland, unexciting metaphors. The word "thing" is overused. It can describe a sex organ, profession or hobby ("doing one's thing"), or a problem. The bland, high-level abstraction that banal lovers often use is "relationship": clinically accurate, but hardly suggestive of any emotion.

Solomon presents other metaphors, including the dramatic model, in which lovers strive for catharsis (often playing before onlookers); the contract model, which emphasizes "commitment" and "obligation"; and the biological metaphor, which stresses that people are "made for each other."

People rarely select a metaphor consciously. In the case of love, the linguistic model we use is likely to come from the models to which we're exposed, both in the media and in our personal experience. Once a metaphorical view of love exists, we tend to behave in ways that support it. We can speculate that one source of difficulty for many couples is the partners' fundamentally different views of how their relationship "ought" to be. What metaphor do you use? Is it appropriate?

Self-concept The words we use to describe people's roles or functions in society can also shape the way they feel about themselves. Much of people's self-esteem is derived from the importance they feel their work has, a perception which often comes from the titles for their roles. For example, a theater owner had trouble keeping ushers working for more than a week or two. The ushers tired quickly of their work, which consisted mostly of taking tickets, selling popcorn, and showing people to their seats. Then, with only one change, the manager ended the personnel problems. The manager simply "promoted" all the ushers to the "new" position of "assistant manager." And believe it or not, the new title was sufficient to make the employees happy. The new name encouraged them to think more highly of themselves and to take new pride in their work.

The significance of words in shaping our self-concept goes beyond job titles. Racist and sexist language greatly affect the self-concepts of the people discriminated against. An article in the *New York Times Magazine* by Casey Miller and Kate Swift (1972) points out some of the aspects of our language that discriminate against women, suggesting women are of lower status than men. Miller and Swift write that, except for words referring to females by definition, such as "mother" and "actress," English defines many nonsexual concepts as male. The underlying assumption is that people in general are men. Also, words associated with males have positive connotations, such as "manly," "virile," "courageous," "direct," "strong," and "independent," whereas words related to females are fewer and have less positive connotations, such as "feminine wiles" and "womanish tears."

Most dictionaries, in fact, define "effeminate" as the opposite of masculine, although the opposite of "feminine" is closer to "unfeminine." Any language expressing stereotyped sexual attitudes or assuming the superiority of one sex over another is sexist, so adding feminine endings to nonsexual words, such as "poetess" for female poet, is as sexist as "separate but equal" is racist.

Whereas sexist language usually defines the world as made up of superior men and inferior women, racist language usually defines it as composed of superior whites and other inferior racial groups. Words and images associated with "white" are usually positive, whether it's the hero-cowboy in white or connotations of white as "pure," "clean," "honorable," "innocent," "bright," and "shiny." The words and images associated with black are often negative, a concept that reaches from the clothes of the villain-cow-

boy to connotations such as "decay," "dirt," "smudge," "dismal," "wicked," "unwashed," and "sinister."

To the extent that our language is both sexist and racist, our view of the world is affected. For example, men are given more opportunity than women to see themselves as "good," and in the same way whites are given more opportunity than blacks. Language shapes the self-concepts of those it labels in such a way that members of the linguistically slighted group see themselves as inferior.

Many linguistic changes beginning in the late 1960s were aimed primarily at teaching speakers and writers a new vocabulary in order to change the destructive connotations that accompany many of our words. For example, "black is beautiful" is an effort to reduce perceived status differences among blacks and whites.

Changes in writing style were also designed to counter the sexual prejudices inherent in language, particularly eliminating the constant use of "he" and introducing

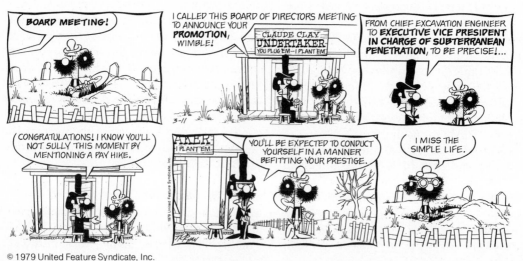

© 1979 United Feature Syndicate, Inc.

various methods either to eliminate reference to a particular sex, or to make reference to both sexes. Words that use "man" generically to refer to humanity at large often pose problems, but only to the unimaginative. Consider the following substitutions: "mankind" may be replaced with "humanity," "human beings," "human race," and "people"; "manmade" may be replaced with "artificial," "manufactured," and "synthetic"; "manpower" may be replaced with "human power," "workers," and "workforce"; and "manhood" may be replaced with "adulthood."

> "Congressmen" are "members of congress."
>
> "Firemen" are "fire fighters."
>
> "Chairmen" are "presiding officers," "leaders," and "chairs."
>
> "Foremen" are "supervisors."
>
> "Policemen" and "policewomen" are both "police officers."
>
> "Stewardesses" and "stewards" are both "flight attendants."

Throughout this book we have used a number of techniques for avoiding sexist language: switching to the sexually neutral plural (they); occasionally using the passive voice to eliminate sexed pronouns; employing the "he or she" structure; carefully balancing individual masculine and feminine pronouns in illustrative material; and even doing total rewrites to delete conceptual sexual bias. Another solution, proposed by Casey Miller and Kate Swift, could be to use *tey* for "he" and "she," *ter(s)* for "his" and "her(s)," and *tem* for "him" and "her." The plural forms remain intact, with the use of "they," "their(s)," and "them." What would happen if we had chosen to implement this solution to the problem?

Language Reflects Our Attitudes

Besides shaping perceptions, language often reflects the speaker's attitudes. In their fascinating book *Language Within Language*, Morton Wiener and Albert Mehrabian (1968) describe several ways in which the forms and structures of verbal expressions offer clues about how people feel and what they believe.

Liking One needn't be a communication scholar to realize that people often express liking or disliking indirectly. We've all sensed another's disapproval or approval without knowing exactly how it was communicated. Wiener and Mehrabian suggest several indirect verbal methods for signifying liking or disliking. The fact that most of them are not chosen consciously doesn't diminish their impact.

Demonstrative pronoun choice While several pronouns can correctly refer to a person, some are more positive than others. Consider the difference between saying, "These people want our help" and the equally accurate, "Those people want our help." Most people would probably conclude that the first speaker is more sympathetic than the second. In the same way, speakers sound more positive when they say "Here's Tom" than if they say, "There's Tom." The difference in such cases is one of grammatical *distance*. People generally suggest attraction by indicating closeness and dislike by linguistically removing themselves from the object of their conversation.

Sequential placement Another way to signify attitude is to place positive items earlier in a sequence. For example, notice the difference between discussing "Jack and Jill" and referring to "Jill and Jack." Or consider

"My hand is doing this movement . . . "

"Is it doing the movement?"

"I am moving my hand like this . . . and now the thought comes to me that . . . "

"The thought 'comes' to you?"

"I have the thought."

"You have it?"

"I think. Yes. I think that I use 'it' very much, and I am glad that by noticing it I can bring it all back to me."

"Bring it back?"

"Bring myself back. I feel thankful for this."

"This?"

"Your idea about the 'it'."

"My idea?"

"I feel thankful towards you."

Claudio Naranjo

---

how people respond to questions about courses they are taking or friends they intend to invite to an upcoming party. In many cases the first person or subject mentioned is more important or better liked than subsequent ones. (Of course, sequential placement isn't always significant. You may put "toilet bowl cleaner" at the top of your shopping list simply because it's closer to the market door than champagne.) Wiener and Mehrabian point out an interesting example of the sequencing principle that often occurs in psychotherapy, where the patient mentions a certain subject first, not because it is more likeable, but because it's the easiest one to discuss. Even here the same principle applies: Positive subjects often precede negative ones.

Negation People usually express liking in a direct, positive manner while they use more negative language with less favorable subjects. Imagine, for instance, that a person asks a friend's opinion about a book, movie, or restaurant. Consider the difference between the response, "It was good" and, "It wasn't bad." In the same way, the positive, "I'd like to get together with you" may be a stronger indication of liking than the more negative, "Why don't we get together?"

Duration The length of time people spend discussing a person or subject can also be a strong indicator of attraction to either the subject or to the person with whom they're talking. If a person asks a new acquaintance about work and receives the brief response, "I'm a brain surgeon" with nothing more, the questioner would probably suspect that either the subject was a sensitive one or that this person wasn't interested in the questioner. Of course, there may be other reasons for short answers, such as preoccupation of the speaker, but one good yardstick for measuring liking is the time others spend communicating with us.

Responsibility Besides indicating liking or interest, language can also reflect a speaker's unconscious willingness to take responsibility for his or her statements, as the following categories show.

The "it" statement Notice the difference between the sentences of each set:

"It bothers me when you're late."

"I'm worried when you're late."

"It's nice to see you."

"I'm glad to see you."

"It's a boring class."

"I'm bored in the class."

"It" statements externalize the subject of the conversation. The subject is neither the person talking nor the one listening, but some "it" that is never really identified. Whenever people hear the word "it" used this way, they should ask themselves what "it" refers to. They inevitably find that the speaker uses "it" to avoid clearly identifying to whom the thought or feeling belongs.

The "you" statement The word "you" also allows the speaker to disown comments that might be difficult to express:

"You get frightened" instead of

"I get frightened . . . "

"You wonder . . . " instead of

"I wonder . . . "

"You start to think . . . " instead of

"I'm starting to think . . . "

The "we" statement The word "we" can sometimes bring people together by pointing out their common beliefs. But in other cases the word becomes a device for diffusing the

■ *Only presidents, editors, and people with tapeworms have the right to use the editorial "we."*

Mark Twain

speaker's responsibility, a device that refers to a nebulous collection of people that doesn't really exist. Just as "you" and "we" often really means "I." "We all believe . . . " means "I believe . . . " and "We ought to . . . " means "I want to . . . " (You might notice that this text uses a lot of "we's." Do you find your beliefs included enough to think the word is justified?)

Questions In the manner of "you" statements, questions often make the other person defensive. They can also be used as a form of flattery ("Where did you get that lovely tie?"), or as a replacement of "I" statements (the most common). Some therapists argue that there are very few *real* questions, that most questions hide some statement that the person does not want to make, possibly out of fear.

"What are we having for dinner?" may hide the statement, "I want to eat out," or "I want to get a pizza."

"How many textbooks are assigned in that class?" may hide the statement, "I'm afraid to get into a class with too much reading."

"Are you doing anything tonight?" can be a less risky way of saying, "I want to go out with you tonight."

"Do you love me?" safely replaces the statement, "I love you," which may be too embarrassing, too intimate, or too threatening for the person to state directly.

In all these cases the questioners avoid the risk of expressing themselves first. Of course, you never use questions this way, do you?

The "but" statement Statements that take the form X-but-Y can be quite confusing. A closer look at this construction explains why. "But" has the effect of cancelling the thought that proceeds it:

"You're a really swell person, but I think we ought to stop seeing each other."

"You've done good work for us, but we're going to have to let you go."

"This paper has some good ideas, but I'm giving it a grade of D because it's late."

These "buts" often mask the speaker's real meaning behind more pleasant-sounding ideas. A more accurate and less confusing way of expressing complex ideas is to replace "but" with "and." In this way you can express a mixture of attitudes without eliminating any of them.

Language reflects attitudes. Language shapes attitudes. Language can clarify or obscure. Symbols stand for ideas, but not always the same ones. Our brief look at language shows that words and things aren't related in the straightforward way that we might assume. Because it's so difficult to understand each other's ideas through words, it's tempting to look for better alternatives. As you'll see in the next chapter, other ways of communicating do exist. But often we're faced with no other choice but to do the best we can with our often inadequate means of verbal expression. Perhaps the most we can do is to proceed with caution, trying our best to understand each other and always realizing that the task is a difficult one.

Sex-roles and language differences So far we have been talking about linguistic patterns that are common for both sexes. In some cases, however, there are significant differences between the way that men and women speak. Many of these differences reflect cultural attitudes regarding the roles of both sexes.

A large body of research (summarized by Berryman and Wilcox, 1980, and Lakoff, 1975) describes the ways in which men and women use language differently. Women, for example, are more likely to speak in a grammatically correct manner. They ask more questions, use more intensifying adverbs and adjectives, more words implying emotion and feeling, make more self-references, utter a higher number of incomplete assertions, and generally talk more than males. Besides behaving in a converse manner, men are more likely to use obscene expressions and expletives.

Most people intuitively recognize the difference between characteristically male and female speech patterns. In one study Cynthia Berryman and James Wilcox (1980) asked students to evaluate statements allegedly made by one group member in a discussion. Actually, there were two different transcripts, each created by the researchers. While the content of the message was the same in both cases, one transcript reflected linguistic features associated with female sex-typed behavior, while the other was characteristic of male language. The "female" message, for example, contained eight intensifiers, six questions, four phrases implying feeling or emotion, and was 384 words long. The "male" version contained no intensifiers, no questions, no phrases implying feeling or emotion, two obscenities, four instances of slang, five instances of incorrect grammar, and was 338 words long.

Subjects were asked to guess the sex of the speaker. Approximately 80 percent of the subjects described the stereotypically male version as having been delivered by a man, while roughly 55 percent guessed that the "female" version was spoken by a woman. Whether subjects identified the speaker as a man or a woman, they saw the source of the "male" message as being more masculine, more commanding, and less accomodating than the source of the "female" message. The authors attribute the impression of lesser command for the "female" version to the use of questions and incomplete assertions. They speculate that the absence of questions and unfinished sentences as well as the inclusion of obscenities probably contributed to the perception of the male sex-typical speaker as more commanding.

Research shows that the language a speaker uses reflects his or her psychological orientation. Donald Ellis and Linda McCallister (1980) used the Bem Sex-Role Inventory described in Chapter 3 (see pages 70–71) to identify subjects as one of the following sex-types: masculine, feminine, or androgynous. They then observed the language behavior of these subjects in group discussions to determine whether each sex-type used a characteristic language pattern.

The results showed that language does, in fact, reflect sex-type. One area in which this became apparent was relational control. Whenever individuals interact their messages have implications for how the power in their relationship will be distributed. Messages can express dominance ("one-up"), submissiveness ("one-down"), or equivalence (mutual identification). Ellis and McCallister found that the masculine sex-type subjects used significantly more dominance language than either feminine or androgynous group members. Feminine members expressed slightly more submissive behaviors and more equivalence behaviors than the androgynous members, and their submissiveness and equivalence were much greater than the masculine subjects.

The patterns of interaction between members were also revealing. Masculine subjects engaged in a pattern that the authors de-scribed as "competitive symmetry": A masculine sex-type would respond to another member's bid for control with a counter-attempt to dominate the relationship, resulting in an almost continuous series of "one-up" interactions. Feminine sex-type subjects responded to another's bid for control unpredictably, using dominance, submission, and equivalence behaviors in an almost random fashion. Androgynous individuals behaved in a more predictable pattern: They most frequently met another's bid for dominance with a symmetrical attempt at control, but then moved quickly toward an equivalent relationship, sometimes acting deferentially during a transitional stage. Ellis and McCallister characterize this approach as more workable and efficient than either the sex-typically masculine or feminine styles.

As you read the foregoing information, it's important to realize that "masculinity" and "femininity" are culturally recognized sex-roles, and are not necessarily gender-related. For instance, at one time or another we have classified some speakers as "feminine men" or "masculine women." It is tempting to quarrel with Bem's use of the terms "masculine" and "feminine," arguing that these terms perpetuate stereotyping. Whatever descriptors one uses, the overriding point remains: Language reflects a speaker's attitudes.

Readings

Alexander, Hubert G. *Meaning in Language.* Glenview, Ill.: Scott, Foresman and Co., 1969.

*Berryman, Cynthia L., and James R. Wilcox. "Attitudes Toward Male and Female Speech: Experiments on the Effects of Sex-Typical Language." *Western Journal of Speech Communication* 44 (1980): 50–59.

Bois, J. Samuel. *The Art of Awareness.* Dubuque, Iowa: Wm. C. Brown, 1973.

Chase, Stuart. *The Tyranny of Words*. New York: Harvest Books, 1938.

Clark, Virginia P., Paul A. Eschholz, and Alfred F. Rosa, eds. *Language: Introductory Readings*, 2nd Ed. New York: St. Martin's Press, 1977.

*Condon, John C. *Semantics and Communication*, 2nd Ed. New York: Macmillan, 1975.

Cook, Robert E. "Pin Cherry Perceptions." *Natural History* 90 (November 1981): 97–102.

Davis, Ossie. "The English Language Is My Enemy." In *Language: Concepts and Processes*, Joseph A. DeVito, ed. Englewood Cliffs, N.J.: Prentice-Hall, 1973.

DeVito, Joseph A., ed. *Language: Concepts and Processes*. Englewood Cliffs, N.J.: Prentice-Hall, 1973.

Donohue, William A. "Development of a Model of Rule Use in Negotiation Interaction." *Communication Monographs* 48 (1981): 106–120.

*Donohue, William A., Donald P. Cushman, and Robert E. Nofsinger, Jr. "Creating and Confronting Social Order: A Comparison of Rules Perspectives." *Western Journal of Speech Communication* 44 (1980): 5–19.

*Eakins, Barbara Westrook, and R. Gene Eakins. *Sex Differences in Human Communication*. Boston: Houghton Mifflin, 1978.

Ellis, Donald G., and Linda McCallister. "Relational Control Sequences in Sex-Typed and Androgynous Groups." *Western Journal of Speech Communication* 44 (1980): 35–49.

Fabun, Don. *Communications: The Transfer of Meaning*. Beverly Hills, Calif.: Glencoe Press, 1968.

Francis, W. Nelson. "Word-Making: Some Sources of New Words." In *Language: Introductory Readings*, 2nd Ed., Virginia P. Clark, Paul A. Eschholz, and Alfred F. Rosa, eds. New York: St. Martin's Press, 1977.

Hayakawa, S. I. *Language in Thought and Action*. New York: Harcourt, Brace and Jovanovich, 1964.

Hayakawa, S. I. *The Use and Misuse of Language*. Greenwich, Conn.: Fawcett Books, 1962.

Hogan, Patricia. "A Woman Is Not a Girl and Other Lessons in Corporate Speech." *Business and Society Review* 14 (1975): 34–38.

Korzybski, Alfred. *Science and Sanity*. Lancaster, Penn.: Science Press Printing Co., 1933.

Lakoff, Robin. *Language and Woman's Place*. New York: Harper Colophon Books, 1975.

Markel, Norman N., Joseph F. Long, and Thomas J. Saine. "Sex Effects in Conversational Interaction: Another Look at Male Dominance." *Human Communication Research* 2 (1976): 356–364.

Miller, Casey, and Kate Swift. "One Small Step for Genkind." *New York Times Magazine* (April 16, 1972). Reprinted in *Language: Concepts and Processes*. Joseph A. DeVito, ed. Englewood Cliffs, N.J.: Prentice-Hall, 1973.

Miller, Casey, and Kate Swift. *Words and Women*. Garden City, N.Y.: Anchor Press, 1976.

Murray, Jim. "Two Sides to Every Sports Cliché." *Albuquerque Journal* (Sunday, December 9, 1979): F–10.

Newman, Edwin. *A Civil Tongue*. Indianapolis: Bobbs-Merrill, 1976.

Ogden, C. K., and I. A. Richards. *The Meaning of Meaning*. New York: Harcourt, Brace, 1923.

Rich, Andrea L. *Interracial Communication*. New York: Harper and Row, 1974.

Ritchie-Key, Mary. *Male/Female Language*. Metuchen, N.J.: Scarecrow Press, 1975.

Rosenfeld, Lawrence B. "The Confrontation Policies of S. I. Hayakawa: A Case Study in Coercive Semantics." *Today's Speech* 18 (1970): 18–22.

Sagarian, Edward. "The High Cost of Wearing a Label." *Psychology Today* (March 1976): 25–27.

*Solomon, Robert C. "The Love Lost in Clichés." *Psychology Today* (October 1981): 83–94.

"The Euphemism: Telling It Like It Isn't." *Time* (September 19, 1969): 26–27.

Whorf, Benjamin Lee. *Language, Thought and Reality*, John B. Carroll, ed. Cambridge, Mass.: M.I.T. Press, 1956.

Wiener, Morton, and Albert Mehrabian. *A Language Within Language: Immediacy, a Channel in Verbal Communication*. New York: Appleton-Century-Crofts, 1968.

*Wood, Barbara S. *Children and Communication: Verbal and Nonverbal Language Development*. Englewood Cliffs, N.J.: Prentice-Hall, 1976.

5

Nonverbal Communication

Rudolph Valentino and Vilma Banky in *Son of the Sheik*. (Museum of Modern Art / Film Stills Archive)

■■■ *After studying the material in this chapter*

You should understand:

1. The five distinguishing characteristics of nonverbal communication.

2. The five functions of nonverbal communication.

3. The various types of nonverbal communication.

You should be able to:

1. Identify and describe the nonverbal behavior of yourself or another person in any situation.

2. Identify examples of nonverbal behavior that repeats, substitutes for, complements, accents, regulates, and contradicts a verbal message.

3. Analyze the emotional message contained in selected examples of your own nonverbal behavior.

4. Share your interpretation of another's nonverbal behavior in a tentative manner when such sharing is appropriate.

"People don't always say what they mean . . . but their body gestures and movements tell the truth!"

"Will he ask you out? Is she encouraging you? Know what is really happening by understanding the secret language of body signals. You can:

    Improve your sex life . . .
    Pick up your social life . . .
    Better your business life . . . "

"Read Body Language *so that you can penetrate the personal secrets, both of intimates and total strangers . . .*

    Does her body say that she's a loose woman?
    Does her body say that she's a phony?
    Does her body say that she's a manipulator?
    Does her body say that she's lonely?"

Unless you've been trapped in a lead mine or doing fieldwork in the Amazon Basin, claims like these are probably familiar to you. Almost every drugstore, supermarket, and airport bookrack has its share of "body language" paperbacks. They promise that, for only a few dollars and a fifth grade reading ability, you can learn secrets that will change you from a fumbling social failure into a self-assured mindreader who can uncover a person's deepest secrets at a glance.

While promises like these do sell lots of books (much more than texts!), they are almost always exaggerations. Don't misunderstand: There *is* a scientific body of knowledge about nonverbal communication, and it *has* provided many fascinating and valuable clues about human behavior. That's what this chapter is about. But it's unlikely the next few pages will instantly turn you into a rich, sexy, charming communication superstar. But don't go away. Even without glamorous promises, a quick look at some facts about nonverbal communication shows that it's an important field to study.

Before explaining any further, we need to define our subject. If *non* means "not" and *verbal* means "words," then it seems logical that nonverbal communication would involve "communication that does not use words." Actually, this definition is not totally correct. As you will soon learn in detail, every spoken message has a vocal element, coming not from *what* we say, but from *how* we say it. For our purposes we will include this vocal dimension along with messages sent by the body and the environment. Our working definition of nonverbal communication, then, includes "those messages expressed by other than linguistic means."

These nonlinguistic messages are important because what we do often conveys more meaning than what we say. Albert Mehrabian (1972), a psychologist working in the area of nonverbal behavior, claims that 93 percent of the emotional impact of a message comes from a nonverbal source, whereas only a paltry 7 percent is verbal. Anthropologist Ray Birdwhistell (1970) describes a 65–35 percent split between words and actions, again in favor of nonverbal messages. While the applicability of these figures is limited (Hegstrom, 1979), the point still remains: Nonverbal communication contributes a great deal to sharing meanings.

You might ask how this can be. At first glance it seems as if meanings come from words. To answer this question, imagine that you've just arrived in a foreign country in which the inhabitants speak a language you don't understand. Visualize yourself on a crowded street, filled with many types of people, from the very rich to the quite poor. In spite of these differences in wealth, there seems to be little social friction, with one exception. On one corner two people seem close to a fight. One man—he seems to be a shopkeeper—is furious at a customer, who seems to be complaining about an item he

> ▬▬ *Fie, fie upon her!*
> *There's language in her eyes,*
>   *her cheek, her lip.*
> *Nay, her foot speaks; her wanton*
>   *spirits look out at every*
> *joint and motive in her body.*
>
> William Shakespeare
> TROILUS AND CRESSIDA

has just bought. Two police officers stroll by and obviously notice the commotion, but walk on unconcerned. Most of the pedestrians are in a great hurry, rushing off to who-knows where . . . all except one couple. They are oblivious to everything but themselves, obviously in love.

In spite of the fact that you've never been here before, you feel comfortable because everyone seems friendly and polite. Shoppers murmur apologetically when they bump into you on the crowded sidewalks, and many people smile when your eyes meet theirs. In fact, you notice that one attractive stranger seems *very* friendly, and quite interested in you. In spite of the fact that you've been warned to watch out for shady characters, you know there's no danger here. "Why not?" you think. "It's a vacation." You smile back and both of you walk toward each other . . .

Aside from being a pleasant daydream, this little experiment should have proved that it's possible to communicate without using words. With no knowledge of the language, you were able to make a number of assumptions about what was going on in that foreign country. You obtained a picture of the economic status of some of its inhabitants, observed some conflicts and speculated about their nature, noticed something about the law enforcement policy, formed impressions about the pace of life, and became acquainted with courtship practices. How did you do all this? By tuning into the many nonverbal channels available: facial expressions, clothing, postures, gestures, vocal tones, and more. Of course, you don't have to travel abroad to recognize nonverbal messages, for they're present all the time. Because we're such a vocal society, we often ignore the other channels through which we all communicate. But they're always there.

Before we take a closer look at each of these channels, let's examine some characteristics that all nonverbal communications share.

Characteristics of Nonverbal Communication

Nonverbal communication exists Our fantasy trip to the foreign country demonstrated this fact. Even without talking it's possible to get an idea about how others are feeling. In fact, you can often learn more about others by noticing what they do than what they say. Sometimes you might suspect people seem friendly, sometimes distant, sometimes tense, excited, bored, amused, or depressed. The point is that without any formal experience you can recognize and to some degree interpret messages that other people send nonverbally. In this chapter we want to sharpen the skills you already have, to give you a a better grasp of the vocabulary of nonverbal language, and to show you how this understanding can help you know yourself and others better.

You can't not communicate The fact that communication without words does take place brings us to the second important feature of nonverbal communication. To understand what we mean here, think back to a re-

■■■ *First of all, he had to make it clear to those potential companions of his holiday that they were of no concern to him whatsoever. He stared through them, round them, over them—eyes lost in space. The beach might have been empty. If by chance a ball was thrown his way, he looked surprised; then let a smile of amusement lighten his face (Kindly Preedy), looked round dazed to see that there* were *people on the beach, tossed it back with a smile to himself and not a smile* at *the people, and then resumed carelessly his nonchalant survey of space.*

But it was time to institute a little parade, the parade of the Ideal Preedy. By devious handlings he gave any who wanted to look a chance to see the title of his book—a Spanish translation of Homer, classic thus, but not daring, cosmopolitan too—and then gathered together his beach-wrap and bag into a neat sand-resistant pile (Methodical and Sensible Preedy), rose slowly to stretch at ease his big frame (Big-Cat Preedy), and tossed aside his sandals (Carefree Preedy, after all).

William Sansom
A CONTEST OF LADIES

---

cent time you spent with another person. Suppose we asked you not to communicate any messages at all while with your partner. What would you have done. Closed your eyes? Withdrawn into a ball? Left the room? You can probably see that even these behaviors communicate messages that mean you're avoiding contact.

Take a minute and try *not* communicating. Find a partner and spend some time trying not to disclose any messages to each other. What happened?

The impossibility of not communicating is extremely significant because it means that each of us is a kind of transmitter that cannot be shut off. No matter what we do, we send out messages that say something about ourselves. If, for instance, someone were observing you now, what nonverbal clues would they get about how you're feeling? Are you sitting forward or reclining back? Is your posture tense or relaxed? Are your eyes wide open or do they keep closing? What does your facial expression communicate now? Can you make your face expressionless? Don't people with expressionless faces communicate something to you?

The fact that we are all constantly sending nonverbal clues is important because it means that we have a constant source of information available about ourselves and others. If you can tune into these signals, you'll be more aware of how others feel and think, and you'll be better able to respond to their behavior.

Nonverbal communication transmits feelings Whereas feelings are communicated quite well nonverbally, thoughts don't lend themselves particularly well to nonverbal channels. Think back to the fantasy you just completed. Do you recall the different messages that you sent and received? Most people find that nonverbal communication

113

"Come on, Zorba," I cried, "teach me to dance!"

Zorba leaped to his feet, his face sparkling . . .

"Watch my feet, boss," he enjoined me. "Watch!"

He put out his foot, touched the ground lightly with his toes, then pointed the other foot; the steps were mingled violently, joyously, the ground reverberated like a drum.

He shook me by the shoulder.

"Now then, my boy," he said. "Both together!"

We threw ourselves into the dance. Zorba instructed me, corrected me gravely, patiently, and with great gentleness. I grew bold and felt my heart on the wing like a bird.

"Bravo! You're a wonder!" cried Zorba, clapping his hands to mark the beat. "Bravo, youngster! To hell with paper and ink! To hell with goods and profits! To hell with mines and workmen and monasteries! And now that you, my boy, can dance as well and have learnt my language, what shan't we be able to tell each other!"

He pounded on the pebbles with his bare feet and clapped his hands.

"Boss," he said. "I've dozens of things to say to you. I've never loved anyone as much before. I've hundreds of things to say, but my tongue just can't manage them. So I'll dance them for you!"

Nikos Kazantzakis
ZORBA THE GREEK

---

expresses how they *feel*, unlike verbal messages, which usually relate what they *think*.

You can test this another way. Here's a list that contains both thoughts and feelings. Try to express each item nonverbally, and see which ones come most easily:

1. You're tired.
2. You're in favor of capital punishment.
3. You're attracted to another person in the group.
4. You think marijuana should be legalized.
5. You're angry at someone in the group.

This experience shows that, short of charades, thoughts don't lend themselves to nonverbal expression, but feelings obviously do.

Nonverbal communication is ambiguous Some words of caution before introducing you to a fourth feature of nonverbal communication: A great deal of ambiguity surrounds nonverbal behavior. To understand what we mean, consider this: How would you interpret silence from your spouse, date, or companion after an evening in which you both laughed and joked a lot? Can you think of at least two possible meanings of this nonverbal behavior? Or suppose that a much-admired person with whom you've worked suddenly begins paying more attention to you than ever before. What could the possible meanings of this be?

The point is that although nonverbal behavior can be extremely revealing, it can have so many possible meanings that it's foolish to think that your interpretations will always be correct. It's important to recognize nonverbal messages as *clues* that need to be checked out for accuracy, and not facts. Popular advice on this subject notwithstanding, it's *not* usually possible to read a person like a book.

Much nonverbal communication is culture-bound Besides nonverbal communication being ambiguous, it also varies from one culture to another. Depending on your background, you may interpret a particular nonverbal behavior differently than someone raised in different circumstances. Also, the meaning you attribute to a particular non-

Peter O'Toole in *Lawrence of Arabia.* (Culver Pictures)

■■■■ *Writer (to movie producer Sam Goldwyn): Mr. Goldwyn, I'm telling you a sensational story. I'm only asking for your opinion, and you fall asleep.*

Goldwyn: Isn't sleeping an opinion?

---

verbal behavior may be the same meaning attributed to some *other* nonverbal behavior by a member of a culture different from yours. Finally, although a particular nonverbal behavior may have meaning for you, in another culture it may be perceived as little more than idiosyncratic or random behavior.

Consider the following three nonverbal behaviors:

1. The little finger pointed straight up.
2. A rapid crossing of the index fingers.
3. The drawing of the index finger over an eyebrow after the finger has been licked briefly.

If you are a member of the predominant American culture, these three behaviors would probably appear meaningless. However, as Morsbach (1973) tells us, in Japan each is meaning-laden. The first gesture refers to a girlfriend, wife, or mistress; the second alludes to a fight; and the third is an indirect way to indicate to someone that he or she is a liar. Three examples of nonverbal behaviors that appear random and meaningless in one culture are recognized as patterned and meaningful in another.

Now, consider the following situation: A teacher is standing in front of her class and talking. Some students maintain eye contact with her while others do not. Which children are conveying respect for the teacher: the ones who maintain eye contact, or the ones who don't? Depending upon your own cultural background, the answer may be the former or the latter. For example, for Anglo children, maintaining eye contact is a sign of respect: Anglo children are taught to keep eye contact when their teacher speaks. Black children, on the other hand, are taught that looking is a sign of *dis*-respect.

Finally, consider the following example: A Japanese businessman sits across from an American businessman as they begin to discuss a trade agreement. The Japanese gentleman sits with his feet flat on the floor, his hands in his lap, and his torso erect. The American perceives that the Japanese is uncomfortable, tense, and likely to disagree with whatever he proposes. The Japanese businessman, on the other hand, recognizes that he has adopted a position identified as relaxed in his culture. The meanings attributed to the same behavior differ according to the cultural backgrounds of the participants.

Verbal and Nonverbal Communication

Although this chapter deals with nonverbal communication, don't get the idea that our words and actions are unrelated. Quite the opposite is true: Verbal and nonverbal communication are interconnected in communication acts, although not always in the same way. Let's take a look at the various relationships between our words and other types of expression (Knapp, 1978).

Repeating First, nonverbal behavior can *repeat* what is said verbally. If someone asked you for directions to the nearest drugstore, you could say, "North of here about two blocks," and then repeat your instructions nonverbally by pointing north. This kind of repetition is especially useful when we're describing an idea that can also be viewed visually, such as size, shape, direction, and other such physically demonstrable concepts.

Substituting   Nonverbal messages may also *substitute* for verbal ones. For example, instead of saying, "North of here about two blocks," you could point north and add, "about two blocks." The usefulness of substitution goes far beyond simply describing physical ideas. For instance, the more you know someone, the easier it is to use nonverbal expressions as a kind of shorthand to substitute for words. When you see a familiar friend wearing a certain facial expression, it isn't necessary to ask, "What kind of day did you have?" In the same way, experience has probably shown you that certain kinds of looks, gestures, and other clues say far better than words, "I'm angry at you," or, "I feel great."

In spite of the usefulness of nonverbal communication as a substitute for words, it's often dangerous to trust your interpretations and unspoken messages entirely. Even with the people you know best there's room for misunderstanding, and the potential for jumping to wrong conclusions increases the less you know the other person. Remember our warning: nonverbal communication is ambiguous.

Complementing   Another way in which verbal and nonverbal messages can relate is called *complementing*. If you saw a student talking to a teacher, and her head was slightly bowed, her voice low and hesitating, and she shuffled slowly from foot to foot, you might conclude that she felt inferior to the teacher, possibly embarrassed about something she did. The nonverbal behaviors you observed provided the context for the verbal behaviors—they conveyed the relationship between the teacher and student.

Complementing nonverbal behaviors signal the attitudes that the interactants hold toward one another.

Accenting   Nonverbal behaviors can also *accent* verbal messages. Just as we use italics in print to underline a word or idea, we can emphasize some part of a face-to-face message in various ways: Pointing an accusing finger adds emphasis to criticism (as well as probably creating defensiveness in the receiver); shrugging one's shoulders accents confusion; and hugging can highlight excitement or affection. As you'll see later in this chapter, the voice plays a big role in accenting verbal messages.

Regulating   Nonverbal behavior also serves to *regulate* verbal behavior. By lowering the voice at the end of a sentence ("trailing off"), we indicate that the other person may speak. We also convey this information through the use of eye contact and by the way we position our bodies. Young children are often yelled at for interrupting adults. What adults fail to understand is that children have not as yet learned all the subtle cues indicating when the other person may speak. Through a rough series of trials and errors (*very* rough in some homes), children finally learn how to "read" other people well enough to avoid interrupting behaviors.

Contradicting   Finally—and often most significantly—nonverbal behavior can often *contradict* the spoken word. If you said, "North of here about two blocks" and pointed south, your nonverbal message would contradict what you said. While sending such incompatible messages might sound foolish at first, there are times when we deliberately do just that. One frequent use of double messages (as they're often called) is to politely but clearly send a mes-

*I suppose it was something you said
That caused me to tighten
And pull away.
And when you asked,
"What is it?"
I, of course, said,
"Nothing."*

*Whenever I say, "Nothing,"
You may be very certain there is
something.
The something is a cold, hard lump of
Nothing.*

Lois Wyse

---

sage that might be difficult to handle if it were expressed in words. For instance, think of a time when you became bored with a conversation while your companion kept rambling on. At such a time the most straightforward statement would be, "I'm tired of talking to you and want to go meet someone else." Although it might feel good to be so direct, this kind of honesty is often considered impolite for anyone over five years of age.

Instead of being blunt, people frequently rely on nonverbal methods of sending the same message. While nodding politely and murmuring "huh-huh" and "no kidding?" at the appropriate times, a communicator can signal a desire to leave by looking around the room, turning slightly away from the speaker, or even making a point of yawning. In most cases clues such as this are enough to end the conversation without the awkwardness of expressing outright what's going on. Courtship is one area in which double messages abound. Even in these liberated times the answer "no" to a romantic proposition may mean "yes." Of course, it may also

really mean an emphatic "no." The success of many relationships has depended on the ability of one partner to figure out—mostly using nonverbal messages—when a double message is being sent, and when to take the words at face value.

So far we've been talking about cases where a communicator deliberately contradicts a verbal message with nonverbal signals. There are other times when we unintentionally say one thing with our words and another with our actions. Have you ever tried to look confident when you were really afraid? Often the facade is almost perfect; then, just when you're convinced that you're looking like a calm, cool character, you notice some behavior that is an obvious signal of your nervousness: shaky knees, sweaty palms, quivering voice. This kind of double message is the downfall of many of us at one time or another: students in beginning public speaking classes, or nervous applicants in job interviews, for example.

As we discuss the different kinds of nonverbal communication, we'll point out a number of ways in which people contradict themselves by either conscious or unconscious behaviors. Thus, by the end of this chapter you should have a better idea of how others feel, even when they can't or won't tell you with their words.

Types of Nonverbal Communication

So far we've talked about the characteristics of nonverbal communication and how our unspoken messages relate to our use of words. Now it's time to look at the many types of nonverbal communication.

The face and eyes The face and eyes are probably the most noticed parts of the body.

This doesn't mean, however, that the nonverbal messages from the face and eyes are the easiest to read. The face is a tremendously complicated channel of expression to interpret for the following reasons:

1. It's hard to describe the number and kind of expressions we commonly produce with our face and eyes. For example, researchers have found that there are at least eight distinguishable positions of the eyebrows and forehead, eight more of the eyes and lids, and ten for the lower face (Ekman and Friesen, 1975). When you multiply this complexity by the number of emotions we experience, you can see why it would be almost impossible to compile a dictionary of facial expressions and their corresponding emotions.

2. Facial expressions change with incredible speed. For example, slow-motion films have been taken that show expressions fleeting across a subject's face in as short a time as a fifth of a second. Also, it seems that different emotions show most clearly in different parts of the face: happiness and surprise in the eyes and lower face; anger in the lower face, brows, and forehead; fear and sadness in the eyes; and disgust in the lower face.

3. We learn to control facial expressions early in life. Thus, most of us are fairly successful at disguising or censoring undesired messages (O'Hair, Cody, and McLaughlin, 1981). In spite of this censoring, the rapid speed at which expressions can change, and the inability of senders to see their own faces and make sure they send the desired messages, means that each of us does convey a great deal of "true" information, whether we want to or not.

Two prominent researchers in this area, Paul Ekman and Wallace Friesen (1975), talk

The face is the mirror of the mind, and eyes without speaking confess the secrets of the heart.

St. Jerome

about three ways in which we falsify messages by controlling our facial expression.

Simulating Sometimes we hide a lack of any feelings at all by *simulating* an expression we don't really feel. For example, suppose someone tells you that a friend you know only casually was in a minor auto accident. You may not be particularly upset by this news, but you feign an expression of upset because you feel the situation calls for it. The real feeling you had was close to neutral, and you created the upset expression to meet the demands of the social situation.

Neutralizing At other times we avoid expressing an undesired emotion by *neutralizing* our expression. For example, suppose the doorbell chimes just as you get into the shower. You have to shut off the water, dry yourself, jump into a robe or some clothing, and rush to the door before the person who rang walks off—all in about twenty seconds. Your expression as you race to the door is probably one of anger, or at least irritation. But just as you open the door you neutralize the expression, tone it down. The neutral mask covers the expression of the real feeling.

Masking A third technique of falsifying involves *masking* a true emotion with one seemingly more appropriate. Boring classes may result in half-closed eyes, frequent yawns, and a dull, glazed-over expression, but they also give rise to a common mask for boredom: an "interested" face, one with wide-open eyes, a brow wrinkled to convey thought, and the expression of other more situation-appropriate responses.

In spite of the complex ways in which we strive to control our facial expressions, you can still pick up messages by watching a person's face. One of the easiest ways is to look for expressions that seem to be overdone. Often when people try to fool themselves or others they'll emphasize their masks to a point where their expressions seem too exaggerated to be true. Another way to detect feelings is by watching for expressions at moments when those displaying them aren't thinking about what their faces are showing. We've all had the experience of glancing into another car while stopped in a traffic jam or looking around at a sporting event and seeing expressions that the wearer would probably never show in more guarded moments. At other times it's possible to watch a micro-expression as it flashes across someone's face. For just a moment we see a flash of emotion quite different from the one a speaker is trying to convey. Finally, you may be able to spot contradictory expressions on different parts of someone's face: Eyes say one thing, but the expression of mouth or eyebrows might be sending quite a different message.

The eyes themselves can send several kinds of messages. Meeting another's glance with your eyes is usually a sign of involvement, whereas looking away signals a desire to avoid contact. This explains why solicitors on the street—panhandlers, salespeople, petitioners—try to catch your eye. Once they've managed to establish contact with a glance it becomes harder for the approached person to draw away. A friend explained how to apply this principle to hitchhiking: "When I'm hitching a ride, I'm always careful to look the drivers in the eye as they come toward me. Most of them will try to look somewhere else as they pass, but if I can catch a driver's eye, the car will almost always stop." Most of us remember trying to avoid a question we didn't understand by glancing away from the teacher. At times like these we usually became very interested in our textbooks, fingernails, the clock—anything but the teacher's stare. Of course, the teacher always seemed to know the meaning of this nonverbal behavior and ended up picking on those of us who signaled our uncertainty.

Eyes also can communicate positive or negative attitudes. When someone glances toward us with the proper facial expression, we get a clear message that the looker is interested in us, thus the expression "making eyes." At the same time, when our long glances toward others are avoided, we can be pretty sure that the others aren't as interested in us as we are in them. (Of course, there are all sorts of courtship games in which the receiver of a glance pretends not to notice any message by glancing away, yet signals interest with some other part of the body.)

The eyes communicate both dominance and submission. We've all played the game of trying to stare down somebody, and in real life there are also times when downcast eyes are a sign of giving in. In some religious orders, for example, subordinate members are expected to keep their eyes downcast when addressing a superior.

Even the pupils of our eyes communicate. E. H. Hess and J. M. Polt (1960) measured the amount of pupil dilation while showing men and women various pictures. The results of the experiment were interesting: A person's eyes grow larger in proportion to the degree of interest he or she has in an object. For example, men's pupils grew about 18 percent larger when looking at pictures of a naked woman, and the rate of dilation of women looking at a naked man's picture was 20 percent. Interestingly enough, the greatest increase in pupil size occurred when women looked at a picture of a mother and infant. A good salesperson can increase profits by being aware of pupil dilation. As Edward Hall (1969) describes, he was once in a Middle East bazaar, where an Arab merchant insisted that a customer looking at his jewelry buy a certain piece to which the shopper hadn't been paying much attention. But the vendor had been watching the pupils of the buyer's eyes and had known what the buyer really wanted.

Posture Another way we communicate nonverbally is through our posture. To see if this is true, stop reading for a moment and notice how you're sitting. What does your position say nonverbally about how you feel? Are there any other people near you now? What messages do you get from their present posture? By paying attention to the postures of those around you, as well as to your own, you'll find another channel of nonverbal communication that can furnish information concerning how people feel about themselves and others.

The English language indicates the deep links between posture and communication. English is full of expressions that tie emotional states with body postures:

"I won't take this lying down!"
"He can't stand on his own two feet."
"She has to carry a heavy burden."
"Take a load off your back."
"You're all wrapped up in yourself."
"Don't be so uptight!"

Such phrases show that an awareness of posture exists for us, even if it's often unconscious. The main reason we miss most posture messages is that they aren't too obvious. It's seldom that people who feel weighed down by a problem hunch over so much that they stand out in a crowd. And when we're bored we usually don't lean back and slump enough to embarrass the person with whom we're bored. In interpreting posture, then, the key is to look for small changes that might be shadows of the way people feel inside.

For example, a teacher who has a reputa-

Why have hands? They are, from time to time, useful. This has been, in many cases, established. They are mankind's only really trustworthy vocabulary, the nerves and muscles of the spirit made manifest.

Kenneth Patchen

---

tion for interesting classes told us how he uses his understanding of micropostures to do a better job:

> Because of my large classes I have to lecture a lot, and that's an easy way to turn students off. I work hard to make my talks entertaining, but you know that nobody's perfect, and I do have my off days. I can tell when I'm not doing a good job of communicating by picking out three or four students before I start my talk and watching how they sit throughout the class period. As long as they're leaning forward in their seats, I know I'm doing okay, but if I look up and see them starting to slump back, I know I'd better change my approach.

Psychologist Albert Mehrabian (1972) has found that other postural keys to feelings are tension and relaxation. He says that we take relaxed postures in nonthreatening situations and tighten up when threatened. Based on this observation he says we can tell a good deal about how others feel simply by watching how tense or loose they seem to be. For example, he suggests that watching tenseness is a way of detecting status differences: the lower-status person is generally the more rigid and tense-appearing, whereas the one with higher status is more relaxed. This situation is the kind that often happens when we picture a "chat" with the boss (or professor or judge) where we sit ramrod straight while our "superior" leans back in a chair.

The same principle applies to social situations where it's often possible to tell who's uncomfortable by looking at pictures. Often you'll see someone laughing and talking as if perfectly at home, while his or her posture shouts nervousness. Some people never relax, and their posture shows it.

Gestures   While we can use our entire body to communicate through postures, we also express feelings with just one body part through gesturing. Like other forms of non-verbal communication, gestures can either reinforce or contradict a speaker's words. We've all seen the reinforcing power that comes from certain body movements. For instance, imagine the gestures that would accompany the following statements:

> "What can I do about it?"
> "I can't stand it anymore!"
> "Now let me tell you something!"
> "Easy now. It'll be all right."

It was easy to envision what gestures should accompany each message, wasn't it? You can see what an important role these movements play by imagining a speaker expressing the same words without gesturing. Somehow the speaker would seem less involved or sincere. In fact, an absence of gestures is usually a good indication that the speaker may be feeling unenthusiastic about the subject being discussed.

Sometimes gestures provide a clue to unspoken feelings—ones that even the sender may be unaware of. Sigmund Freud, pioneer explorer of the subconscious, recognized this in 1905 when he wrote, "He that has eyes to see and ears to hear may convince himself that no mortal can keep a secret. If his lips are silent, he chatters with his fingertips; betrayal oozes out of him at every pore." The report of one psychotherapist (Wachtel, 1967) gives a dramatic example of how gestures can provide clues to inner feelings:

Lon Chaney and Lila Lee. (Culver Pictures)

Mrs. L sat leaning back, with one hand holding the other. Her hands seemed to be acting out a struggle to prevent expression through gesturing, mildly reminiscent of the efforts of Dr. Strangelove to prevent his arm from making a Hitler salute. The hand being held continued to begin movements which were prevented by the holding hand.

Of course, such telltale gesturing isn't restricted to the psychiatrist's office. One clear example of someone whose feelings show up through gestures is the fidgeter, who assures us that "everything is fine" while almost ceaselessly biting a fingernail, flicking a cigarette, or bending a paperclip. Even when the fidgeter is aware of these gestures and tries to control them, the nervousness usually finds another way of leaking out, such as toe tapping, leg crossing and uncrossing, or other restless movements.

Besides nervousness, you can often detect other emotions from a person's gestures. It's possible to observe anger by looking beyond a smile and noticing whitened knuckles and clenched fists. When a person would like to express friendship or attraction, but for some reason feels inhibited, you can sometimes notice a slight reaching out and maybe even an opening of hands. We've even seen those who proclaim to all how open and honest they want to be while their gestures suggest something different: talking from behind a hand, folding their arms across their chests, or turning away from us. In one article, Paul Scheflen (1974), a psychiatrist, tells how a person's sexual feelings can be signaled through gestures. He describes "preening behaviors" that draw attention to the sender's body and advertise a "come-on" message. Movements such as stroking or combing the hair, glancing in a mirror, and rearranging the clothing are often signals of sexual interest in another person.

Ekman and Friesen (1975) describe another kind of double message—the "lie of omission." Deceivers nonverbally show true feelings by failing to accompany words with appropriate gestures. This is the kind of behavior we see from people who say they are excited or happy while sitting almost motionless with hands, arms, legs, and posture signaling boredom, discomfort, or fatigue.

Touch Besides being the earliest means we have of making contact with others, touching is essential to our healthy development. During the nineteenth and early twentieth centuries a large percentage of children born every year died from a disease then called *marasmus*, which translated from Greek means "wasting away." In some orphanages the mortality rate was nearly 100 percent, but even children in the most "progressive" homes, hospitals, and other institutions died

regularly from the ailment (Halliday, 1948). When researchers finally tracked down the causes of this disease, they found that the infants suffered from lack of physical contact with parents or nurses, rather than from lack of nutrition, medical care, or other factors. The infants hadn't been touched enough, and died as a result. From this knowledge came the practice of "mothering" children in institutions—picking the baby up, carrying it around, and handling it several times each day. At one hospital that began this practice, the death rate of infants fell between 30 and 35 percent to below 10 percent. (Bakwin, 1949).

As children develop, their need for being touched continues. In his excellent book *Touching: The Human Significance of the Skin* (1971), Ashley Montagu describes research suggesting that allergies, eczema, and other health problems are in part caused by a person's lack of mother-contact while an infant. Although Montagu says that these problems develop early in life, he also cites cases where adults suffering from conditions as diverse as asthma and schizophrenia have been successfully treated by psychiatric therapy that uses extensive physical contact.

Touch seems to increase a child's mental functioning as well as physical health. L. J. Yarrow (1963) conducted surveys showing that babies who have been given plenty of physical stimulation by their mothers have significantly higher IQs than those receiving less contact.

Touch also plays a large part in how we respond to others and to our environment (see Willis and Hamm [1980] for a review of research on this subject). For example, touch increases self-disclosure, verbalization of psychiatric patients, and the preference children have for their counselors. Touch also increases compliance. In a study by Chris Kleinke (1977), subjects were approached by

We can turn now to the safer and more tender intimacies of the dance-floor. At parties, discotheques, dance-halls, and ballrooms, adults who are strangers to one another can come together and move around the room in an intimate frontal embrace. Individuals who are already friendly can also use the situation to escalate a non-touching relationship into a touching one. This special role that social dancing plays in our society is that it permits, in its special context, a sudden and dramatic increase in body intimacy in a way that would be impossible elsewhere. If the same full frontal embrace were performed between strangers, or partial strangers, outside the context of the dance-floor, the impact would be entirely different. Dancing, so to speak, devalues the significance of the embrace, lowering its threshold to a point where it can lightly be indulged in without fear of rebuff. Having permitted it to occur, it then gives a chance for it to work its powerful magic. If the magic fails to work, the formalities of the situation also permit retreat without ignominy.

Desmond Morris
INTIMATE BEHAVIOR

---

a female confederate who requested the return of a dime left in the phone booth from which they had just emerged. When the request was accompanied by a light touch on the subject's arm, the probability that the subject would return the dime increased significantly. In a similar experiment (Willis and Hamm, 1980), subjects were asked by a male or female confederate to sign a petition or complete a rating scale. Again, subjects were more likely to cooperate when they were touched lightly on the arm. In the rating scale variation of the study, the results were especially dramatic: 70 percent of those who were touched complied, while only 40 percent of the untouched subjects were willing to cooperate (indicating a predisposition not to comply).

Despite the importance of touch, our society places less importance on this sense than less immediate ones, such as sight or hearing. Our language is full of visual and aural figures of speech, such as: "Seeing is believing"; "I'll be hearing from you"; "Here's looking at you"; and "Sounding something out." As Bernard Gunther (1968) points out, when leaving someone we say, "See you later," not "touch," "smell," or "taste" you later.

In spite of the need for making physical contact with others, North American society discourages much touching. Anyone who has traveled to other countries, particularly in Latin America, southern Europe, and parts of Africa, has noticed the differences in the amount of contact between citizens there and in the United States, Canada, and northern Europe.

For most Americans, the amount of touching decreases with age (Knapp, 1978, pp. 244–246). Sixth-graders touch each other less than first-graders. Parents touch their older children less often than their younger ones. Within our culture there are differences between the touching behavior of various groups. For instance, men touch each other much less than they touch women. While this might seem perfectly natural to someone brought up in a culture holding that touch between members of the same sex suggests homosexuality, a look at other cultures shows that prolonged hand contact, embracing, and even types of kissing goes on between the most masculine of men and the most feminine of women.

What touching does go on between adults in North America culture is highly prescribed by unwritten social rules. In the 1960s Sidney Jourard (1966) conducted a survey exploring touching behavior. He first divided the body into fourteen areas (such as top of head, face, hands, thighs, etc.), and asked 300 students in which areas they gave and received touches most often when interacting with parents, same-sex friends, and opposite-sex friends.

Jourard found that body contact occurs most frequently between friends of the opposite sex, and is usually confined to upper portions of the body. The data for Jourard's report was collected during 1963 and 1964. During the intervening years there has been

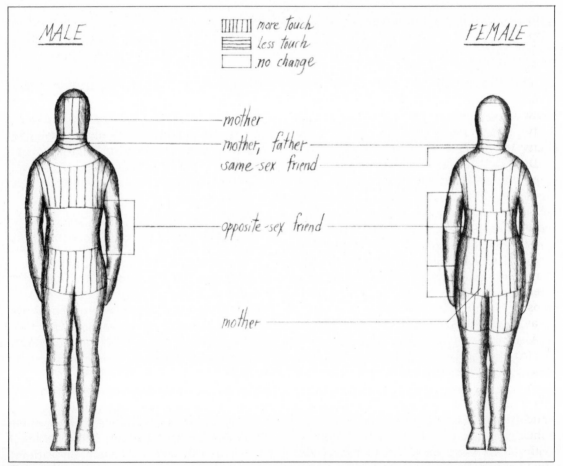

Figure 5–1

much talk about the need for more touch. But has the actual amount of contact changed? Is one group more accessible to touch now than in 1964? Are different body parts more accessible? Do certain people have greater access to others? To answer these questions, Rosenfeld, Kartus, and Ray (1976) repeated Jourard's study twelve years later.

A large number of unmarried male and female undergraduate students between eighteen and twenty-two years old completed a questionnaire asking how often and where on their bodies during the previous twelve months they were touched by their mother, father, closest same-sex friend, and closest opposite-sex friend. The body diagram presented to the subjects was divided into fourteen areas, starting with 1 at the top of the head, and ending with 14 at the toes (see Figure 5–1). Touching remained about the same between parents and their children and also between same-sex friends. However, touch between opposite-sex friends increased.

Data such as these paint a clear, if depressing, view of touching in our society. As young children, most Americans receive at least a modest amount of physical love and intimacy from their parents. The next time most can expect to receive this level of physical caring won't come until they have chosen a partner. Even then, the nurturing seemingly brought by physical contact will most often come only from that partner—a heavy demand for one person to carry.

Associated with (but not always the same as) the kind of love and intimacy we've been discussing is the sexual side of touching. It's obvious that sex can be one way of expressing care for a partner. But especially in a touch-starved culture, sex can also serve another purpose not necessarily connected with intimate love or affection: It may simply be a socially acceptable way of touching and being touched by another human being. While it's possible to argue that there's nothing wrong with making this kind of contact, it's sad to think that a sexual act is one of the very few ways to touch another person acceptably in a manner more personal than a handshake. While we're only speculating, see if this idea makes sense to you: If we lived in a culture where physical contact was more acceptable, perhaps many people could achieve the touching they seem to need without resorting to sex out of desperation. Then sex would be able to exist in its proper role, as one form of contact, to be valued and enjoyed when the time is right instead of being sometimes overused by people who see it as the only way to bridge the gap between themselves and others.

Voice The voice itself is another channel of nonverbal communication. If you think about it for a moment, you'll realize that a certain way of speaking can give the same word or words many meanings. For example, look at the possible meanings from a single sentence just by changing the word emphasis:

This is a fantastic communication book. (Not just any book, but *this* one in particular.)

This is a *fantastic* communication book. (This book is superior, exciting.)

This is a fantastic *communication* book. (The book is good as far as communication goes; it may not be so great as literature or drama.)

This is a fantastic communication *book*. (It's not a play or record, it's a book.)

It's possible to get an idea across without ever expressing it outright by accenting a certain word in a sentence. In *Nonverbal Communication in Human Interaction*, Mark

Knapp (1978) quotes an example from *Newsweek* on how this is done. It describes how Robert J. McCloskey, a State Department official in the Nixon Administration, was able to express the government's position in an off-the-record way:

> McCloskey has three distinct ways of saying, "I would not speculate": spoken without accent, it means the department doesn't know for sure; emphasis on the "I" means "I wouldn't, but you may—and with some assurance"; accent on "speculate" indicates that the questioner's premise is probably wrong (p. 322).

The voice communicates in many other ways—through its tone, speed, pitch, number, and lengths of pauses, volume, and nonfluencies (such as stammering, use of "uh," "um," and "er"). All these factors together can be called *paralanguage,* and they can do a great deal to reinforce or contradict the message our words convey.

Sarcasm is one instance in which we use both emphasis and tone of voice to change a statement's meaning to the opposite of its verbal message. Experience this yourself with the following three statements (first time through say them literally, and then say them sarcastically):

1. "Darling, what a beautiful little gown!"
2. "I really had a wonderful time on my blind date."
3. "There's nothing I like better than calves' brains on toast."

Albert Mehrabian (1972) and others have conducted experiments indicating that when the vocal factors (tone of voice, nonfluencies, emphasis, and so forth) contradict the verbal message (words), the vocal factors carry more meaning. They had subjects evaluate the degree of liking communicated by a message in which vocal clues conflicted with the words and found that the words had

little effect on the interpretation of the message.

Communication through paralanguage isn't always intentional. Often our voices give us away when we're trying to create an impression different than our actual feelings. For example, you've probably had experiences of trying to sound calm and serene when you were really exploding with inner nervousness. Maybe your deception went along perfectly for a while—just the right smile, no telltale fidgeting of the hands, posture appearing relaxed— and then, without being able to do a thing about it, right in the middle of your relaxed comments your voice squeaked! The charade was over.

In addition to reinforcing or contradicting messages, some vocal factors influence the way a speaker will be perceived by others. For example, breathiness in a man causes him to be perceived as artistic, and in a woman causes her to be perceived as petite, pretty, yet shallow. Both men and women suffer being viewed as the same stereotypes when they speak with a flat voice: They are perceived as sluggish, cold, and withdrawn. And both men and women suffer stereotyping associated with an increase in speaking rate: They are perceived as more animated and extroverted. Nasality is probably the most socially offensive vocal cue, giving rise to a host of perceived undesirable characteristics.

The degree to which vocal factors communicate is extensive, as Lawrence Rosenfeld and Jean Civikly have pointed out in *With Words Unspoken: The Nonverbal Experience* (1976). From vocal cues *alone* (people in these studies could not see the person speaking), we can determine age, differentiate "big" from "small" people, and judge personality characteristics, such as dominance, introversion, sociability, and certain emotions (although fear and nervousness, love and sadness, and pride and satisfaction are often confused). Interestingly, from vocal cues alone we can determine a person's status—and we can do this on the basis of *single word cues* (we don't need more than a few seconds worth of a speech sample).

Proxemics and territoriality Proxemics is the study of how people and animals use the space around them. Before we discuss this facinating area of research, try the following experiment.

Choose a partner, go to opposite sides of the room, and face each other. Very slowly begin walking toward each other while carrying on a conversation. You might simply talk about how you feel as you experience the activity. As you move closer, try to be aware of any change in your feelings. Continue moving slowly toward each other until you are only an inch or so apart. Remember how you feel at this point. Now, while still facing each other, back up until you're at a comfortable distance for carrying on your conversation.

During this experiment your feelings will most likely change at least three times. During the first phase, when you were across the room from your partner, you probably felt unnaturally far away. Then, as you neared a point about three feet distant, you probably felt like stopping; this is the distance at which two people in our culture normally stand while conversing socially. If your partner wasn't someone you're emotionally close to, you probably began to feel quite uncomfortable as you moved through this normal range and came closer; it's possible that you had to force yourself not to move back. Some people find this phase so uncomfortable that they can't get closer than twenty inches or so to their partner.

The reason for your discomfort has to do with your spatial needs. Each of us carries

▇▇ *Once I heard a hospital nurse describing doctors. She said there were beside-the-bed doctors, who were interested in the patient, and foot-of-the-bed doctors, who were interested in the patient's condition. They unconsciously expressed their emotional involvement—or lack of it—by where they stood.*

Edward Hall

around a sort of invisible bubble of *personal space* wherever we go. We think of the area inside this bubble as our own—almost as much a part of us as our own bodies. As you moved closer to your partner, the distance between your bubbles narrowed and at a certain point disappeared altogether: Your space had been invaded, and this is the point at which you probably felt uncomfortable. As you moved away again, your partner retreated out of your bubble, and you felt more relaxed.

Of course, if you were to try this experiment with someone close to you— your husband, wife, girlfriend or boyfriend—you might not have felt any discomfort at all, even while touching. On the other hand, if you'd been approaching someone who made you uncomfortable—a total stranger or someone you disliked—you probably would have stopped farther away from them. The reason for this is that our personal bubbles vary in size according to the person we're with and the situation we're in. And it's precisely the varying size of our personal space—the distance that we put between ourselves and others—that gives a nonverbal clue about our feelings. For example, in a recent study by Edgar O'Neal and his associates (1980), the body-buffer zones of male undergraduates increased after they were insulted by experimenters.

Fury, 1936. (Museum of Modern Art / Film Stills Archive)

Anthropologist Edward T. Hall (1969) has defined four distances we use in our everyday lives. He says that we choose a particular one depending upon how we feel toward others at a given time, and that by "reading" which distance people take, we can get some insight into their feelings.

Intimate distance The first of Hall's zones begins with skin contact and ranges out to about eighteen inches. We usually use intimate distance with people who are emotionally very close to us, and then mostly in private situations—making love, caressing, comforting, protecting. By allowing someone

to move into our intimate distance we let them enter our personal space. When we do this voluntarily, it's usually a sign of trust: We've willingly lowered our defenses. On the other hand, when someone invades this most personal area without our consent, we usually feel threatened. This explains the feeling you may have had during the last exercise when your partner intruded into your space without any real invitation from you. It also explains the discomfort we sometimes feel when forced into crowded places such as buses or elevators with strangers. At times like these the standard behavior in our society is to draw away or tense our muscles and avoid eye contact. This is a nonverbal way of signaling, "I'm sorry for invading your territory, but the situation forced it."

In courtship situations a critical moment usually occurs when one member of a couple first moves into the other's intimate zone. If the partner being approached does not retreat, this usually signals that the relationship is moving into a new stage. On the other hand, if the reaction to the advance is withdrawal to a greater distance, the initiator should get the message that it isn't yet time to get more intimate. We remember from our dating experiences the significance of where on the car seat our companions chose to sit. If they moved close to us, it meant one thing; if they stayed jammed against the passenger's door, we got quite a different message.

Personal distance This second spatial zone ranges from eighteen inches at its closest point to four feet at its farthest. Its closer phase is the distance at which most couples stand in public. But if someone of the opposite sex stands this near one partner at a party, the other partner is likely to feel uncomfortable. This "moving in" often is taken to mean that something more than casual conversation is taking place. The far range of personal distance runs from about two-and-a-half to four feet. It's the zone just beyond the other person's reach. As Hall puts it, at this distance we can keep someone "at arm's length." This choice of words suggests the type of communication that goes on at this range: The contacts are still reasonably close, but they're much less personal than the ones that occur a foot or so closer.

Test this for yourself. Start a conversation with someone at a distance of about three feet, and slowly move a foot or so closer. Do you notice a difference? Does this distance affect your conversation?

Social distance This third zone ranges from four to about twelve feet out. Within it are the kinds of communication that usually occur in business situations. Its closer phase, from four to seven feet, is the distance at which conversations usually occur between salespeople and customers and between people who work together. Most people feel uncomfortable when a salesclerk comes as close as three feet, whereas four or five feet nonverbally signals, "I'm here to help you, but I don't mean to be too personal or pushy."

We use the far range of social distance— seven to twelve feet—for more formal and impersonal situations. This is the range at which we sit from our boss (or other authority figures) as he or she stares across the desk at us. Sitting at this distance signals a far different and less relaxed type of conversation than if we were to pull a chair around to the boss's side of the desk and sit only three or so feet away.

Public distance This is Hall's term for the furthest zone, running outward from twelve feet. The closer range of public distance is the one that most teachers use in the classroom. In the further reaches of public space—twenty-five feet and beyond—two-way communication is almost impossible. In some cases it's necessary for speakers to use public distance due to the size of their audience, but we can assume that anyone who voluntarily chooses to use it when he or she could be closer is not interested in having a dialogue.

When our spatial bubble is invaded, we respond with what are called *barrier behaviors*, behaviors designed to create a barrier (or fix a broken one) between ourselves and other people. You may wish to invade someone's personal space and note the reaction. At first the person is most likely to simply back away, probably without realizing what is happening. Next your partner might attempt to put an object between you, such as a desk, a chair, or some books clutched to the chest, all in an effort to get some separation. Then, the other person will probably decrease eye contact (the "elevator syndrome," in which we can crowd in and even touch one another so long as we avoid eye contact). Furthermore, your reluctant partner might sneeze, cough, scratch, and exhibit any variety of behaviors to discourage your antisocial behavior. Finally, in the end, if none of these behaviors achieve the desired goal of getting some space between the two of you the other person might "counterattack," gently at first ("Move back, will you?"), but then more forcefully (probably with a shove).

Writers sometimes confuse personal space with a related concept: *territoriality.* Whereas personal space is the invisible bubble we carry around, the bubble that serves as an extension of our physical being, territory remains stationary. Any geographical area, such as a room, house, neighborhood, or country to which we assume some kind of "rights" is our territory. What's interesting about territoriality is that there is no real basis for assumption of proprietary rights of "owning" some area, but the feeling of "owning" exists nonetheless. My room in my house is *my room* whether I'm there or not (unlike my personal space which is carried around with me) and it's my room because I say it's my room. Although I could probably make a case for my room *really being* my room (as opposed to belonging to another family member or to the mortgage holder on the house), what about the desk I sit at in each class? I feel the same about the desk. It's *my desk,* even though it's certain that the desk is owned by the school and is in no way really mine.

How can you tell if you are territorial? Ask yourself: Is there perhaps some piece of land, some area, which you would defend against others? Are you uncomfortable when someone comes into your room uninvited, or when you're not there? Does the thought of your neighborhood showing an increase in crime make you want to fight back? Does the thought of defending your country sound like a good idea? Ethographers (people who study animal behavior and attempt to make parallels with human behavior) argue that we are, indeed, territorial *in nature;* that is, like other animals, we human beings are biologically programmed to defend our territory.

Territoriality in animals serves a number of functions, such as providing a defended area for food and mating, and a place to hide from enemies. A territory also aids in regulation of population density since only those controlling certain parts of the territory (usually the best pieces of land) tend to mate, thereby keeping the population in balance.

It is difficult to determine the advantages territoriality has for humans as a species. However, certain advantages do exist for individuals, especially for those with high status. Generally we grant people with higher status more personal territory and greater privacy. We knock before entering our supervisor's office, whereas he or she can usually walk into our work area without hesitating. In traditional schools professors have offices, dining rooms, and even toilets that are private, whereas the students, who are presumably less important, have no such sanctuaries. In the military greater space and privacy usually come with rank: Privates sleep forty to a barracks, sergeants have their own private rooms, and generals have government-provided houses.

Physical attractiveness The importance of beauty has been emphasized in the arts for centuries. More recently, social scientists have begun to measure the degree to which physical attractiveness affects interaction between people. Recent findings, summarized by Knapp (1978), Berscheid and Walster (1978), and Rosenfeld (1979), indicate that women who are perceived as attractive have more dates, receive higher grades in college, persuade males with greater ease, and receive lighter court sentences. Both men and women who others view as attractive are rated as being more sensitive, kind, strong, sociable, and interesting than their less fortunate brothers and sisters. And who is most likely to succeed in business? Place your bet with the attractive job applicant. For example, shorter men have more difficulty finding jobs in the first place, and men over 6′2″ receive starting salaries that average 12.4 percent higher than comparable applicants under six feet.

The influence of attractiveness begins early in life. Preschoolers, for example, were shown photographs of children their own age and asked to choose potential friends and enemies. The researchers found that children as young as three agreed as to who was attractive ("cute") and unattractive ("homely"). Furthermore, they evaluated their attractive counterparts—both of the same and opposite sex—more highly. Also, preschool children rated by their peers as pretty were most liked, and those identified as least pretty were least liked. Children who were interviewed rated good-looking children as having positive social characteristics ("He's friendly to other children"), and unattractive children negatively ("He hits other children without reason").

Teachers, unfortunately, share this prejudice. Teachers rated identical school reports, some with an attractive child's photo attached and others with an unattractive child's, differently: Unattractive children were given lower grades, presumed to have lower I.Q.'s, and thought to get along less well with their peers.

Fortunately, attractiveness is something we can control without having to call the plastic surgeon. We view others as beautiful or ugly, not just on the basis of the "original equipment" they come with, but also on *how they use that equipment*. Posture, gestures, facial expressions, and other behaviors can increase the attractiveness of an otherwise unremarkable person. Exercise can improve the way each of us looks. And finally, the way we dress can make a significant difference in the way others perceive us, as you'll now see.

Clothing The way we dress tells others something about us. The armed forces, for instance, have developed uniforms partly as a way of showing who has what particular job and who's in charge. Thus, uniforms are a sort of nonverbal badge that describes the wearer's place in the military social system. Although many have a tendency to criticize the military as a rigid system that puts people into strictly defined classes, in many ways we also use clothing to categorize people.

Think about the people you know. Can you tell anything about their political or social philosophies by the way they dress? A good place to begin your survey is with the faculty at your school. Is there any relationship between the way instructors dress and their teaching style? Take a look at your friends. Do you find that the people who spend time together share the same ideas about clothing? Is there a "uniform" for political radicals and one for conservatives? Is there a high fashion "uniform" that tells the public who's in style and who's out of it?

One setting in which dress is significant is in the employment interview. The impor-

If one wears a shoe known to be a runner's shoe, those knowledgeable in these matters can recognize another of their kind. Shoes are ranked in terms of status in the runner's culture, but for the purposes of achieving recognition as a member, it is sufficient merely to be sporting a running shoe; an Interval 305 New Balance or Brooks 270 will do the job.

Although any running shoe suffices to communicate "I am a runner," the kind of shoe worn does articulate the message further. For example, a person sporting a pair of Eugen Brutting Marathons, a shoe with a distinctive diamond embossed with the letters EB, communicates that his or her commitment to running is serious. These shoes cost approximately $12 more than other popular running shoes. They are known for their ultralight yet substantive construction. A person wearing them communicates that he or she knows a great deal about shoes, that he or she trains long and hard and for fast times.

Jeffrey E. Nash
DECODING THE RUNNER'S WARDROBE

---

tance of this situation has led to many books and articles describing how to behave in a way that will result in a job offer. In a chapter titled "Forget Your Leisure Suit, but Not Your Bra," W. Pierson Newall (1979) concludes that dressing too differently from the interviewer can cast doubt on an applicant's qualifications. In H. Anthony Medley's *The Neglected Art of Being Interviewed* (1978), the author argues that 80 percent of the interviewer's opinion is formed before the first word is spoken. John P. Molloy (1976) refers to a survey of 17 major industries which suggests that any clothing other than the most conservative style can result in a negative rating from interviewers.

In a recent study conducted by Janelle Johnson (1981), 38 personnel representatives involved in recruiting and interviewing in the southwest were asked several questions regarding their attitudes toward applicants' appearance. One question was "What is the most predominant factor influencing your initial impression of interviewees?" Choices

were: physical attractiveness, résumé, appearance (dress), and manners. The majority of respondents (45 percent) indicated appearance as the most influential factor (followed by résumé with 33 percent and the other two items with 11 percent each).

Another question asked was how the first impression created by the applicant affected the rest of the interview. Choices were: not at all, not significantly, significantly, and it is the most important factor affecting the rest of the interview. The majority of respondents indicated that their first impression affected the rest of the interview, either somewhat (42 percent) or significantly (37 percent).

At this point you might be thinking of the old saying, "You can't judge a book by its cover." How valid is such a statement? In an attempt to answer this, psychologist Lewis Aiken (1963) conducted a study focusing on "wearer characteristics." His goal was to see if there was any relationship between the type of clothing a person chooses to wear and personality. Aiken focused his study on female subjects and found that clothes do offer some clues about the characteristics of the wearer. For instance, Aiken found that women who had a high concern for decoration and style in dress also scored above average on traits such as conformity, sociability, and nonintroversion. Women who dressed for comfort also scored high in the areas of self-control and extroversion. A great interest in dress correlated positively with compliance, stereotypic thinking, social conscientiousness, and insecurity. Those who dressed in high conformity to style also rated above average on social conformity, restraint, and submissiveness. And finally, women who stressed economy in their dress rated high on responsibility, alertness, efficiency, and precision.

To see if Aiken's results held for men as well as women and to bring his research up to date, Lawrence Rosenfeld and Tim Plax (1977) conducted a follow-up investigation. They gave a battery of psychological examinations to a large number of male and female college students, and also administered

Drawing by Richter; © 1968 The New Yorker Magazine, Inc.

"A general! Goodness gracious, you don't look like a general!"

a test that measured the subjects' attitudes toward clothes on four dimensions: clothing consciousness, exhibitionism, practicality, and the desire to design clothes.

Upon analyzing the results, some definite relationships between personality type and approach to clothing did emerge. For instance, both men and women who were not especially conscious of clothing style proved to be more independent than their more stylish counterparts. Highly exhibitionistic males were less sympathetic than other groups, and exhibitionistic women were more detached in their relationships. Men who dressed in a highly practical manner rated low on leadership orientation and were less motivated toward friendship relationships, whereas those less concerned with practicality were more success oriented and forceful.

Results such as these are facinating, for they show that to some degree we *can* get an idea about human "books" by their covers. At the same time it's important to remember that research results are generalizations, and that not every clothes-conscious or exhibitionistic dresser fits into the pattern just described. Again, the best course is to treat your nonverbal interpretations as hunches that need to be checked out and not as absolute facts.

Environment   To conclude our look at nonverbal communication we want to emphasize the ways in which physical settings, architecture, and interior design affect our communication. Begin your thinking by recalling for a moment the different homes you've visited lately. Were some of these homes more comfortable to be in than others? Certainly a lot of these kinds of feelings are shaped by the people you were with, but there are some houses where it seems impossible to relax, no matter how friendly the hosts. We've spent what seemed like endless evenings in what Mark Knapp (1978) calls "unliving rooms," where the spotless ashtrays, furniture coverings, and plastic lamp covers seemed to send nonverbal messages telling us not to touch anything, not to put our feet up, and not to be comfortable. People who live in houses like this probably wonder why nobody ever seems to relax and enjoy themselves at their parties. One thing is quite certain: They don't understand that the environment they have created can communicate discomfort to their guests.

There's a large amount of research that shows how the design of an environment can shape the kind of communication that takes place in it. In one experiment at Brandeis University, Maslow and Mintz (1956) found that the attractiveness of a room influenced the happiness and energy of people working in it. The experimenters set up three rooms: an "ugly" one, which resembled a janitor's closet in the basement of a campus building; an "average" room, which was a professor's office; and a "beautiful" room, which was furnished with carpeting, drapes, and comfortable furniture. The subjects in the experiment were asked to rate a series of pictures as a way of measuring their energy and feelings of well-being while at work. Results of the experiment showed that while in the ugly room, the subjects became tired and bored more quickly and took longer to complete their task. Subjects who were in the beautiful room, however, rated the faces they were judging higher, showed a greater desire to work, and expressed feelings of importance, comfort, and enjoyment. The results teach a lesson that isn't surprising: Workers generally feel better and do a better job when they're in an attractive environment.

Many business people show an understanding of how environment can influence communication. Robert Sommer, a leading environmental psychologist, described several such cases. In *Personal Space: The Behavioral Basis for Design* (1969), he points out that dim lighting, subdued noise levels, and comfortable seats encourage people to spend more time in a restaurant or bar. Knowing this, the management can control the amount of customer turnover. If the goal is to run a high-volume business that tries to move people in and out quickly, it's necessary to keep the lights shining brightly and not worry too much about soundproofing. On the other hand, if the goal is to keep customers in a bar or restaurant for a long time, the proper technique is to lower the lighting and use absorbent building materials that will keep down the noise level.

Furniture design can control the amount of time a person spends in an environment too. From this knowledge came the Larsen chair, which was designed for Copenhagen

Conrad Nagel and Aileen Pringle in *Three Weeks*, 1924. (Museum of Modern Art / Film Stills Archive)

> Campuses are full of conscious and unconscious architectural symbolism. While the colleges at Santa Cruz evoke images of Italian hill towns as they might have been if the peasants had concrete, the administration building is another story. It appears to anticipate the confrontations between students and administration that marked the sixties. At Santa Cruz, administrative offices are located in a two-story building whose rough sloped concrete base with narrow slit windows gives it the look of a feudal shogun's palace. The effect is heightened by the bridge and landscaped moat that one crosses to enter the building. "Four administrators in there could hold off the entire campus," joked one student.
>
> Sym Van Der Ryn *(Chief Architect, State of California)*

restaurant owners who felt their customers were occupying their seats too long without spending enough money. The chair is constructed to put an uncomfortable pressure on the sitter's back if occupied for more than a few minutes. (We suspect that many people who are careless in buying furniture for their homes get much the same result without trying. One environmental psychologist we know refuses to buy a chair or couch without sitting in it for at least half an hour to test the comfort.)

Sommer also describes how airports are designed to discourage people from spending too much time in waiting areas. The uncomfortable chairs, bolted shoulder to shoulder in rows facing outward, make conversation and relaxation next to impossible. Faced with this situation, travelers are forced to move to restaurants and bars in the terminal, where they're not only more comfortable but where they're likely to spend money.

Casino owners in places such as Las Vegas also know how to use the environment to control behavior. To keep gamblers from noticing how long they've been shooting craps, playing roulette and blackjack, and feeding slot machines, they build their casinos without windows or clocks. Unless wearing a wristwatch, the customer has no way of knowing how long he or she has been gambling, or, for that matter, whether it's day or night.

In a more therapeutic and less commercial way physicians have also shaped environments to improve communications. One study showed that simply removing a doctor's desk made patients feel almost five times more at ease during office visits. Sommer found that redesigning a convalescent ward of a hospital greatly increased the interaction between patients. In the old design seats were placed shoulder to shoulder around the edges of the ward. By grouping the chairs around small tables so that patients faced each other at a comfortable distance, the amount of conversations doubled.

Even the design of an entire building can shape communication among its users. Architects have learned that the way housing projects are designed will control to a great extent the contact neighbors will have with each other. People who live in apartments near stairways and mailboxes have many more neighbor contacts than do those living in less heavily traveled parts of the building, and tenants generally have more contacts with immediate neighbors than with people even a few doors away. Architects now use this information to design buildings that either encourage communication or increase privacy, and house hunters can use the same knowledge to choose a home that gives them the neighborhood relationships they want.

So far we've talked about how designing an environment can shape communication, but there's another side to consider. Watching how people use an already existing environment can be a way of telling what kind of relationships they want. For example, Sommer watched students in a college library and found that there's a definite pattern for people who want to study alone. While the library was uncrowded, students almost always chose corner seats at one of the empty rectangular tables. Finally each table was occupied by one reader. New readers would then choose a seat on the opposite side and far end of an occupied table, thus keeping the maximum distance between themselves and the other readers. One of Sommer's associates tried violating these "rules" by sitting next to and across from other female readers when more distant seats were available. She found that the approached women reacted defensively, either by signaling their discomfort through shifts in posture, gesturing, or by eventually moving away.

Research on classroom environments is rather extensive. Probably the most detailed study was conducted by Raymond Adams and Bruce Biddle (1970). Observing a variety of classes from grades one, six, and eleven, the principal finding was that the main determinant of whether a student was actively and directly engaged in the process of classroom communication was that student's seating position. This finding held even when

students were assigned seats, indicating that location, and not personal preferences, determined interaction.

Other studies by Robert Sommer and his colleagues (1978) found that students who sit opposite the teacher talk more, and those next to the teacher avoid talking at all. Also, the middle of the first row contains the students who interact most, and as we move back and to the sides of the classroom, interaction decreases markedly.

With an overwhelming lack of imagination we perpetuate a seating arrangement reminiscent of a military cemetery. This type of environment communicates to students that the teacher, who can move about freely while they can't, is the one who is important in the room, is the only one to whom anyone should speak, and is the person who has all the information. The most advanced curriculum has little chance of surviving without a physical environment that supports it.

As we draw this discussion of nonverbal communication to a close, there are some points we'd like to reemphasize.

1. In a normal two-person conversation the words or verbal components of the message may carry far less of the social meaning of the situation than do the nonverbal components. This statistic may have been difficult for you to believe when we cited it at the beginning of the chapter, but by this time you know how many channels nonverbal communication includes. Our hope is that the information and experiences of the chapter have placed some importance on nonverbal communication in your life.

2. When compared with verbal language, nonverbal behavior is very limited. Our nonverbal communication is concerned mostly with the expression of feelings, likings, or preferences, and these usually *reinforce, contradict,* or *accent* our verbal message.

3. Although nonverbal behaviors are more powerful in expressing feelings than are words, they're ambiguous and difficult to "read" accurately. Nonverbal behaviors always bear checking out.

4. Many gestures, glances, postures, and other behaviors are culturally learned. They do not necessarily apply to other cultures or even to subcultures within our society. At this point most research on nonverbal behaviors has been done on middle- and upper-middle-class college students and shouldn't be automatically generalized to other groups.

5. Remember the importance of congruency—the matching of your verbal and nonverbal expressions. Contradicting messages from two channels are a pretty good indication of deliberate or unconscious deception, and matching signals reinforce a message.

We haven't tried to teach you *how* to communicate nonverbally in this chapter—you've always known this. What we do hope you've gained here is a greater *awareness* of the messages you and others send, and we further hope that you can use this new awareness to understand your relationships, improve them, and make them more interpersonal.

Readings

Adams, Raymond, and Bruce Biddle. *Realities of Teaching: Explorations with Video Tape.* New York: Holt, Rinehart and Winston, 1970.

Aiken, Lewis R. "The Relationship of Dress to Selected Measures of Personality in Undergraduate Women." *Journal of Social Psychology* 80 (1963): 119–128.

Ardrey, Robert. *The Territorial Imperative.* New York: Dell, 1966.

Baker, Ellen, and Marvin E. Shaw. "Reactions to Interpersonal Distance and Topic Intimacy: A Comparison of Strangers and Friends." *Journal of Nonverbal Behavior* 5 (1980): 80–91.

Bakker, Cornelius B., and Marianne Bakker-Rabadau. *No Trespassing! Explorations in Human Territory.* San Francisco: Chandler and Sharp, 1973.

Bakwin, H. "Emotional Deprivation in Infants." *Journal of Pediatrics* 35 (1949): 512–521.

*Berscheid, Ellen, and Elaine Hatfield Walster. *Interpersonal Attraction*, 2nd Ed. Reading, Mass.: Addison-Wesley, 1978.

Birdwhistell, Ray L. *Kinesics and Context.* Philadelphia: University of Pennsylvania Press, 1970.

Burgoon, Judee, and Thomas Saine. *The Unspoken Dialogue.* Boston: Houghton Mifflin, 1978.

Byers, P., and H. Byers. "Nonverbal Communication and the Education of Children." In *Functions of Language in the Classroom*, C. B. Cazden, V. P. John, and D. Hymes, eds. New York: Teachers College Press, 1972.

Deasy, C. M. "When Architects Consult People." *Psychology Today* 3 (March 1970): 10.

*Ekman, Paul, and Wallace V. Friesen. *Unmasking the Face: A Guide to Recognizing Emotions from Facial Expressions.* Englewood Cliffs, N.J.: Prentice-Hall, 1975.

Ellyson, Steve L., John F. Dovidio, and Randi L. Corson. "Visual Behavior Differences in Females as a Function of Self-Perceived Expertise." *Journal of Nonverbal Behavior* 5 (1981): 164–171.

Exline, Ralph V., Steve L. Ellyson, and B. Long. "Visual Behavior as an Aspect of Power Role Relationships." In *Advances in the Study of Communication and Affect*, Vol 2., P. Pilner, L. Krames, and T. Alloway, eds. New York: Plenum Press, 1975.

Feldman, Saul D. "The Presentation of Shortness in Everyday Life. Height and Heightism in American Society: Toward a Sociology of Stature." In *Lifestyles: Diversity in American Society*, 2nd Ed., S. D. Feldman and G. W. Thielbar, eds. Boston: Little, Brown and Company, 1975.

Gunther, Bernard. *Sense Relaxation: Below Your Mind.* New York: Macmillan, 1968.

*Hall, Edward T. *The Hidden Dimension.* Garden City, N.Y.: Anchor Books, 1969.

Halliday, J. L. *Psychosocial Medicine: A Study of the Sick Society.* New York: Norton, 1948.

Hegstrom, Timothy G. "Message Impact: What Percentage Is Nonverbal?" *Western Journal of Speech Communication* 43 (1979): 134–142.

Hess, E. H., and J. M. Polt. "Pupil Size as Related to Interest Value of Visual Stimuli." *Science* 132 (1960): 349–350.

Johnson, Janelle M. "The Significance of Dress in an Interview." Unpublished paper, University of New Mexico, 1981.

Jourard, Sidney M. "An Exploratory Study of Body Accessibility." *British Journal of Social and Clinical Psychology* 5 (1966): 221–231.

Keyes, Ralph. "The Height Report." *Esquire* (November 1979): 31–43.

Kleinke, Chris R. "Compliance to Requests Made by Gazing and Touching Experimenters in Field Settings." *Journal of Experimental Social Psychology* 13 (1977): 218–223.

*Knapp, Mark L. *Nonverbal Communication in Human Interaction,* 2nd Ed. New York: Holt, Rinehart and Winston, 1978.

*La France, Marianne, and Clara Mayo. "A Review of Nonverbal Behaviors of Women and Men." *Western Journal of Speech Communication* 43 (1979): 96–107.

Leathers, Dale G. *Nonverbal Communication Systems.* Boston: Allyn and Bacon, 1978.

Maslow, A., and N. Mintz. "Effects of Aesthetic Surroundings: Initial Effects of Those Aesthetic Surroundings upon Perceiving 'Energy' and 'Well-Being' in Faces." *Journal of Psychology* 41 (1956): 247–254.

Medley, H. Anthony. *The Neglected Art of Being Interviewed.* Belmont, Calif: Wadsworth, 1978.

Mehrabian, Albert. *Nonverbal Communication.* Chicago: Aldine-Atherton, 1972.

Molloy, John T. *Dress for Success.* New York: Wyden, 1975.

Molloy, John T. *The Men's and Women's Dress for Success Book.* Englewood Cliffs, N.J.: Prentice-Hall, 1976.

Montagu, Ashley. *Touching: The Human Significance of the Skin.* New York: Harper and Row, 1971.

Morsbach, H. "Aspects of Nonverbal Communication in Japan." *Journal of Nervous and Mental Disease* 157 (1973): 262–277.

Newall, W. Pierson. *One on One.* New York: Focus Press, 1979.

Noller, Patricia. "Gaze in Married Couples." *Journal of Nonverbal Behavior* 5 (1980): 115–129.

O'Hair, Henry D., Michael J. Cody, and Margaret L. McLaughlin. "Prepared Lies, Spontaneous Lies, Machiavellianism, and Nonverbal Communication." *Human Communication Research* 7 (1981): 325–339.

O'Neal, Edgar C., Mark A. Brunault, Michael S. Carifio, Robert Troutwine, and Jaine Epstein. "Effect of Insult Upon Personal Space Preferences." *Journal of Nonverbal Behavior* 5 (1980): 56–62.

Rosenfeld, Lawrence B. "Beauty and Business: Looking Good Pays Off." *New Mexico Business Journal* (April 1979): 22–26.

*Rosenfeld, Lawrence B., and Jean M. Civikly. *With Words Unspoken: The Nonverbal Experience.* New York: Holt, Rinehart and Winston, 1976.

Rosenfeld, Lawrence B., Sallie Kartus, and Chett Ray. "Body Accessibility Revisited." *Journal of Communication* 26 (1976): 27–30.

Rosenfeld, Lawrence B., and Timothy G. Plax. "Clothing as Communication." *Journal of Communication* 27 (1977): 24–31.

*Rosenthal, Robert, and Bella M. DePaulo. "Expectancies, Discrepancies, and Courtesies in Nonverbal Communication." *Western Journal of Speech Communication* 43 (1979): 76–95.

Scheflen, Albert E. *How Behavior Means.* Garden City, N.Y.: Anchor Books, 1974.

Smith, David E., Frank N. Willis, and Joseph A. Gier. "Success and Interpersonal Touch in a Competitive Setting." *Journal of Nonverbal Behavior* 5 (1980): 26–34.

*Sommer, Robert. *Personal Space: The Behavioral Basis of Design.* Englewood Cliffs, N.J.: Prentice-Hall, 1969.

Sommer, Robert. *Tight Spaces.* Englewood Cliffs, N.J.: Prentice-Hill, 1978.

Taylor, Anne P., and George Vlastos. *School Zone: Learning Environments for Children.* New York: Van Nostrand Reinhold, 1975.

Taylor, H. M. "American and Japanese Non-verbal Behavior." In *Papers in Japanese Linguistics* 3, J. V. Neustupny, ed. Melbourne: Monash University, 1974.

Thompson, James J. *Beyond Words: Nonverbal Communication in the Classroom.* New York: Citation Press, 1973.

Wachtel, P. "An Approach to the Study of Body Language in Psychotherapy." *Psychotherapy* 4 (1967): 97–100.

Willis, Frank N., and Helen K. Hamm. "The Use of Interpersonal Touch in Securing Compliance." *Journal of Nonverbal Behavior* 5 (1980): 49–55.

Wilson, Glenn, and David Nias. "Beauty Can't Be Beat." *Psychology Today* 10 (September 1976): 96–98, 103.

Yarrow, L. J., "Research in Dimensions of Early Maternal Care." *Merrill-Palmer Quarterly* 9 (1963): 101–122.

6

Listening

■ *After studying the material in this chapter*

You should understand:

1. Three common myths about listening and their errors.

2. The four components to listening.

3. Four functions of listening.

4. Five causes of ineffective listening.

5. Nine poor listening habits.

6. Twelve guidelines for effective listening.

7. Six styles of listening that can be used to help others with problems.

You should be able to:

1. Identify specific instances when you listen for information reception, empathy, criticism and discrimination, and other-affirmation.

2. Identify the circumstances (with whom and in what circumstances) you listen ineffectively.

3. Identify the poor listening habits you exhibit in each ineffective listening situation.

4. Use the guidelines listed in the section of this chapter titled "Listening More Effectively" to develop a plan for improving your own listening behavior.

5. Identify the response style(s) you commonly use when responding to others' problems, and describe the combination of listening styles you could use to respond more effectively to these problems.

In a world where almost everyone acknowledges the importance of better communication, the experience of not being listened to is all too common. The problem is especially bad when you realize that listening is the most frequent type of communication behavior. This fact was established as early as 1926 when Paul Rankin surveyed a group of businesspersons, asking them to record the percentage of time they spent speaking, reading, writing, and listening. Rankin found that his subjects spent more time listening than in any other communciation activity, devoting 42 percent of their time to it.

Fifty years later, Rudolph Verderber and his associates (1976) discovered that the frequency of time spent listening is, if anything, higher now than it was in the past. These researchers surveyed a number of college students, asking them to record their various communication interactions for several days. The students proved to spend almost 61 percent of their waking hours communicating, with 63 percent of that time devoted to some type of listening to others.

Listening, then, is one of the most frequent activities in which we engage. Despite this fact, our experience shows that much of the listening we and others do is not at all effective. We misunderstand others and are misunderstood in return. We become bored and feign attention while our minds wander. We engage in a battle of interruptions where each person fights to speak without hearing the other's ideas.

As you'll soon read, some of this poor listening is inevitable. But in other cases we can be better receivers by learning a few basic listening skills. The purpose of this chapter is to help you become a better listener by teaching you some important information about the subject. We'll talk about some common misconceptions concerning listening and show you what really happens when

listening takes place. We'll discuss some poor listening habits and explain why they occur. Finally, we'll introduce you to some more effective alternatives, both to increase your own understanding and to help others.

Myths about Listening

In spite of its importance, listening is misunderstood by most people. Since these misunderstandings so greatly affect our communication, let's take a look at three common misconceptions that many communicators hold.

1. Listening and hearing are the same thing. *Hearing* is the process wherein sound waves strike the eardrum and cause vibrations that are transmitted to the brain. *Listening* occurs when the brain reconstructs these electrochemical impulses into a representation of the original sound, and then gives them meaning. Barring illness, injury, or cotton plugs, hearing cannot be stopped. Your ears will pick up sound waves and transmit them to your brain whether you want them to or not.

Listening, however, is not so automatic. Many times we hear but do not listen. Sometimes we deliberately do not listen. Instead of paying attention to words or other sounds, we avoid them. This most often occurs when we block irritating sounds, such as a neighbor's power lawnmower or the roar of nearby traffic. We also stop listening when we find a subject unimportant or uninteresting. Boring stories, TV commercials, and nagging complaints are common examples of messages we avoid.

There are also cases when we honestly believe we're listening although we're merely hearing. For example, recall times when you think you've "heard it all before." It's likely that in these situations you might claim you were listening when in fact you had closed your mental doors to new information.

People who confuse listening with hearing often fool themselves into thinking that they're really understanding others when in fact they're simply receiving sounds. As you'll see by reading this chapter, true listening involves much more than the passive act of hearing.

2. Listening is a natural process. Another common myth is that listening is like breathing: a natural activity that people do well. "After all," this common belief goes, "I've been listening since I was a child. Why should I have to study the subject in school?"

This attitude is understandable considering the lack of attention most schools devote to listening in comparison with other communication skills. From kindergarten to college most students receive almost constant training in reading and writing. Every year the exposure to literature continues, from Dick and Jane through Dostoyevsky. Likewise, the emphasis on writing continues without break. You could probably retire if you had a dollar for every composition, essay, research paper, and bluebook you have written since the first grade. Even spoken communication gets some attention in the curriculum. It's likely that you had a chance to take a public speaking class in high school and another one in college.

Compare all this training in reading, writing, and speaking with the almost total lack of instruction in listening. Even in college, there are few courses devoted exclusively to the subject. This state of affairs is especially ironic when you consider the fact that over 60 percent of our communication involves listening.

The truth is that listening is a skill much like speaking: Virtually everyone listens, though few people do it well. Your own ex-

perience should prove that communication often suffers due to poor listening. How many times have others misunderstood directions or explanations because they didn't seem to be receiving your ideas clearly? And how often have you failed to accurately understand others because you weren't receiving their thoughts accurately? The answers to these questions demonstrate the need for effective training in listening.

3. All listeners receive the same message. When two or more people are listening to a speaker, we tend to assume that they are each hearing and understanding the same message. In fact, such uniform comprehension isn't the case. Communication is *proactive*: Each person involved in a transaction of ideas or feelings responds uniquely. Recall our discussion of perception in Chapter 3, where we pointed out the many factors that cause each of us to perceive an event in a different manner. Physiological factors, social roles, cultural background, personal interests, and needs all shape and distort the raw data we hear into uniquely different messages.

Components of Listening

In his book *Listening Behavior*, Larry Barker (1971) describes the process of listening as having four components: hearing, attending, understanding, and remembering.

1. Hearing. As we already discussed, *hearing* is the physiological aspect of listening. It is the nonselective process of sound waves impinging on the ear and, insofar as these waves range between approximately 125 and 8,000 cycles per second (frequency) and 55 to 85 decibels (loudness), the ear can respond. Hearing is also influenced by background noise. If a background noise is the same frequency as the speech sound, then the speech sound is said to be masked; however, if the background noise is of a different frequency than speech, it is called "white noise," and may or may not detract greatly from our ability to hear. Hearing is also affected by auditory fatigue, a temporary loss of hearing caused by continuous exposure to the same tone or loudness. People who spend an evening in a discotheque may experience auditory fatigue and, if they are exposed often enough, permanent hearing loss may result.

2. Attending. After the sounds are converted into electrochemical impulses and trans-

mitted to the brain, a decision—often unconscious—is made whether to focus on what was heard. While the listening process started as a physiological one, it quickly became a psychological one. An individual's needs, wants, desires, and interests determine what is *attended to*. If you're hungry, you are more likely to attend to the message about restaurants in the neighborhood from the person next to you than the competing message on the importance of communication from the speaker in front of the room.

3. Understanding. The component of understanding is composed of several elements.

■ *And, contrary to popular belief, it is usually the good talker who makes the best listener. A good talker (by which I do not mean the egomaniacal bore who always talks about himself) is sensitive to expression, to tone and color and inflection in human speech. Because he himself is articulate, he can help others to articulate their half-formulated feelings. His mind fills in the gaps, and he becomes, in Socrates' words, a kind of midwife for ideas that are struggling to be born.*

This is why a competent psychiatrist is worth his weight in gold—and generally gets it. His listening is keyed for the half-tones and the dissonances that escape the untrained ear. For it is the mark of the truly good listener that he knows what you are saying often better than you do; and his playback is a revelation, not a recording.

Sydney J. Harris

First, understanding a message involves some recognition of the grammatical rules used to create that message. We find the children's books by Dr. Seuss amusing because he breaks the rules of grammar and spelling in interesting ways, and we are familiar enough with the rules to recognize this. Second, understanding depends upon our knowledge about the source of the message—whether the person is sincere, prone to lie, friendly, an adversary, and so on. Third, there is the social context. The time and place, for example, helps us decide whether to take a friend's insults seriously or as a joke. Understanding depends, generally, upon sharing common assumptions about the world. Consider the following sentences used by Jerrold Katz and Jerry Foder (1971):

   a. I bought alligator shoes.
   b. I bought horse shoes.

Both sentences can be interpreted the same way since they have the same grammatical structure, and may be uttered by the same person (the first two components of understanding). Both could indicate that a person bought two pairs of shoes, one made from alligator, the other from horse, or that two pairs of shoes were purchased, one for an alligator, the other for a horse. However, because of the common assumptions we share about the world, we understand that the first sentence refers to shoes made *from* alligator hides, and that the second refers either to shoes *for* horses or for playing a game.

Finally, understanding often depends on the ability to organize the information we hear into recognizable form. As early as 1948, Ralph Nichols related successful understanding to a large number of factors, most prominent among which were verbal ability, intelligence, and motivation.

A more recent investigation completed in 1979 by Tim Plax and Lawrence Rosenfeld examined the relationship of a large number of ability, personality, and motivational variables to the comprehension of organized and disorganized messages. They found that people who were successful at comprehending organized spoken messages were generally less intelligent, yet more secure, more sensitive to others, and more willing to try to understand them. People who were successful at comprehending disorganized spoken messages proved to be insightful and versatile in their thinking, yet somewhat unchanging and inflexible in their view of themselves. People who were not successful at comprehending disorganized spoken messages were flexible, comfortable in unfamiliar situations, and of average or less than average intelligence.

While it is difficult to draw all these diverse results into a neat package, it seems reasonable to conclude that people who are good listeners are generally more intelligent and less flexible than those who are not good listeners. Also, people who are not good listeners are more comfortable with new situations and more willing to work to understand other people than are good listeners.

It may seem odd that inflexibility is associated with successful listening, at least listening for information. However, most of the research done on the characteristics of good listeners (as little as there is) has used students as subjects. Once we realize that intelligence in students is often measured by the ability to absorb, memorize, and repeat information, then the connection between "inflexibility" and "successful *student* listening" becomes clearer. Students are trained to listen for the information most likely to appear on comprehension tests. There is little emphasis on the student critically analyzing that information.

4. Remembering. The ability to recall information once we've understood it is a function of several factors: The number of times the information is heard or repeated; how much information there is to store in the brain; and whether the information may be "rehearsed" or not.

Research conducted during the 1950s (Barker, 1971) revealed that people remember only about half of what they hear *immediately* after hearing it. This is true even if people work hard at listening. This situation would probably not be too bad if the half remembered right after was retained, but it isn't. Within two months, half of the half is forgotten, bringing what we remember down to about 25 percent of the original message. This loss, however, doesn't take two months: People start forgetting immediately (within eight hours the 50 percent remembered drops to about 35 percent). Given the amount of information we process every day—from teachers, friends, the radio, TV, and other sources—the *residual message*

At a Lecture—Only 12 Percent Listen

Bright-eyed college students in lecture halls aren't necessarily listening to the professor, the American Psychological Association was told yesterday.

If you shot off a gun at sporadic intervals and asked the students to encode their thoughts and moods at that moment, you would discover that:

• About 20 percent of the students, men and women, are pursuing erotic thoughts.

• Another 20 percent are reminiscing about something.

• Only 20 percent are actually paying attention to the lecture; 12 percent are actively listening.

• The others are worrying, daydreaming, thinking about lunch or–surprise–religion (8 percent).

This confirmation of the lecturer's worse fears was reported by Paul Cameron, 28, as assistant professor at Wayne State University in Detroit. The annual convention, which ends Tuesday, includes about 2000 such reports to 10,000 psychologists in a variety of meetings.

Cameron's results were based on a nine-week course in introductory psychology for 85 college sophomores. A gun was fired 21 times at random intervals, usually when Cameron was in the middle of a sentence.

SAN FRANCISCO SUNDAY EXAMINER AND CHRONICLE

(what we remember) is a small fraction of what we hear.

So far we have used the term "remembering" in connection with the long-term retention of information. Some, but not all types of listening involve this long-term recall. There are actually two types of memory: short-term, limited in capacity and lasting from 20 seconds to one minute; and long-term, virtually unlimited in capacity (Wolvin and Coakley, 1982, pp. 42-43). It is possible to move information from short- to long-term memory by rehearsing, or repeating it, as you probably do when you mentally repeat the name of an important person to whom you have just been introduced.

The results of short- and long-term memory differ. A series of studies by Robert Bostrom (Bostrom and Bryant, 1980; Bostrom and Waldhart, 1980) demonstrated that while long-term "lecture" listening is an excellent predictor of performance on a written examination (with little gain contributed by short-term listening), the opposite proved true for oral performance. In other words, short-term listening ability is closely related to measures of oral performance, whereas long-term comprehension is closely related to general measures of mental ability. These studies show that different types of listening skills are applicable in different contexts. "Listening," when used in the context of classroom performance, refers to long-term retention of information; but in the context of a conversation it most likely refers to short-term use of data. This difference helps explain why our feelings about a speaker often change when we need to listen for more than a half minute: We are forced to put what we hear into long-term memory. This might also explain why some students who participate actively in class discussions do not achieve outstanding test scores. Their short-term listening skills are fine, but their long-term recall skills are poorly developed.

Functions of Listening

"All right," you might respond. "So I don't listen to everything I hear, I don't understand everything I listen to, and I don't remember everything I understand. I still seem to get along well enough. Why should I worry about becoming a better listener?" Author Rob Anderson (1979) suggests four benefits that can come from improving your listening skills.

1. Information reception. People who can understand and retain more information have a greater chance of becoming successful, however you define that term. In school the advantages of listening effectively are obvious. Along with the skills of effective writing and reading, the ability to receive and understand the spoken word is a major key to academic success. The same holds true in the business and professional worlds. Understanding the instructions and advice of superiors and colleagues, learning about the needs and reactions of subordinates, and discovering the concerns of clients and other members of the public are important in virtually every job.

Even in one's personal life, the ability to receive and understand information is a key to success. Being a good listener can help you learn everything from car repair to first aid for houseplants to the existence of cheap restaurants. And socially, everyone knows the benefits of being able to hear and remember information about others whom we'd like to know better.

2. Empathy. A listener who was *only* able to receive and recall large amounts of information efficiently would be hardly more likeable or valuable as a friend than a computer would be. While the ability to receive data might be admirable, personally helpful listeners are also able to empathize: to understand and "feel with" the emotions and thoughts of a speaker. An impressive body of research supports the idea that the ability to empathize is an important element in effective communication for many social roles: business supervisors, teachers, therapists and counselors, and of course friends.

It's obvious that listening empathically can be a valuable way to help someone with a problem. But developing the ability to empathize can also have personal payoffs for you as a listener. The most obvious one is the reward of having helped solve another person's problems. But in addition, as an empathic listener, you can broaden your own understanding, and in doing so often learn how to deal with issues in your own life. Just as it's helpful to hear the pleasures and problems of traveling to a new place before going there yourself, listening to another person's experiences in personal issues can teach you what to think and do when you encounter similar circumstances.

3. Criticism and discrimination. In their interesting book *Teaching as a Subversive Activity*, Neil Postman and Charles Weingartner (1969) discuss this function of listening in their chapter on "Crap Detecting." They define a crap detector as someone who not only functions in a society, but *observes* it, noting its obsessions, fears, strengths, and weaknesses. Critical listeners are able to hear a speaker's words and understand the ideas without necessarily accepting them totally. The ability to listen analytically and critically differs radically from the kind of empathic reception just discussed, but it is equally as important. Critical listeners can help individuals and societies understand themselves and recognize the accuracy of their ideas.

4. Other-affirmation. As Chapter 1 notes, a basic human need is to be recognized and acknowledged by others. Listening is one of the most fundamental means of giving this kind of acknowledgement. The act of listening, of *choosing* to listen, is itself an affirmation of the speaker. Whenever you listen to another person you are sending a nonverbal message suggesting that he or she is important. Of course, there are varying degrees of importance, and there are also various degrees of listening intensity reflecting this range of valuing. A brief affirmation can come from pausing to exchange a few minutes of chit-chat with an acquaintance, while a much stronger message of acknowledgment is reflected in your willingness to spend hours hearing a friend talk over a personal problem.

Why We Listen Ineffectively

Given the importance of receiving information, building empathy, critically discriminating, and affirming others, it's obvious that listening well can be valuable for both the

MOMMA by Mell Lazarus. Courtesy of Mell Lazarus and Field Newspaper Syndicate.

receiver and the speaker. Yet in spite of this fact, we often do not listen with much energy or concern. Why? Sad as it may be, it's impossible to listen *all* the time, for several reasons.

Hearing problems   If a person suffers from a physical impairment that prevents either the hearing of sounds at an adequate volume or the receiving of certain auditory frequencies, then listening will obviously suffer. Once a hearing problem has been diagnosed it's often possible to treat it. The real tragedy occurs when a hearing loss goes undiagnosed. In such cases both the person with the defect and those surrounding can become frustrated and annoyed at the ineffective communication that takes place. If you suspect that you or someone you know might have a hearing loss, it's wise to have a physician or audiologist perform an examination.

Amount of input   The sheer amount of speech most of us encounter every day makes it impossible to carefully listen to everything we hear. According to the study cited earlier, many of us spend almost half the time we're awake listening to verbal messages—from teachers, coworkers, friends, family, salespeople, and total strangers. This means we often spend five or more hours a day listening to people talk. If you add these hours to those where we listen to radio and TV, you can see that it's virtually impossible for us to keep our attention totally focused for this length of time. Therefore, we periodically let our attention wander.

Personal concerns   A third reason we don't always listen carefully is that we're often wrapped up in personal concerns of more immediate importance to us than the message others are sending. It's hard to pay attention to someone else when you're anticipating an upcoming test or thinking about the wonderful time you had last night with good friends. Yet we still feel we have to "listen" politely to others, and so we continue with our charade.

Rapid thought   Listening carefully is also difficult for a physiological reason. Although we're capable of understanding speech at rates up to 600 words per minute (Goldhaber, 1970), the average person speaks between 100 and 140 words per minute. Thus, we have a lot of "spare time" to spend with our minds while someone is talking. And the temptation is to use this time in ways that don't relate to the speaker's ideas, such as thinking about personal interests, daydreaming, planning a rebuttal, and so on. The trick is to use this spare time to understand the speaker's ideas better, rather than letting your attention wander.

"Noise"   Finally, the physical and mental worlds in which we live often present distractions that make it hard to pay attention to others. The sound of traffic, music, and the speech of others, as well as the kind of psychological noise discussed in Chapter 10 all interfere with out ability to hear well. Also, fatigue or other forms of discomfort can distract us from paying attention to a speaker's remarks. Consider, for example, how the efficiency of your listening decreases when you are seated in a crowded, hot, stuffy room full of moving people and other noises. In such circumstances even the best intentions aren't enough to ensure cogent understanding.

Before going any further we want to make it clear that we aren't suggesting that it's always desirable to listen intently, even when the circumstances permit. Given the number of messages to which we're exposed, it's impractical to expect yourself to listen well 100 percent of the time. This fact becomes even more true when you consider how many of the messages sent at us aren't especially worthwhile: boring stories, deceitful commercials, and remarks we've heard many times before. Given this deluge of relatively worthless information, it's important to realize that nonlistening behaviors are often reasonable. Our only concern is that you have the ability to be an accurate receiver when it really does matter.

Poor Listening Habits

Although it may not be necessary or desirable to listen effectively all the time, it's sad to realize that most people possess one or more bad habits that keep them from understanding truly important messages. As you read the following list of these poor listening behaviors, see which ones describe you.

Pseudolistening Pseudolistening is an imitation of the real thing. "Good" pseudolisteners give the appearance of being attentive: They look you in the eye, nod and smile at the right times, and even may answer you occasionally. Behind that appearance of interest, however, something entirely different is going on, for pseudolisteners use a polite facade to mask thoughts that have nothing to do with what the speaker is saying. Often pseudolisteners ignore you because of something on their mind that's more important to them than your remarks. Other times they may simply be bored, or think that they've heard what you have to say before, and so tune out your remarks. Whatever the reasons, the significant fact is that pseudolistening is really counterfeit communication.

To be able to really listen, one should abandon or put aside all prejudices, preformulations, and daily activities. When you are in a receptive state of mind, things can be easily understood; you are listening when your real attention is given to something. But unfortunately most of us listen through a screen of resistance. We are screened with prejudices, whether religious or spiritual, psychological or scientific; or with our daily worries, desires, and fears. And with these for a screen, we listen. Therefore, we listen really to our own noise, to our own sound, not to what is being said.

J. Krishnamuriti
THE FIRST AND LAST PERSONAL FREEDOM

Stage hogging Stage hogs are only interested in expressing their ideas and don't care about what anyone else has to say. These people will allow you to speak from time to time, but only so they can catch their breath, use your remarks as a basis for their own babbling, or to keep you from running away. Stage hogs really aren't conversing when they dominate others with their talk—they're making a speech and at the same time probably making an enemy.

Selective listening Selective listeners respond only to the parts of a speaker's remarks that interest them, rejecting everything else. All of us are selective listeners from time to time, as for instance when we screen out media commercials and music as we keep an ear cocked for a weather report or an announcement of time. In other cases selective listening occurs in conversations with people who expect a thorough hearing, but only get their partner's attention when

At the end of my university studies, when I was leaving for my first professional teaching job, I went to say goodby to a teacher, William Trent, who said, "I can give you no theoretical advice in pedagogy, but I'll tell you one thing from experience. It will frequently happen when you are holding forth that somebody in class will disagree. He will probably shake his head violently. You will be tempted to go after him and convert him then and there. Don't do it. He is probably the only one who is listening to you."

John Erskine

the subject turns to their favorite topic—perhaps money, sex, a hobby, or some particular person. Unless and until you bring up one of these pet subjects, you might as well talk to a tree.

Filling in gaps People who fill in the gaps like to think that what they remember makes a whole story. Since we remember half or less of what we hear, these people manufacture information so that when they retell what they listened to, they can give the impression they "got it all." Of course, filling in the gaps is as dangerous as selective listening: The message that's left is only a distorted (not merely incomplete) version of the message that could have been received.

Assimilation to prior messages We all have a tendency to interpret current messages in terms of similar messages remembered from the past. This phenomenon is called *assimilation to prior input*. A problem arises for those who go overboard with this and push, pull, chop, squeeze, and in other ways mutilate messages they receive to *make sure* they are consistent with what they

heard in the past. This unfortunate situation occurs when the current message is in some way different from past beliefs.

Insulated listening Insulated listeners are almost the opposite of their selective listening cousins. Instead of looking for something, these people avoid it. Whenever a topic arises they'd rather not deal with, insulated listeners simply fail to hear, or acknowledge it. You remind them about a problem—perhaps an unfinished job, poor grades, or the like—and they'll nod or answer you and then promptly forget what you've just said.

Defensive listening Defensive listeners take innocent comments as personal attacks. Teenagers who perceive parental questions about friends and activities as distrustful snooping are defensive listeners, as are insecure breadwinners who explode anytime their mates mention money, or touchy parents who view any questioning by their children as a threat to their authority and parental wisdom. It's fair to assume that many defensive listeners are suffering from shaky public images, and avoid admitting this by projecting their own insecurities onto others.

Ambushing Ambushers listen carefully to you, but only because they're collecting information that they'll use to attack what you have to say. The cross-examining prosecution attorney is a good example of an ambusher. Needless to say, using this kind of strategy will justifiably initiate defensiveness on the other's behalf.

Insensitive listening Insensitive listeners offer the final example of people who don't receive another person's messages clearly. As we've said before, people often don't express their thoughts or feelings openly but instead communicate them through subtle and unconscious choice of words and/or nonverbal clues. Insensitive listeners aren't able to look beyond the words and behavior to understand hidden meanings. Instead, they take a speaker's remarks at face value.

It's important not to go overboard in labeling listeners as insensitive. Often a seemingly mechanical comment is perfectly appropriate. This most often occurs in situations involving *phatic* communication, in which a remark derives its meaning totally from context. For instance, the question, "How are you?" doesn't call for an answer when you pass an acquaintance on the street. In this context the statement means no more than, "I acknowledge your existence and I want to let you know that I feel friendly toward you." It is not an inquiry about the state of your health. While insensitive listening is depressing, you would be equally discouraged to hear a litany of aches and pains every time you asked, "How's it going?"

Listening More Effectively

After reading this far you probably recognize the need for better listening in many contexts. What steps can you yourself take to become a better receiver?

Stop talking Zeno of Citium put it most succinctly: "We have been given two ears and but a single mouth, in order that we may hear more and talk less." It is difficult to listen and talk at the same time. This includes the silent debating, rehearsing, and retorting that often goes on in our minds. The first step to better listening, then, is to keep quiet when another person speaks.

Put the speaker at ease Help the speaker feel free to talk to you by working to create a

*When we speak we do not listen, my
    son and I.
I complain of slights, hurts inflicted on
    me.
He sings a counterpoint, but not in
    harmony.
Asking a question, he doesn't wait to
    hear.
Trying to answer, I interrupt his
    refrain.
This comic opera excels in disharmony
    only.*

Lenni Shender Goldstein

supportive communication climate. Besides telling the speaker that you care about what is being said, look and act interested. Nonverbal cues associated with caring appear to be more important than a listener's verbal response. Good eye contact, a forward lean of the torso, and a warm tone of voice are three nonverbal expressions of empathy; together they seem to be twice as important as the words that accompany these behaviors (Haase and Tepper, 1972). Of course, the only way that such behaviors will be convincing over the length of a conversation is if you are sincerely interested in the speaker.

React appropriately In order to help the speaker realize that you might be having problems understanding, offer positive and negative feedback. These behaviors can include nonverbal facial expressions: nodding, shaking your head, and so on, as well as verbal statements.

Concentrate on what is being said Focus your attention on the words, ideas, and the feelings of the speaker. Use the "extra" time you have listening to put the speaker's ideas

Edgar Bergen, Charlie McCarthy, Adolphe Menjou, and Vera Zorina in *The Goldwyn Follies,* 1938. (Culver Pictures, Inc.)

into your own words, relate them to your experience, and think about any questions you might have.

Get rid of distractions   Avoid fidgeting with your pen, playing with a paperclip you've found, doodling, or writing the letter home that's been on your mind. Whenever possible, pick a listening environment that minimizes distractions such as passersby, telephone calls, loud noises, and so on. When you are stuck in a distracting setting, do your best to tune it out.

Don't give up too soon   Avoid interrupting until the other person expresses a complete thought: Clarity may be on the way! Statements that first seem obscure often make sense if you let the speaker talk for a while.

Avoid making assumptions   If you disagree with what you hear, don't assume that the speaker is "uninformed," "lying," or otherwise behaving dishonorably.

Don't argue mentally   Give the speaker a fair hearing; control your anger. If you argue mentally, you lose the opportunity to concentrate on what the speaker is saying. Also, it is often the case that when we mentally argue, we tend to place the other person in a fixed category, and thus cease responding to a unique person, albeit a unique person with whom we disagree.

Listen for main points and supporting evidence Critical listening will show that a speaker almost always advances one or more main points and backs them up with examples, stories, analogies, and other types of supporting material. One key to successful listening is to search for these main points, and then see if the speaker's support bears them out. A far less productive method is to dwell on an interesting story or comment while forgetting the speaker's main idea.

Share responsibility for the communication Remember that communication is a transaction, that we are simultaneously senders and receivers. Just as a good marriage requires both partners to give 100 percent of their effort, so a successful conversation demands the energy and skill of both parties.

Ask questions Thus far we have been discussing listening methods basically passive in nature; that is, those that can be carried out silently. It's also possible to verify or increase your understanding in a more active way by asking questions to be sure you are receiving the speaker's thoughts and feelings accurately.

Although the suggestion to ask questions may seem so obvious as to be trivial, honestly ask yourself whether you take full advantage of this simple but effective method. It's often tempting to remain silent instead of being a questioner for two reasons. Sometimes you may be reluctant to show your ig-

norance by asking for further explanation of what seems as if it should be an obvious point. This reluctance is especially strong when the speaker's respect or liking is important to you. At such times it's a good idea to remember a quote attributed to Confucius: "He who asks a question is a fool for five minutes. He who does not ask is a fool for life."

A second reason people are often disinclined to ask questions is that they think they already understand a speaker. But do we in fact understand others as often or as well as we think? You can best answer by thinking about how often people misunderstand *you* while feeling certain that they know what you've meant. If you are aware that others should ask questions of you more often, then it's logical to assume that the same principle holds true in reverse.

Use active listening Questioning is often a valuable tool for increasing understanding. Sometimes, however, it won't help you receive a speaker's ideas any more clearly, and it can even lead to further communication breakdown. To see how this can be so, consider the common example of asking directions to a friend's home. Suppose the instructions you've received are to, "Drive about a mile and then turn left at the traffic signal." Now imagine that a few common problems exist in this simple message. First, suppose that your friend's idea of a mile differs from yours: Your mental picture of the distance is actually closer to two miles, where your friend's is closer to 300 yards. Next, consider the likely occurrence that "traffic signal," really meant "stop sign"; after all, it's common for us to think one thing and say another. Keeping these problems in mind, suppose you tried to verify your understanding of the directions by asking. "After I turn at the light, how far should I go?"

Walter Matthau and George Burns in *The Sunshine Boys*, 1975.

to which your friend replied that the house is the third from the corner. Clearly, if you parted after this exchange, you would encounter a lot of frustration before finding the elusive residence.

What was the problem here? It's easy to see that questioning might not have helped you, for your original idea of how far to drive and where to turn were mistaken. And contained in such mistakes is the biggest problem with questioning, for such inquiries

don't tell you whether you have accurately received the information that has *already* been sent.

Now consider another kind of feedback—one that would tell you whether you understand what had already been said before you asked additional questions. This sort of feedback involves restating in your own words the message you thought the speaker has just sent, without adding anything new. In the example of seeking directions we've been using, such rephrasing might sound like, "So you're telling me to drive down to the traffic light by the high school and turn toward the mountains, is that it?" Immediately sensing the problem your friend could then reply, "Oh no, that's way too far. I meant that you should drive to the four-way stop by the park and turn there. Did I say stop light? I always do that when I mean stop sign!"

This simple step of restating what you thought the speaker said before going on is commonly termed *active listening*, and it is an important tool for effective listening. Remember that what is significant in active listening is to *paraphrase* the sender's words, not to parrot them. In other words, restate what you think the speaker has said in your own terms as a way of cross-checking the information. If you simply repeat the speaker's comments *verbatim*, you'll sound as if you're foolish or hard of hearing, and just as importantly, you still might be misunderstanding what's been said.

Because it's an unfamiliar way of responding, active listening may feel awkward when you first begin to use it. But by paraphrasing occasionally at first and then gradually increasing the frequency of such responses, you can begin to learn the benefits of this method without feeling foolish or sounding odd to others.

Listening to Help

So far we've talked about how becoming a better listener can help you to understand other people more often and more clearly. If you use the skills presented so far, you should be rewarded by communicating far more accurately with others every day. But there's another way in which listening can improve your relationships. Strange as it may sound, you can often help other people solve their own problems simply by learning to listen—actively and with concern.

Before we introduce various methods of listening as a method of helping, read the following situations and think about how you would respond in each of them.

1. You're speaking with a friend who has just been rejected from getting a badly wanted job. "I don't know what to do," your friend tells you. "I studied and worked two years to get that job, and it's all been for nothing."
2. Another friend confesses, "My marriage seems to be on the rocks. We hardly talk anymore. And everything triggers off a fight. We're in a rut, and it seems to be getting worse."
3. While at work or school, an acquaintance approaches you and says, "I can't decide whether to stay here or move up north. I have plenty of friends here and things are pretty good. On the other hand, I'd hate to give up a good job opportunity and find out it was a mistake. What do you think I should do?"

There are several ways in which you could have responded to these problems, none inherently good or bad. If often happens, however, that we use these ways in situations when they aren't best suited to helping others solve their problems. There's a proper time and place for each kind of response. The problem, though, usually occurs when we use these ways in the wrong situations or else depend upon one or two styles of responses for all situations.

As you read the following descriptions of ways of responding, see which ones you most frequently used in the previous exercise, and notice the results that probably would have occurred from your response.

It is always a silly thing to give advice, but to give good advice is absolutely fatal.

Oscar Wilde

Advising   When approached with another's problem, the most common tendency is to try to help by offering a solution. While such a response is sometimes valuable, it often isn't as helpful as people generally think.

Your suggestion may not offer the best course to follow, in which case it can even be harmful. There's a temptation to tell others how *we* would behave in their place, but it's important to realize that what's right for one person may not be right for another. A related consequence of advising is that it often allows others to avoid responsibility for their decisions. If, for example, a partner follows your suggestion and things don't work out, the blame can always be pinned on you. Finally, people simply may not want advice—they may not be ready to accept it, wanting instead simply to talk out their thoughts and feelings.

Judging   A judging response evaluates the sender's thoughts or behaviors in some way. The judgment may be favorable ("That's a good idea"; "You're on the right track now"), or unfavorable ("An attitude like that won't get you anywhere"). In either case this response implies that the person doing the judging is in some way qualified to pass judgment on the speaker's thoughts or actions.

Judgmental or evaluative language is likely to make someone defensive. Thus, responding in this way might tend to put the speaker on guard and in so doing end the conversation and the possibility of helping.

Analyzing   The analyzer's response suggests that the receiver understands the sender better than the sender understands his or her own message ("What's bothering you is . . . "; "What you really think is . . . "). In a sense, the analyzer tries to read the speaker's mind or provide a lesson in psychology.

There are two problems with analyzing. First, your interpretation may not be correct, in which case the sender may become even more confused by accepting it. Second, even if your analysis is accurate, sharing it with the sender might not be useful. There's a chance that it will create defensiveness (since analyzing implies superiority and the authority to evaluate).

There are times when analyzing can be a way of helping people to see their "blind spots," but this style of responding is one many of us use too often.

Questioning   Although questioning is often a helpful way for you to understand the unclear parts of a person's statements, it can also be used as a tool to direct the other's thoughts. We've all been questioned by a parent, teacher, or other authority figure who seemed to be trying to trap us. In this way questioning is a strategy, and often implies that the person doing the asking already has some idea of what direction the discussion should take.

Supporting   Sometimes a person needs encouragement, and in these cases a supporting response might be best. But in many cases this kind of help isn't helpful at all. Telling a person who's obviously upset that "everything's all right" or joking about a problem can communicate a message that you don't accept the other's feelings as valid or that there isn't justification in the problem for feeling that way.

All these responses may be helpful at times, but they often confuse people asking for help, making them feel worse than before they shared a problem or making them defensive. Good intentions aren't always helpful.

Active listening In active listening the receiver makes a paraphrasing statement that reflects both the *feelings* and the *thoughts* of the speaker. Imagine that a friend complained about a recent assignment: "I killed myself working on that paper. I deserved more than a lousy B-minus." An active listening response to such a comment would paraphrase both the speaker's ideas and the underlying emotions: "Sounds like you're really disappointed because the professor didn't appreciate the work you did."

Reflecting back a speaker's ideas and feelings in this way can be surprisingly helpful. First, it helps clarify the other person's concerns. If your paraphrasing is accurate, the speaker has a clear picture of the problem; and if you guess wrong the speaker will correct you, and in doing so clarify the situation. In addition, your mention of the speaker's emotions can open up an important, unexplored area of concern. The emotional responses we have to problems are often more important than the problems themselves. For example, the grade on the paper mentioned above might only be a small part of your companion's problem, and focusing the discussion on that assignment might cause you both to ignore the other related areas of concern. On the other hand, encouraging the speaker to talk about his or her frustration, anger, or disappointment lets the actual subject of the problem surface.

Besides the actual act of paraphrasing, a key element of active listening is empathy, or as an unknown writer put it, "To see with the eyes of another, to hear with the ears of another, to feel with the heart of another." The purpose of expressing empathy is, according to Byrnes and Yamamota (1981), "to create an atmosphere of reassurance and understanding so that the feelings of the client [or any other person with whom you are interacting] may be expressed without mistrust or fear" (p. 343).

George Gazda and his associates (1977, p. 64) describe four types of response that they use to train teachers to respond empathically to students. The four levels are:

1. An irrelevant or hurtful response that does not appropriately attend to the surface feelings of the other person.
2. A response that only partially communicates an awareness of the surface feelings of the other person.
3. A response conveying that the other person is understood at the level he or she is expressing himself or herself. Surface feelings, in other words, are accurately reflected.
4. A response conveying that the other person is understood beyond his or her level of immediate awareness. Underlying feelings are identified and reflected.

You can practice identifying each level of response by picturing the following situation, presented by Gazda: One of your married friends, a student in several classes with you, tells you the following: "It's getting tough to stay in school with what's happening at home. My family is losing out. With all the school work piled on, I have no time to just be with them and relax." Rate each of the following responses on a 1 (not empathic) to 4 (highly empathic) scale.

_____ 1. "Rearrange your schedule so you can be home more."

_____ **2.** "You feel like an inadequate father and husband—as if you aren't really a part of the family because you don't have enough time to spend with them. That must feel terrible."

_____ **3.** "You feel like you're spreading yourself too thin, taking on too much and missing out on your family life."

_____ **4.** "You feel down because you're not with your family as much as you'd like because of school."

The first response is rated 1 on the empathy scale. It ignores surface feelings, is criticizing, and is probably irrelevant since the schedule is already set. The third response rates a 2: It suggests only a partial awareness of the other's feelings and ignores much of the other's statement. The fourth response rates a 3 on the empathy scale. It communicates an awareness of the surface feeling ("down"), and neither adds nor subtracts from what was said. This response says "I heard what you said and am attempting to understand how you feel." The second response earns a rating of 4. It goes beyond the speaker's present awareness and conveys an understanding of the underlying problem—feeling like an inadequate family member—as well as reflecting the content of what was said.

There are several reasons why active listening works so well. First, it takes the burden off you as a friend. Simply being there to understand what's on someone's mind often makes it possible for him or her to clarify the problems. This means you don't have to know all the answers to help. Also, helping by active listening means you don't need to guess at reasons or solutions that might not be correct. Thus, both you and your friend are saved from going on a wild goose chase after incorrect solutions.

A second advantage of active listening is that it's an efficient way to get through layers of hidden meanings. Often people express their ideas, problems, or feelings in strangely coded ways. Active listening can sometimes help cut through to the real meaning. Not too long ago a student came to an instructor and asked, "How many people get Ds and Fs in this class?" The instructor could have taken the question at face value and answered it, but instead he tried active listening. He replied by saying, "Sounds like you've got some fears of doing poorly in here." After a few minutes of listening the instructor learned that the student was afraid that getting a low grade in a communication class would be equal to failing as a person.

The third advantage of active listening is that it's usually the best way to encourage people to share more of themselves with you. Knowing that you're interested will make them feel less threatened, and many will be willing to let down some of their defenses. In this sense active listening is simply a good way to learn more about someone, and a good foundation on which to build a relationship.

Regardless of the advantages, active listening isn't appropriate in all situations when someone wants help. Sometimes people are simply looking for information and not trying to work out their feelings. At times like this active listening would be out of place. If someone asks you for the time of day, you'd do better to simply give the information than to respond by saying, "You want to know what time it is." If you're fixing dinner and someone wants to know when it will be ready, it would be exasperating to reply, "You're interested in knowing when we'll be eating."

However, people do often hide an important feeling behind an innocent sounding statement or question, and in such cases active listening on your part can usually bring their real concern into the open. But don't go overboard with the technique. Usually, if there's a feeling hidden behind a question you'll recognize some accompanying non-verbal clue—a change in your friend's facial expression, tone of voice, posture, and so on. But it takes attention, concentration, and caring on your part.

You should realize that success in using active listening will depend on the attitude you bring to a situation. Too often people will think of active listening as a kind of gim-mick they can use when some unpleasant sit-uation arises. If you think about the tech-nique this way it is almost sure to fail. In fact, unless you truly mean what you say,

you'll come across as being manipulative, phony, and uncaring. So as you practice this listening skill try to keep these points in mind:

1. Don't actively listen unless you truly want to help the person. There's nothing wrong with being too preoccupied to help. But you'll be doing both yourself and the other person a disservice if you pretend to care when you really don't.

2. Don't try to listen actively if you're not willing to take the necessary time. Listening with feedback isn't easy. If you're willing to make the effort, you'll probably be re-warded, but you'll only lose the speaker's trust if you commit yourself and then don't follow through.

© 1978 United Feature Syndicate, Inc.

3. Don't try to impose your ideas on the other person. Active listening means accepting other people's feelings and trusting that they can find their own solutions. If you try to moralize, to suggest, or to change the speaker, you won't really be actively listening, and it's less likely that you'll be of much help.

4. Keep your attention focused on the sender. Sometimes, as you listen to others share feelings, it's easy to become defensive, to relate their thoughts to your own life, or to busy yourself thinking of an answer. Remember that active listening is a form of helping someone else. Keep your energy focused on this goal.

Readings

Anderson, Rob. *Students as Real People: Interpersonal Communication and Education.* Rochelle Park, N.J.: Hayden, 1979.

Axline, Virginia M. *Dibs: In Search of Self.* New York: Ballantine Books, 1967.

*Baddeley, Alan D. *The Psychology of Memory.* New York: Basic Books, 1976.

*Barker, Larry L. *Listening Behavior.* Englewood Cliffs, N.J.: Prentice-Hall, 1971.

Beier, Ernst G., and Evans G. Valens. *People-Reading: How We Control Others, How They Control Us.* New York: Stein and Day, 1975.

Bostrom, Robert N., and Carol L. Bryant. "Factors in the Retention of Information Presented Orally: The Role of Short-Term Listening." *Western Journal of Speech Communication* 44 (1980): 137–145.

*Bostrom, Robert N., and Enid S. Waldhart. "Components in Listening Behavior: The Role of Short-Term Memory." *Human Communication Research* 6 (1980): 221–227.

Brynes, D. A., and K. Yamamoto. "Some Reflections of Empathy." *School Counselor* 28 (1981): 343–345.

Cleveland, B. "Active Listening Yields Better Discussion." *Social Studies* 7 (1980): 218–221.

Dittmann, Allen T. "Developmental Factors in Conversational Behavior." *Journal of Communication* 22 (1972): 404–423.

Foulke, Emerson, and Thomas Stricht. "Review of Research in Time-Compressed Speech." In *Time-Compressed Speech,* Sam Duker, ed. Metuchen, N.J.: Scarecrow Press, 1974.

*Gazda, George M., Frank R. Asbury, Fred J. Balzer, William C. Childers, and Richard P. Walters. *Human Relations Development: A Manual for Educators,* 2nd Ed. Boston: Allyn and Bacon, 1977.

Goldhaber, Gerald M. "Listener Comprehension of Compressed Speech as a Function of the Academic Grade Level of Subjects." *Journal of Communication* 20 (1970): 167–173.

Haney, William V. *Communication and Interpersonal Relations: Text and Cases,* 4th Ed. Homewood, Ill.: Richard D. Irwin, Inc., 1979.

Haase, R. F., and D. T. Tepper. "Non-Verbal Components of Empathic Communication." *Journal of Counseling Psychology* 19 (1972): 417–424.

Katz, Jerrold J., and Jerry A. Foder. "The Structure of a Semantic Theory." In *Readings in the Philosophy of Language,* Jay F. Rosenberg and Charles Travis, eds. Englewood Cliffs, N.J.: Prentice-Hall, 1971.

Kelley, Charles M. "Empathic Listening." In *Small Group Communication: A Reader,* 2nd Ed., Robert Cathcart and Larry Samovar, eds. Dubuque, Iowa: Wm. C. Brown, 1974.

Nichols, Ralph G. "Factors in Listening Comprehension." *Speech Monographs* 15 (1948): 154–163.

*Nichols, Ralph G., and L.A. Stevens. *Are You Listening?* New York: McGraw-Hill, 1957.

Palamatier, Robert A., and George McNinch. "Source of Gains in Listening Skill: Experimental or Pre-Test Experience?" *Journal of Communication* 22 (1972): 70–76.

Plax, Timothy G., and Lawrence B. Rosenfeld. "Receiver Differences and the Comprehension of Spoken Messages." *Journal of Experimental Education* 48 (Fall 1979).

Postman, Neil, and Charles Weingartner. *Teaching as a Subversive Activity.* New York: Delacorte Press, 1969.

Rogers, Carl R. *On Becoming a Person.* Boston: Houghton-Mifflin, 1961.

Rossiter, Charles M. "Sex of the Speaker, Sex of the Listener, and Listening Comprehension." *Journal of Communication* 22 (1972): 64–69.

Verderber, Rudolph, Ann Elder, and Ernest Weiler. *A Study of Communication Time Usage by College Students.* Unpublished study, University of Cincinnati, 1976.

Weaver, Carl. *Human Listening: Processes and Behavior.* Indianapolis: Bobbs-Merrill, 1972.

*Wolvin, Andrew, and Carolyn Coakley. *Listening.* Dubuque, Iowa: Wm. C. Brown, 1982.

7

Self-Disclosure

■■■■ *After studying the material in this chapter*

You should understand:

1. How self-disclosure is defined.

2. How the Johari Window represents the degrees of self-disclosure is a dyadic relationship.

3. The criteria receivers use to judge whether another's message is self-disclosing.

4. Four types of nondisclosing communication.

5. How sex differences affect self-disclosure.

6. Eight reasons people self-disclose.

7. Reasons people fear self-disclosure.

You should be able to:

1. Identify the degree to which you engage in self-disclosure with individuals in your life and the circumstances in which you do so.

2. Identify the types of nondisclosing communication you practice and the circumstances in which you do so.

3. List the benefits and costs of your present level of self-disclosure.

4. Use the guidelines in this chapter to identify how you might improve the amount and content of your self-disclosing communication in your important relationships.

The dream is a common one. You suddenly find yourself without clothes—on the street, at work, at school, or maybe in a crowd of strangers. Everyone else is fully dressed, while you stand alone, naked and vulnerable. Maybe others see you and respond with curiosity or hostility or laughter. Or possibly you seem to be invisible, searching for shelter before you are recognized. Whatever the details, dreams of this sort are usually disturbing.

You needn't be a psychoanalyst to figure out that the nakedness here is symbolic, representing the fear of disclosing oneself in other ways: dropping the masks and facades that we often show to the world. Laughter hides pain, a relaxed pose covers tension, a veneer of certainty masks confusion. And we fear being found out.

Why are we often afraid of being real, of letting others know who we really are? In his thoughtful book, *What Are You Afraid Of?: A Guide to Dealing With Your Fears*, John T. Wood (1976) suggests an answer:

> I am afraid to be who I am with you . . . I am afraid to be judged by you, I am afraid you will reject me. I am afraid you will say bad things about me. I am afraid you will hurt me. I am afraid, if I really am myself, you won't love me—and I need your love so badly that I will play the roles you expect me to play and be the person that pleases you, even though I lose myself in the process.

There probably isn't a person over the age of six who wouldn't understand these words. At one time or another all of us are afraid to be real with others. As Wood suggests, the biggest reason for hiding our true selves is usually fear of rejection. As we'll soon see, there are other reasons as well. Because the issue of self-disclosure is such a crucial one in interpersonal communication, we want to spend this chapter looking at it in detail.

We'll talk about what self-disclosure is and how it differs from other types of communication, we'll see how one's sex influences disclosure. We will look at the benefits and apparent drawbacks of disclosing. Finally, we'll offer some suggestions for when self-disclosure is appropriate. Let's begin by defining our terms.

What Is Self-Disclosure?

A model of self-disclosure To *disclose* means to show, make known, reveal. *Self-disclosure*, then is the act of making yourself known to another person, showing yourself in a way so that others can perceive you. (We'll offer a more detailed definition shortly.)

One way to illustrate how self-disclosure operates in communication is to look at a device called the *Johari Window*, developed by Joseph Luft and Harry Ingham (Luft, 1969).

Imagine a frame that contains everything there is to know about you: your likes and dislikes, your goals, your secrets, your needs—everything.

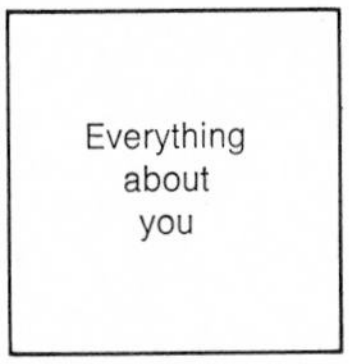

Figure 7–1

Of course, you aren't aware of everything about yourself. Like most people you're probably discovering new things about yourself all the time. To represent this aspect, we can divide the frame containing everything about you into two parts: the part you know about, and the part of which you are not aware (see Figure 7-2).

169

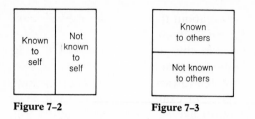

Known to self	Not known to self

Figure 7–2

Known to others
Not known to others

Figure 7–3

Part 1 represents the person of which both you and others are aware. This area is labeled your *open area*. Part 2 represents the part of you that you yourself are not aware of, but others are. This is called your *blind area*. Part 3 represents your *hidden area*; you're aware of this part of yourself, but you don't allow others to know it. Part 4 represents the part of you that is known neither to you nor to others and is therefore referred to as the *unknown area*.

We can also divide the frame containing everything about you in another way. In this division one part represents the things about you that others know, and the second part contains the things about you that you keep to yourself. Figure 7-3 represents this view.

When we place these two divided frames one atop the other, we have a Johari Window. By looking at Figure 7-4 you can see that Johari divides everything about you into four parts.

Interpersonal communication of any significance is virtually impossible if the individuals involved have little open area. And taking this a step further, you can see that a relationship is limited by the individual who is less open, that is, who possesses the smaller open area. Figure 7-5 illustrates this situation with Johari Windows.

We've set up *A's* window in reverse so that the Number 1 areas of both *A's* and *B's* Joharis appear next to each other. Note that the amount of successful communication (represented by the arrows connecting the two open areas) is dictated by the size of the smaller open area of *A*. The arrows originating from *B's* open area and being turned aside by *A's* hidden and blind areas represent unsuccessful attempts to communicate.

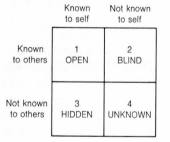

	Known to self	Not known to self
Known to others	1 OPEN	2 BLIND
Not known to others	3 HIDDEN	4 UNKNOWN

Figure 7–4

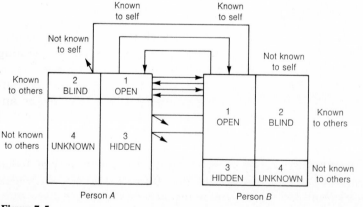

Figure 7–5

170

Can you put yourself into one of the windows in Figure 7-5? Have you had the experience of not being able to "really get to know" someone because he or she was too reserved or closed? Or perhaps you've frustrated another person's attempts to build a relationship with you in the same way. Whether you picture yourself as more like Person *A* or Person *B* in Figure 7-5, the fact is that self-disclosure is necessary for the success of any interpersonal relationship.

A definition of self-disclosure You might argue that aside from secrets, it's impossible *not* to make yourself known to others. After all, every time you open your mouth to speak you're revealing your tastes, interests, desires, opinions, beliefs, or some other bit of information about yourself. Even when the subject isn't a personal one, your choice of what to speak about tells the listener something about who you are. And, if you recall Chapter 5, you'll remember that each of us communicates nonverbally even when we're not speaking at all. For instance, a yawn might mean that you're tired or bored, a shrug of your shoulders might indicate uncertainty or indifference, and how close or how far you choose to stand from your listener may be taken as a measure of your friendliness or comfort with him or her.

If every verbal and nonverbal behavior in which you engage is self-revealing, how can self-disclosure be distinguished from any other act of communication? According to psychologist Paul Cozby (1973) there is a difference. In order for a communication act to be considered self-disclosing it must meet the following criteria: (1) it must contain personal information about the sender; (2) the sender must verbally communicate this information; and (3) another person must be the target. Put differently, the content of self-disclosing communication is the *self*, and in-

formation about the self is *purposefully communicated to another person.*

Although this definition is a start, it ignores the fact that some messages intentionally directed toward others are not especially revealing. For example, telling a companion that you dislike eating clams is quite different from announcing that you dislike some aspect of her or him. Let's take a look at several factors that further distinguish self-disclosure from other types of communication.

Honesty It almost goes without saying that true self-disclosure has to be honest. It's not revealing to say, "I've never felt this way about anyone before" to every Saturday night date, or to preface every lie with the statement, "Let me be honest . . . "

What about cases where individuals do not know themselves well enough to present accurate information? Are these unintentionally false statements self-disclosing? For our purposes, the answer is yes. As long as you are honest and accurate to the best of your knowledge, the communication can qualify as an act of self-disclosure. On the other hand, both painting an incomplete picture of yourself (telling only part of what's true), or avoiding saying anything at all about yourself, are not self-disclosive acts.

Depth A self-disclosing statement is generally regarded as being personal—containing relatively "deep" rather than "surface" information. Of course, what is personal and intimate for one person may not be for another. For example, Lawrence, Ron, and Neil might respond differently to a question about their undergraduate grade point averages, depending on how intimate or personal each feels the information is. For Lawrence it might be highly personal (it was a lousy average), whereas for Ron and Neil it may

Woody Allen in *Bananas*, 1971. (Culver Pictures)

come under the heading of surface information. Even simple statements such as a response to the question "How old are you?" can be extremely revealing for some people.

Availability of information Several researchers in the area of self-disclosure are concerned with the question of what makes a given act of communication qualify as self-disclosure. They argue that such messages must contain information the other person is not likely to know at the time or be able to obtain from another source without a great deal of effort, if at all.

For example, describing your conviction for a drunk driving accident might feel as if it were an act of serious disclosure, for the information concerns you, is offered intentionally, is honest and accurate, and considered personal. However, if the other person could obtain that information elsewhere without much trouble—from a glance at the morning newspaper or from various gossips, for example—your communication would not be an act of self-disclosure.

Context of sharing Sometimes the self-disclosing nature of a statement comes from the setting in which it is uttered. For instance, relatively innocuous information about family life seems more personal when a teacher shares it with her class. This sort of sharing creates a more personal atmosphere because it changes the relationship from a purely "business" level to a more intimate one.

We can summarize our definitional tour by saying that an act of self-disclosure: (1) has the self as content; (2) is intentional; (3) is directed at another person; (4) is honest; (5) is revealing; (6) contains information unavailable from other sources; and (7) gains much of its intimate nature from the context in which it is expressed.

The receiver's perception of disclosing behavior So far we have been looking at self-disclosure from the sender's (discloser's) viewpoint. After all, a receiver can't always be certain whether a given act of communication is truly intentional, honest, revealing, and containing information unavailable elsewhere. Suppose, for example, that at a party you met someone who remarked, "I've never felt comfortable in places like this." Is your companion disclosing? The content of the communication concerns the self and is directed at another person (you); but is the statement intentional, honest, revealing, and unavailable elsewhere? You might guess at the answers to these questions, but you could not know for sure.

While the sender may be best suited to judge whether a message is self-disclosive, the receiver of the message also makes judgments about the communication. What characteristics of a message or sender impress receivers as being most disclosive? Recent investigations have begun to answer this question.

In a series of studies conducted by Gor-

> ■ *Letting people in is largely a matter of not expending energy to keep them out.*

Hugh Prather

don Chelune (1981; Chelune, Skiffington, and Williams, 1981), subjects were asked to rate the degree to which they believed a speaker was self-disclosing from 0 (indicating the speaker totally withheld personal information) to 100 (indicating total disclosure). These ratings were then compared to a number of objective behaviors exhibited by the speakers:

self-references: statements descriptive of the speaker

self-reference percent: number of self-references divided by the total number of statements made

positive self-reference percent: percentage of statements describing favorable attributes of the speaker

negative self-reference percent: percentage of statements describing unfavorable attributes of the speaker

intimacy: depth of verbal content, measured on a 5-point scale

affective manner of presentation: degree of congruence between the intimacy level and the manner in which it was presented

rate of disclosure: number of self-references per minute

Results indicate that all of these factors shape a receiver's evaluation of how much self-disclosure a sender is exhibiting. The single best predictor of subjects' ratings was intimacy, with rate of disclosure and congruent affective manner the next most influential factors. Chelune also found, interestingly, that men were consistently seen as being more disclosing than women (this was true for both male and female raters), possibly reflecting the stereotyped notion that men do not self-disclose very much; hence, any disclosure is "a lot."

Other elements of a communication situation also affect the receiver's perception of another's self-disclosure. Chris Kleinke (1979) discusses variables such as social context (the location, subject, people), the appropriateness of the information disclosed (highly intimate disclosure early in a relationship is usually viewed as inappropriate), attributions made about the discloser's motives ("Why is she telling me this?"), and individual characteristics of both the sender and receiver (self-image, dogmatism, neuroticism, anxiety, and need for approval). All of these factors need to be considered when determining how much and what kind of self-disclosure is appropriate.

Nondisclosing Communication

After looking at the preceding characteristics, it's clear that relatively few acts of communication are truly self-disclosing. Since we spend so little time engaging in this kind of sharing, let's take a look at the messages that do make up the bulk of our communicating. We'll start at the "bottom," with the activity that is least revealing, and move toward increasingly disclosive types of messages.

Rituals   Much of our communication is designed to keep people at a distance. Rituals are a prime example of this variety. They are uninvolving acts of communication which have highly predictable outcomes. There is little, if any, risk in performing a ritual. There is also very little payoff in terms of

developing a relationship with the other person:

"Hi, how are you?"
"Fine, how are you?"
"See ya."
"Sure."

Rituals, although not revealing, serve a variety of functions. For example, the "hello–how are you–fine" ritual allows us to acknowledge each other's existence in a short and simple interaction, something of importance in superficial relationships.

Activities   These are the behaviors that help define most of our social roles and that occupy much of our time. Studying, working on the job, shopping, and the hundreds of other well-defined behaviors we seem to accomplish without conscious effort all fall into this category. As with rituals, it's possible to carry out many activities without becoming personally involved with others. The impersonal lectures of a professor, the mechanical behavior of a grocery checker, and the seemingly uninterested examinations of some busy physicians are all examples of nondisclosing activities.

Of course, it is possible to be more personal when carrying out activities. We've all had the occasional surprising pleasure of having real person-to-person contact in our activity-based interactions. But most of the time it seems as if our activities would be just as successful—and rewarding—if we carried them out with efficient machines.

Pastimes   These consist of the chitchat that passes for conversation. More varied than rituals, pastimes serve many of the same functions: They acknowledge the other person's presence and indicate liking, or at least goodwill. And, as their name implies, pas-

> ▇▇▇ *The personality of man is not an apple that has to be polished, but a banana that has to be peeled. And the reason we remain so far from one another, the reason we neither communicate nor interact in any real way, is that most of us spend our lives in polishing rather than peeling.*
>
> *Man's lifelong task is simply one, but it is not simple: To remove the discrepancy between his outer self and his inner self, to get rid of the "persona" that divides his authentic self from the world.*
>
> *This persona is like the peeling on a banana: It is something built up to protect from bruises and injury. It is not the real person, but sometimes (if the fear of injury remains too great) it becomes a lifelong substitute for the person.*
>
> *The "authentic personality" knows that he is like a banana, and knows that only as he peels himself down to his individuated self can he reach out and make contact with his fellows by what Father Goldbrunner calls "the sheer maturity of his humanity." Only when he himself is detached from his defensive armorings can he then awaken a true response in his dialogue with others.*
>
> *Most of us, however, think in terms of the apple, not the banana. We spend our lives in shining the surface, in making it rosy and gleaming, in perfecting the "image." But the image is not the apple, which may be wormy and rotten to the taste.*
>
> *Almost everything in modern life is devoted to the polishing process, and little to the peeling process. It is the surface personality that we work on— the appearance, the clothes, the manners, the geniality. In short, the salesmanship: We are selling the package, not the product.*
>
> Sydney J. Harris

---

times provide a way of relating together when there doesn't seem to be anything else to do. Also, pastimes serve an important role in the early stages of relational development. While discussing relatively superficial, non-threatening topics, the communicators make decisions about whether each wishes to continue the interaction.

Pastimes can be risky if you don't want to play by the rules. We know a woman who learned this when she was invited to join a morning coffee group in her neighborhood. She just moved in and had a month before her job started, so she viewed the invitation as an opportunity to meet the neighbors. The pastime for the morning was, "What my husband did most recently that was horrible." When her turn to talk came she told the others that their complaining was a waste of time, and that they should be doing something more productive with the morning. She broke the rules by not playing along. And some potential friends became immediate enemies.

███ *Something there is that doesn't
    love a wall,
That sends the frozen-ground-swell
    under it,
And spills the upper boulders in the
    sun;
And makes gaps even two can pass
    abreast.*

    *. . . The gaps I mean,
No one has seen them made or heard
    them made,
But at spring mending-time we find
    them there.
I let my neighbor know beyond the
    hill;
And on a day we meet to walk the line
And set the wall between us once
    again.
We keep the wall between us as we go.
To each the boulders have fallen to
    each.*

*We wear our fingers rough with
    handling them.
Oh, just another kind of outdoor game,
One on a side. It comes to little more:*

*There where it is we do not need the
    wall:
He is all pine and I am apple orchard.
My apple trees will never get across
And eat the cones under his pines, I tell
    him.*

*He only says, 'Good fences make good
    neighbors.'*

*Spring is the mischief in me, and I
    wonder
If I could put a notion in his head:
'Why do they make good neighbors?
    Isn't it
Where there are cows? But here there
    are no cows.*

*Before I built a wall I'd ask to know
What I was walling in or walling out,
And to whom I was like to give
    offense.
Something there is that doesn't love a
    wall,
That wants it down.'*

    *. . . I see him there
Bringing a stone grasped firmly by the
    top
In each hand, like an old-stone savage
    armed.
He moves in darkness as it seems to
    me,
Not of woods only and the shade of
    trees.
He will not go behind his father's
    saying,
And he likes having thought of it so
    well
He says again, 'Good fences make good
    neighbors.'*

Robert Frost
MENDING WALL

Games These are the riskiest kinds of non-disclosing communication. Whereas rituals, activities, and pastimes are often honest, if superficial, ways of relating, games are highly structured interactions based on ulte-rior motives. And most significantly, most of these motives involve ill feelings.

As the well-known psychiatrist and author Eric Berne (1964) pointed out, typical games are designed to prove that the other person is wrong and should be blamed ("If it weren't for you . . . "); saved ("I'm only trying to help you . . . "); belittled ("My _____ is better than your _____"); or the object of revenge ("Now I've got you, you sonofabitch"). In another class of games the ulterior motive is to prove that you're wrong, and probably deserve sympathy. This can be achieved through put-down games ("Gee, I'm stupid"), or cop-out games ("Why does this always happen to me?"). While activities of this sort might gain the player some kind of support, we'll soon see that their costs outweigh their gains.

Sex Differences in Self-Disclosure

Are men and women equally willing to communicate in a disclosing way? Sidney Jourard (1971) was one of the first researchers to explore this question. Using his Self-Disclosure Questionnaire he found that females disclose more than males. He explained his results by discussing what he called the "lethal male role"—that is, males are socialized not to disclose and so build up more tension in their daily lives, which results in early death—and the notion that females are socialized to be open and self-disclosing.

More recent research isn't as certain: Some studies support Jourard's early findings, some indicate that there is no difference between the amount males and females disclose, and a few studies indicate that males disclose more (although these are fewest in number). It appears as if the relationship between sex and self-disclosure is not a simple, clear-cut one. For example, males disclose more about their family relationships, interests, and tastes. Also, males appear to disclose less negative and more neutral information about themselves than females. And finally, Cash and Soloway

To reveal myself openly and honestly takes the rawest kind of courage.

John Powell

(1975) found that males who perceive themselves as attractive self-disclose more than other males, whereas females who perceive themselves as attractive disclose less than other females.

In clarifying the relationship between sex and self-disclosure, Lawrence Rosenfeld, Jean Civikly, and Jane Herron (1979) found that the relationship is indeed a complex one, calling for the consideration of a number of variables before any conclusions can be drawn. In general, they found that males disclose *more* to *strangers* than females, and are more willing to disclose *superficial* things about themselves, such as their work, attitudes, and opinions. Males are also less intimate and less personal than females. One clear finding is that both men and women generally prefer self-disclosure with members of the opposite sex (Rosenfeld, 1982).

When the target of disclosure is a friend and not a stranger it's very difficult to predict how either males or females will self-disclose. Is the revealer alone or in a group? Is the topic an intimate one, or one that is rather impersonal? At least these two questions must be answered before any predictions can be made.

Self-disclosure in families differs according to sex. A study by Victor Daluiso (1972) reported that daughters received the lion's share of disclosure from the parents and, probably as a consequence, had a more accurate perception of their parents. Sons received less disclosure than they gave, and they gave less than their sisters. This information suggests that the pattern for later life may be established in the family: Males have a tendency to disclose less intimate information about themselves than females.

Adrienne Abelman (1976) uncovered some fascinating connections between self-disclosure and family relationships. Among her many conclusions were the following: (1) Mutual self-disclosure exists, but primarily between the parents and their children of the same sex; (2) A daughter's satisfaction with her family is related to her father's degree of self-disclosing to his wife; (3) Men seem to rely on self-disclosing with their wives to obtain family satisfaction, whereas women seem to rely on self-disclosing with their children in order to obtain the same thing (which may account for why a father's disclosure to his wife is a determinant of their daughter's satisfaction); (4) Information family members have about each other is related to the degree to which each family member self-discloses.

Men and women differ in their self-disclosing behaviors, but do they *avoid* opening up for the same or different reasons? Rosenfeld (1979) investigated this question in a recent study in which men and women in beginning speech courses were asked to respond to reasons why people might avoid self-disclosure. Before reading the results of the survey you might want to complete the instrument for yourself. Simply indicate on a scale from 1 to 5 (1 = almost always; 2 = often; 3 = sometimes; 4 = rarely; and 5 = almost never) the extent to which you use each reason to avoid self-disclosing.

_____ 1. I can't find the opportunity to self-disclose with this person.
_____ 2. If I disclosed I might hurt the other person.
_____ 3. If I disclosed I might be evaluating or judging the other person.
_____ 4. I cannot think of topics that I would disclose.
_____ 5. Self-disclosure would give the other person information that he/she might use against me at some time.
_____ 6. If I self-disclose it might cause me to make personal changes.
_____ 7. Self-disclosure might threaten relationships I have with people other than the close acquaintance to whom I disclose.
_____ 8. Self-disclosure is a sign of weakness.
_____ 9. If I self-disclose, I might lose control over the other person.
_____ 10. If I self-disclose, I might discover I am less than I wish to be.
_____ 11. If I self-disclose, I might project an image I do not want to project.
_____ 12. If I self-disclose, the other person might not understand what I was saying.
_____ 13. If I self-disclose, the other person might evaluate me negatively.
_____ 14. Self-disclosure is a sign of some emotional disturbance.
_____ 15. Self-disclosure might hurt our relationship.
_____ 16. I am afraid that self-disclosure might lead to an intimate relationship with the other person.
_____ 17. Self-disclosure might threaten my physical safety.
_____ 18. If I self-disclose, I might give information that makes me appear inconsistent.
_____ 19. Any other reason: _____.

An analysis of responses to the questionnaire indicated that there is a great deal of similarity between why males and females avoid self-disclosure. The reason most commonly identified by both men and women was, "If I disclose I might project an image I do not want to project."

Important differences exist, too. For males, subsequent reasons (in order of importance) included: "If I self-disclose, I might give information that makes me appear inconsistent"; "If I self-disclose, I might lose control over the other person"; and "Self-disclosure might threaten relationships I have with people other than the close acquaintance to whom I disclose." Taken as a group, these reasons provide insight into the predominant reason why men avoid self-disclosure: "If I disclose to you I might project an image I do not want to, which could make me look bad and cause me to lose control over you. This might go so far as to affect relationships I have with people other than you." *The object is to maintain control,* which may be hampered by self-disclosure.

For females, reasons in addition to, "If I disclose I might project an image I do not want to project" included (in order of importance): "Self-disclosure would give the other person information that he/she might use against me at some time"; "Self-disclosure is a sign of some emotional disturbance"; and "Self-disclosure might hurt our relationship." Taken as a group, these reasons add up to the following: "If I disclose to you I might project an image I do not want to, such as my being emotionally ill, which you might use against me and which might hurt our relationship." *The object is to avoid personal hurt and problems with the relationship,* both of which may result from self-disclosure.

The results of other analyses have supplemented these results. In general, it appears as if most males avoid self-disclosure to avoid loss of control, and to avoid having to face aspects about themselves that might force them to make changes. A fear of intimacy, and the fear of negative evaluations from others, supports the notion that males generally avoid self-disclosure because they

i think of my poems and songs
as hands
and if i don't hold them out to you
i find i won't be touched

if i keep them
in my pocket
i would never get to see you
seeing me
seeing you

and though i know from experience
many of you
for a myriad of reasons
will laugh
and spit
and walk away unmoved
still
to meet those of you
who do reach out
is well worth the risk
        the pain

so
here are my hands
do what you will

Ric Masten

---

are afraid of the other person. This may relate to the control issue: Males may perceive their relationships primarily as battles for control; hence, others are adversaries, people to fear.

Females, on the other hand, generally do not perceive control as the key issue in their relationships. Rather, the issue is the avoidance of hurt, defined as poor interpersonal relationships or some threat to physical well-being.

Greta Garbo in *The Torrent*, 1926. (Culver Pictures, Inc.)

Reasons for Self-Disclosure

Although the amount of self-disclosure varies from one person to another, almost everyone shares important information about themselves at one time or another. But why? For what reasons? Derlega and Grzelak (1979) present a variety of reasons a person might have for disclosing in any particular situation. We can build upon their work and divide these reasons into several categories.

Catharsis Sometimes you might disclose information in an effort to "get it off your chest." In a moment of candor you might, for instance, share your regrets about having behaved badly in the past.

Self-clarification Sometimes you can clarify your beliefs, opinions, thoughts, attitudes, and feelings by talking about them with another person. This sort of "talking the problem out" occurs in many psychotherapies, but it also goes on in other contexts, all the way from good friends to bartenders or hairdressers.

Self-validation If you disclose information ("I think I did the right thing . . .") with the hope of seeking the listener's agreement, you are seeking validation of your behavior—confirmation of a belief you hold about yourself. On a deeper level, this sort of self-validating disclosure seeks confirmation of important parts of your self-concept.

Reciprocity A well-documented conclusion from research is that one act of self-disclosure begets another (Derlega and Chaikin, 1975). Thus, in some situations you may choose to disclose information about yourself to encourage another person to begin sharing.

Impression formation In some situations you may choose to self-disclose to create a particular impression of yourself. Dating behavior, particularly on the first few dates, is often aimed at creating a favorable impression. To do this, we sometimes share selected bits of information about ourselves—for example, our accomplishments or goals.

Relationship maintenance and enhancement Relationships need disclosure to stay healthy and develop. If a partner doesn't know how you're feeling about him or her—not to mention other parts of your life—then the subjects of your interaction become limited and shallow.

Social control   Revealing personal information may increase your control over the other person, and sometimes over the situation in which you and the other person find yourselves. For example, an employee who tells his boss that he's been courted by another firm probably will have an increased chance of getting raises and other improvements in his working conditions.

Manipulation   Although most of the preceding reasons might strike you as being manipulative, they often aren't premeditated strategies. There are cases, however, when an act of self-disclosure is calculated in advance to achieve a desired result. Of course, if a discloser's hidden motive ever becomes clear to the receiver, the results will most likely be quite unlike the intended ones.

Why We Fear Self-Disclosure

The case for self-disclosure seems overwhelming. Why is it, then, such a small part of our total communication? Why do we have a problem doing it? As John Powell (1968) asks, "Why am I afraid to tell you who I am?"

Self-disclosing behavior, according to Paul Cozby (1973)

> . . . may be seen as the product of two opposing forces, one operating to increase disclosure, the other operating to inhibit disclosure. The first force is the one studied most extensively by disclosure researchers. There are also factors which operate to inhibit disclosure. These might be termed discretion, or a need for privacy, and have been neglected in research on self-disclosure.

Though little empirical research has been done on self-disclosure avoidance, many good explanations have been offered.

Sometimes a neighbor whom we have disliked for a lifetime for his arrogance and conceit lets fall a single commonplace remark that shows us another side, another man, really; a man uncertain, puzzled, and in the dark like ourselves.

Willa Cather

Personal reasons   Focusing on interaction in the organizational setting, Fritz Steele discusses six overlapping causes of low disclosure:

1. Self-disclosure might lead to negative evaluations and rejection, a loss of both self-esteem and esteem from those to whom the self-disclosures are made.

A: *I earned a C average last semester.*
B: *Really? You must be a real dummy!*

2. If a particular self-disclosure alienates or angers the other person, it could lead to a decrease in the satisfaction that might be obtained from the relationship.

A: *At the reunion I met my old sweetheart, and we made love.*
B: *You have fifteen minutes to pack your bags and be out of here!*

3. Self-disclosure might lead to a loss of control over some future situation. Suppose, for instance, that in a moment of candor you confess to a friend that your critical sarcasm is often a way of hiding your feelings of inferiority to the object of your criticism. From that time on, you've sacrificed the usefulness of sarcasm as a way of fooling this person. Thus, your control over another's view of you has been diminished.
4. A possible drawback of self-disclosure is the risk that your honesty might hurt another person.

A: *Well, since you asked, I have been bored lately when we've been together.*
B: *I know. It's my fault. I don't see how you can stand me at all!*

5. Self-disclosure might lead to the projection of a negative image. You might look less "perfect" than you care to. Admitting that you've been unfair, acted foolishly, or are unsure of yourself might indicate that you're human, but in a world where a good public image seems important, revealing one's imperfections is often threatening.

6. Lying often appears to have a greater benefit for the listener than does telling the truth. Steele calls this the "Great Lie Theory." Statements such as "I'm not going to tell you because you'll be better off not knowing" fall into this category. Another example of avoiding self-disclosure to prevent pain is the "I love you" pledge uttered only to make the other person feel better. (Needless to say, confessions such as this have a way of creating much grief in the long run.) Of course, telling the truth usually does more to help the other person than does telling a lie. But this is not what most of us were taught. And that leads to several more reasons for avoiding self-disclosure.

Sociological reasons Gerard Egan (1970), viewing self-disclosure from a sociological perspective, argues that there are two forces in our society that work against greater self-disclosure. The first is a kind of cultural ban against intimate self-disclosure based on a view that open sharing is a sign of weakness, exhibitionism, or mental illness. The second force is a societywide cultivation of the "lie" as a way of life. This force is related to the belief that misrepresentation is necessary to achieve or maintain power and wealth in our society. Unfortunately, the underlying justification for this reason is that how you present

yourself to others must be different from how you really conceive of yourself because if your self-presentation was true to your self-conception, failure would surely result!

Paradoxical as it sounds, a third social force discouraging self-disclosure is precisely the fact that such open behavior does lead to increased awareness. Self-help books and human relations training notwithstanding, a society that uses advertising to promote appearance over reality and that equates material success with satisfaction can't stand too much self-examination and still survive. Thus, it's difficult to be open with one's self and others and "play the game" at the same time. As L.J. Sherrill (1945) put it, "The human organism seems capable of enduring anything in the universe except a clear, complete, fully conscious view of one's self as he actually is." Because self-disclosure leads to self-awareness and the revelation, in front of one or more others, that changes in behavior or goals are necessary, a commitment to *do something* becomes apparent. Self-disclosure demands a willingness to assume responsibility for making any changes revealed as important. The flight from this responsibility, which may appear both awesome and painful, is the avoidance of self-disclosure.

Another force acting against disclosure is the reluctance of many people in our society to truly communicate with others. You may not fear getting in touch with yourself, yet you may fear letting *others* get in touch with *you*. As already mentioned, self-disclosure increases trust, liking, attraction, and may lead to an intimate relationship. Eric Berne's thesis in his book *Games People Play* (1964) is that intimacy frightens many people, which is why they play games. Games keep people apart and reduce the likelihood of intimate contact.

Reasons for avoiding self-disclosure may be best summarized by John Powell, who answers the question posed in the title of his book, *Why Am I Afraid to Tell You Who I Am?* (1968), this way:

> I am afraid to tell you who I am, because, if I tell you who I am, you may not like who I am, and it's all that I have.

Without your facade (that is, the mask others see, the mask that doesn't reflect the inner you), the risk of personal rejection is high indeed. And if you reveal your inner self, what excuses can you muster to overcome the rejection that might tear you apart? No, the risk is too great, so you convince yourself that avoiding self-disclosure altogether is the best answer.

And the cycle begins: loneliness, depression, self-alienation, the loss of community. A high price to pay, but some—maybe you—perceive rejection an even higher price. If you don't share yourself with others, you stand little chance of establishing meaningful relationships with others. Without sharing yourself, it's difficult for others to help meet your basic social needs of belonging, being accepted, and being loved. Once you understand the connection between sharing knowledge of self and meaningful interpersonal relationships, it becomes apparent that you must take the risk that comes with self-disclosure. The question then becomes when to open up and when to remain quiet.

When to Self-Disclose?

One fear we've had while writing this chapter is that a few over-enthusiastic readers may throw down their books after reading half of what we've written and rush away to

> *Which of us has known his brother?*
> *Which of us has looked into his*
> *   father's heart:*
> *Which of us has not remained forever*
> *   prison-bent?*
> *Which of us is not forever a stranger*
> *   and alone?*
>
> Thomas Wolfe

begin sharing every personal detail of their lives to whomever they can find. As you can imagine, this kind of behavior isn't an example of effective interpersonal communication.

Self-disclosure is a special kind of sharing, not appropriate for every situation. Let's take a look at some guidelines that can help you recognize how to express yourself in a way that's rewarding for you and the others involved.

1. Is the other person important to you? There are several ways in which someone might be important. Perhaps you have an ongoing relationship deep enough so that sharing significant parts of yourself justifies keeping your present level of togetherness intact. Or perhaps the person to whom you're considering disclosing is someone with whom you've previously related on a less personal level. But now you see a chance to grow closer, and disclosure may be the path toward developing that personal relationship.

There's still another category of "important person" to whom self-disclosure is sometimes appropriate: Strangers who are players in what has been called the "bus rider phenomenon." This occurs when we meet a total stranger whom we'll probably never see again (on a bus, plane, etc.) and reveal the most intimate parts of our lives. It's sometimes possible to call such strangers "important people" because they provide a safe outlet for expressing important feelings which otherwise would go unshared. A friend of ours tells the following story of how a total stranger can be a party to self-disclosure:

> I was traveling with my husband (we had been married for two weeks) back east to have him meet all the relatives, especially my mother who couldn't make it out for the wedding. We sat three across on the plane; the third person was an old woman. I was very "into" being a new bride, and so did not notice that the woman made several attempts to talk

to us. My husband noticed (thankfully!) and asked the usual question, "Where are you traveling?" She shared with us how her husband, who was back east, had just died there. She was going to take care of the necessary arrangements. It was a crisis unparalleled in her life. And she needed to tell someone, to have someone cry with her for a moment—even two strangers on a plane.

2. Is the risk of disclosing reasonable? Take a realistic look at the potential risks of self-disclosure. Even if the probable benefits are great, opening yourself up to almost certain rejection may be asking for trouble. For instance, it might be foolhardy to share your important feelings with someone you know

© United Feature Syndicate, Inc.

■■■ *"What is REAL?" asked the Rabbit one day, when they were lying side by side near the nursery fender, before Nana came to tidy the room.*

"Does it mean having things buzz inside you and a stick-out handle?"

"Real isn't how you are made," said the Skin Horse, "it's a thing that happens to you. When a child loves you for a long, long time, not just to play with, but REALLY loves you, then you become Real."

"Does it hurt?" asked the Rabbit.

"Sometimes," said the Skin Horse, for he was always truthful. "When you are Real you don't mind being hurt."

"Does it happen all at once, like being wound up," he asked, "or bit by bit?"

"It doesn't happen all at once," said the Skin Horse. "You become. It takes a long time. That's why it doesn't often happen to people who break easily, or have sharp edges, or who have to be carefully kept. Generally, by the time you are Real, most of your hair has been loved off, and your eyes drop out and you get loose in the joints and very shabby. But these things don't matter at all, because when you are Real you can't be ugly, except to people who don't understand."

Margery Williams
THE VELVETEEN RABBIT

---

is likely to betray your confidences or ridicule them. On the other hand, knowing that your partner is trustworthy and supportive makes the prospect of speaking out more reasonable. In anticipating risks, be sure that you are realistic. It's sometimes easy to indulge in catastrophic expectations, in which you begin to imagine all sorts of disastrous consequences of your opening up, when in fact such horrors are quite unlikely to occur.

3. Is the amount and type of disclosure appropriate? A third point to realize is that there are degrees of self-disclosure, so that telling others about yourself isn't an all-or-nothing decision you must make. It's possible to share some facts, opinions, or feelings with one person while reserving riskier ones for others. In the same vein, before sharing important information with someone who does matter to you, you might con-

sider testing their reactions by disclosing less personal data. In a recent study by Lange and Grove (1981), it was found that in initial encounters, individuals who disclose moderately are evaluated more positively than those who disclose very little or a great deal. It was also found that this may be because high levels of disclosure cause the target to become anxious, and low levels of disclosure are not sufficiently stimulating.

4. Is the disclosure relevant to the situation at hand? Self-disclosure doesn't require long confessions about your past life or current thoughts unrelated to the now. On the contrary, it ought to be directly pertinent to your present conversation. It's ludicrous to picture the self-disclosing person as someone who blurts out intimate details of every past experience. Instead, our model is someone who, when the time is appropriate, trusts us

By Mell Lazarus

enough to share the hidden parts of herself that affect our relationship.

Usually, then, the subject of appropriate self-disclosure involves the present, the "here and now" as opposed to "there and then." "How am I feeling now?" "How are we doing now?" These are appropriate topics for sharing personal thoughts and feelings. There are certainly times when it's relevant to bring up the past, but only as it relates to what's going on in the present.

5. Is the disclosure reciprocated? There's nothing quite as disconcerting as talking your heart out to someone only to discover that the other person has yet to say anything to you that is half as revealing as what you've been saying. And you think to yourself: "What am I doing?!" Unequal self-disclosure creates an imbalanced relationship, one doomed to fall apart.

There are few times when one-way disclosure is acceptable. Most of them involve formal, therapeutic relationships in which a client approaches a trained professional with the goal of resolving a problem. For instance, you wouldn't necessarily expect your physician to begin sharing his or her personal ailments with you during an office visit. Nonetheless, it's interesting to note that one frequently noted characteristic of effective psychotherapists, counselors, and teachers is

a willingness to share their feelings about a relationship with their clients.

6. Will the effect be constructive? Self-disclosure can be a vicious tool if it's not used carefully. Psychologist George Bach suggests that every person has a psychological "beltline." Below that beltline are areas about which the person is extremely sensitive. Bach says that jabbing at a "below the belt" area is a sure-fire way to disable another person, though usually at great cost to the relationship. It's important to consider the effects of your candor before opening up to others. Comments such as, "I've always thought you were pretty unintelligent" or, "Last year I made love to your best friend" *may* sometimes resolve old business and thus be constructive, but they also can be devastating—to the listener, to the relationship, and to your self-esteem.

7. Is the self-disclosure clear and understandable? When expressing yourself to others, it's important that you share yourself in a way that's intelligible. This means describing the *sources* of your message clearly. For instance, it's far better to describe another's behavior by saying, "When you don't answer my phone calls or drop by to visit anymore . . ." than to vaguely complain "When you avoid me . . ."

It's also vital to express your *thoughts* and

feelings explicitly. "I feel worried because I'm afraid you don't care about me" is more understandable than "I don't like it . . . " We'll have more to say about thoughts and feelings in Chapter 8.

We hope these guidelines—and this chapter—have given you a better picture of the importance of self-disclosure in interpersonal communication. We've tried to acknowledge that self-disclosure is difficult and risky. Like you, we know that hiding from others is usually easier, and certainly less risky in the short run. But as our dreams of nakedness tell us, avoiding self-disclosure has consequences that can be more painful and risky than wearing masks.

Readings

Abelman, Adrienne K. "The Relationship Between Family Self-Disclosure, Adolescent Adjustment, Family Satisfaction, and Family Congruence." *Dissertation Abstracts International* 36 (1976): 4248A.

Berne, Eric. *Games People Play*. New York: Grove Press, 1964.

Burke, Ronald J., Tamara Weir, and Denise Harrison. "Disclosure of Problems and Tensions Experienced by Marital Partners." *Psychological Reports* 38 (1976): 531–542.

Cash, T.F., and D. Soloway. "Self-Disclosure Correlates of Physical Attractiveness: An Exploratory Study." *Psychological Reports* 36 (1975): 579–586.

*Chelune, Gordon J., ed. *Self-Disclosure*. San Francisco: Jossey-Bass, 1979.

Chelune, Gordon J. "Toward an Empirical Definition of Self-Disclosure: Validation in a Single Case Design." *Western Journal of Speech Communication* 45 (1981): 269–276.

Chelune, Gordon J., Stephen T. Skiffington, and Connie Williams. "A Multidimensional Analysis of Observers' Perceptions of Self-Disclosing Behavior." *Journal of Personality and Social Psychology* 41 (1981): 599–606.

*Cozby, Paul C. "Self-Disclosure: A Literature Review." *Psychological Bulletin* 79 (1973): 73–91.

Daluiso, Victor E. "Self-Disclosure and Perception of that Self-Disclosure Between Parents and Their Teen-Age Children." *Dissertation Abstracts International* 33 (1972): 420B.

Derlega, Valerian J., and Alan L. Chaikin. "Privacy and Self-Disclosure in Social Relationships." *Journal of Social Issues* 33 (1978): 102–115.

*Derlega, Valerian J., and Alan L. Chaikin. *Sharing Intimacy: What We Reveal to Others and Why*. Englewood Cliffs, N.J.: Prentice-Hall, 1975.

Derlega, Valerian J., Bonnie Durham, Barbara Gockel, and David Sholis, "Sex Differences in Self-Disclosure: Effects of Topic Content, Friendships, and Partner's Sex." *Sex Roles* 7 (1981): 433–448.

Derlega, Valerian J., and Janusz Grzelak. "Appropriateness of Self-Disclosure." In *Self-Disclosure*, Gordon J. Chelune, ed. San Francisco: Jossey-Bass, 1979.

Derlega, Valerian J., Midge Wilson, and Alan L. Chaikin. "Friendship and Disclosure Reciprocity." *Journal of Personality and Social Psychology* 34 (1976): 578–582.

Egan, Gerard. *Encounter: Group Processes for Interpersonal Growth*. Belmont, Calif.: Brooks/Cole, 1970.

Gergen, Kenneth J. *The Concept of Self*. New York: Holt, Rinehart and Winston, 1971.

Giffin, Kim, and Bobby R. Patton. *Personal Communication in Human Relations*. Columbus, Ohio: Charles E. Merrill, 1974.

Gilbert, Shirley J. "Self-Disclosure, Intimacy and Communication in Families." *Family Coordinator* 25 (1976): 221–231.

Gilbert, Shirley J., and Gale G. Whiteneck. "Toward a Multidimensional Approach to the Study of Self-Disclosure." *Human Communication Research* 2 (1976): 347–355.

Goodstein, Leonard D., and Virginia M. Reinecker. "Factors Affecting Self-Disclosure: A Review of the Literature." In *Progress in Experimental Personality Research*, VII, Brendan A. Maher, ed. New York: Academic Press, 1974.

Harris, Thomas A. *I'm O.K., You're O.K.* New York: Harper and Row, 1967.

Johnson, David W. *Reaching Out.* Englewood Cliffs, N.J.: Prentice-Hall, 1972.

Jourard, Sidney M. *Disclosing Man to Himself.* Princeton, N.J.: Van Nostrand, 1968.

Jourard, Sidney M. "Healthy Personality and Self-Disclosure." *Mental Hygiene* 43 (1959): 499–507.

*Jourard, Sidney M. *The Transparent Self,* 2nd Ed. Princeton, N.J.: Van Nostrand, 1971.

Kleinke, Chris L. "Effects of Personal Evaluations." In *Self-Disclosure,* Gordon J. Chelune, ed. San Francisco: Jossey-Bass, 1979.

Lange, Jonathon I., and Theodore G. Grove. "Sociometric and Autonomic Responses to Three Levels of Self-Disclosure in Dyads." *Western Journal of Speech Communication* 45 (1981): 355–362.

Luft, Joseph. *Of Human Interaction.* Palo Alto, Calif.: National Press Books, 1969.

Lyons, Arthur. "Personality of High and Low Self-Disclosers." *Journal of Humanistic Psychology* 18 (1978): 83–86.

Moriwaki, Sharon Y. "Self-Disclosure, Significant Others and Psychological Well-Being in Old Age." *Journal of Health and Social Behavior* 14 (1973): 226–232.

Mowrer, Orval Hobart. "Loss and Recovery of Community: A Guide to the Theory and Practice of Integrity Therapy." In *Innovations to Group Psychotherapy,* George M. Gazda, ed. Springfield, Ill.: Charles C. Thomas, 1968.

*Pearce, W. Barnett, and Stewart M. Sharp. "Self-Disclosing Communication." *Journal of Communication* 23 (1973): 409–425.

Powell, John. *Why Am I Afraid To Tell You Who I Am?* Niles, Ill.: Argus Communications, 1968.

*Rosenfeld, Lawrence B. "Self-Disclosure Avoidance: Why Am I Afraid To Tell You Who I Am?" *Communication Monographs* 46 (1979): 63–74.

Rosenfeld, Lawrence B. "Self-Disclosure and Target Characteristics." Unpublished manuscript, University of New Mexico, 1981.

Rosenfeld, Lawrence B. "Why We Self-Disclose: A Preliminary Investigation." Unpublished manuscript, University of North Carolina, 1982.

Rosenfeld, Lawrence B., Jean M. Civikly, and Jane R. Herron. "Anatomical Sex, Psychological Sex, and Self-Disclosure." In *Self-Disclosure,* Gordon J. Chelune, ed. San Francisco: Jossey-Bass, 1979.

Rubin, Zick. "Lovers and Other Strangers: The Development of Intimacy in Encounters and Relationships." *American Scientist* 62 (1974): 182–190.

Sherrill, L.J. *Guilt and Redemption.* Richard, Va.: John Knox Press, 1945.

Steele, Fritz. *The Open Organization: The Impact of Secrecy and Disclosure on People and Organizations.* Reading, Mass.: Addison-Wesley, 1975.

Walker, Lilly S., and Paul H. Eright. "Self-Disclosure in Friendship." *Perceptual and Motor Skills* 42 (1976): 735–742.

Wheeless, Lawrence R., and Janis Grotz. "The Measurement of Trust and Its Relationship to Self-Disclosure." *Human Communication Research* 3 (1977): 250–257.

Williams, Margery. *The Velveteen Rabbit.* New York: Avon, 1975.

Wood, John T. *What Are You Afraid Of?: A Guide to Dealing with Your Fears.* New York: Spectrum Books, 1976.

8

Emotions

■■■■ *After studying the material in this chapter*

You should understand:

1. The four components of emotion.

2. The factors that influence expression of emotion in contemporary society.

3. The benefits of appropriate expression of emotions.

4. The characteristics of facilitative and debilitative emotions.

5. The relationship between activating events, thoughts, and emotions.

6. Seven fallacies that result in unnecessary, debilitative emotions.

7. The steps in the rational-emotive approach to coping with debilitative feelings.

You should be able to:

1. Identify physical and cognitive manifestations of the emotions you experience.

2. Label your own emotions accurately.

3. Identify the degree to which you express your emotions and the consequences of this level of expression.

4. Identify which of your emotions are facilitative and which are debilitative.

5. Identify the fallacious beliefs that result in the debilitative emotions you experience.

6. Apply the rational-emotive approach as a way of managing your own debilitative emotions.

At one time or another you've probably imagined how different life would be if you became disabled in some way. The thought of becoming blind, deaf, or immobile is certainly frightening, and though a bit morbid, it can remind you to appreciate the faculties you do have. But have you ever considered how life would be if you somehow lost your ability to experience emotions?

While life without feelings certainly wouldn't be as dramatic or crippling as other disabilities, consider its effect. Never again would you experience the excitement of Christmas or the first sunny day of spring. You would never enjoy a movie, book, or piece of art—or even find it interesting. Your life would be empty of chuckles, giggles, and smiles, not to mention belly laughs. Happiness, confidence, and love would be nothing but words to you. Of course, an emotionless life would also be free of boredom, frustration, fear, and loneliness, too—but most of us would agree that giving up pleasure is too steep a price to pay for freedom from pain.

This fantasy demonstrates the important role that emotions play in our relationships as well as in other parts of life. Because feelings play such a fundamental role in interpersonal communication, we will take a close look at them in this chapter. We'll explore exactly what feelings are, discuss the ways in which they are handled in contemporary society, and see how recognizing and

"What the hell was that? Something just swept over me— like contentment or something."

Drawing by Weber. © 1981 The New Yorker Magazine, Inc.

James Dean in *Rebel Without a Cause*, 1955. (The Museum of Modern Art/Film Stills Archive)

expressing them can improve relationships. We'll explore a method for coping with troublesome, debilitating feelings that can inhibit rather than help your communication. And finally, we'll look at some guidelines which should give you a clearer idea of when and how to express your emotions effectively.

What Are Emotions?

Suppose that a visitor from the planet Vulcan or Ork asked you to explain emotions. What would you say? You might start by saying that emotions are things that we feel. But this doesn't say much, since you would probably describe feelings as being synonymous with emotions. Social scientists who study the role of feelings generally agree that there are four components to our emotions.

Physiological changes   When a person experiences strong emotions, many bodily changes occur. For example, the physical aspects of fear include an increased heartbeat, a rise in blood pressure, an increase in adrenaline secretions, an increase in blood sugar, a slowing of digestion, and a dilation of the pupils. Some of these changes are recognizable to the person experiencing them. These sensations are terms *proprioceptive stimuli*, meaning they are activated by movement of internal tissues. Proprioceptive messages can offer a significant clue to our emotions once we become aware of them. For instance, one woman we know began focusing on her internal messages and learned that every time she returned to the city from a vacation she felt an empty feeling in the pit of her stomach. From what she'd already learned about herself, she knew that this sensation always accompanied things she dreaded. She then realized she was much happier in the country. Now she is trying to find a way to make the move she knows is right for her.

Another friend of ours had always appeared easygoing and agreeable, even in the most frustrating circumstances. But after focusing on internal messages, he discovered his mild behavior contrasted strongly with the tense muscles and headaches that he got during trying times. This new awareness led him to realize that he did indeed experience frustration and anger—and that he somehow needed to deal with these feelings if he was going to feel truly comfortable.

Nonverbal manifestations   A quick comparison between the emotionless Mr. Spock of *Star Trek* and full-blooded humans tells us that feelings show up in many nonverbal behaviors. Postures, gestures, facial expression, body positioning and distance, all provide clues suggesting our emotional state.

One of the first social scientists to explore the relationship between emotion and behavior was Charles Darwin. In 1872 Darwin published *The Expression of Emotion in Man and Animals,* which asserted that humans and certain other creatures seemed to behave in similar ways when enraged. Later researchers confirmed the premise that among humans, at least, the most basic emotional expressions are universal. A.G. Gitter and his colleagues (1972) found that people from a variety of cultures all agreed on the facial expressions that indicate emotions such as fear, sadness, happiness, and pain. (Chapter 5 discusses the value of observing nonverbal messages as clues to emotion.)

Cognitive interpretations The physiological aspects of fear, such as a racing heart, perspiration, tense muscles, and a boost in blood pressure, are surprisingly similar to the physical changes that accompany excitement, joy, and other emotions. In other words, from measuring the physical condition of someone experiencing a strong emotion, it would be difficult to determine whether the person was trembling with fear or quivering with excitement. The recognition that the bodily components of most emotions are similar led some psychologists (see Schachter and Singer, 1967; Valins, 1967) to conclude that the experience of fright, joy, or anger comes primarily from the *label* that we give to the same physical symptoms. This cognitive explanation of emotion has been labeled *attribution theory.* Psychologist Philip Zimbardo (1977) offers a good example of attribution in action:

> I notice I'm perspiring while lecturing. From that I infer I am feeling nervous. If it occurs often, I might even label myself a "nervous person." Once I have the label, the next question I must answer is "Why am I nervous?" Then I start to search for an appropriate ex-

Half our mistakes in life arise from feeling where we ought to think, and thinking where we ought to feel.

John Churton Collins

planation. I might notice some students leaving the room, or being inattentive. I am nervous because I'm not giving a good lecture. That makes me nervous. How do I know it's not good? Because I'm boring my audience. I am nervous because I am a boring lecturer and I want to be a good lecturer. I feel inadequate. Maybe I should open a delicatessen instead. Just then a student says, "It's hot in here. I'm perspiring and it makes it tough to concentrate on your lecture." Instantly, I'm no longer "nervous" or "boring."

In his book *Shyness,* Zimbardo (1977) discusses the consequences of making inaccurate or exaggerated attributions. In a survey of more than 5,000 subjects, over 80 percent described themselves as having been shy at some time in their lives, while more than 40 percent considered themselves presently shy. Most significantly, the "not shy" people behaved in virtually the *same way* as their shy counterparts. They would blush, perspire, and feel their hearts pounding in certain social situations. The biggest difference between the two groups seemed to be the label with which they described themselves. This difference is significant. Someone who notices the symptoms we've described and thinks, "I'm such a shy person!" will most likely feel more uncomfortable and communicate less effectively than a person with the same symptoms who thinks, "Well, I'm a bit shaky here, but that's to be expected."

Verbal expression The fourth component of emotion is verbal expression. As Gerard

affectionate
afraid
alarmed
alienated
alone
angry
anxious
apathetic
appreciated
attractive
awkward
beaten
beautiful
bewildered
brave
calm
caring
closed
comfortable
committed
compassionate
competent
concerned
confident
confused
contented
cowardly
creative
cruel
curious
cut off from others
defeated
defensive
dejected
dependent
depressed
deprived
desperate
disappointed
domineering
eager
easygoing
embarrassed

envious
evasive
evil
excited
exhilarated
fatalistic
fearful
feminine
flirtatious
friendly
frigid
frustrated
generous
genuine
gentle
giddy
glad
grateful
grudge-bearing
guilty
gutless
happy
hateful
homicidal
hopeful
hopeless
hostile
humorous
hurt
hyperactive
ignored
immobilized
impatient
inadequate
incompetent
indecisive
inferior
inhibited
insecure
insincere
involved
isolated
jealous

joyful
judgmental
lively
lonely
lovable
loved
loving
masculine
masked
masochistic
melancholy
misunderstood
needy
old
optimistic
out of control
overcontrolled
oversexed
paranoid
passionate
peaceful
persecuted
pessimistic
phoney
pitiful
playful
pleased
possessive
preoccupied
prejudiced
pressured
protective
proud
quiet
rejected
religious
remorseful
repelled
repulsive
restrained
sad
sadistic
secure

seductive
self-pitying
self-reliant
sexually aroused
shallow
shy
silly
sincere
sinful
sluggish
soft
sorry for self
stubborn
stupid
suicidal
superior to others
supported
supportive
suspicious
sympathetic
tender
terrified
threatened
tolerant
torn
touchy
triumphant
two-faced
ugly
unsure
understanding
unresponsive
uptight
useless
vindictive
violent
weary
weepy
wishy-washy
youthful

Egan (1977) points out, there are several ways to verbally express a feeling. The first is through single words: I'm angry, excited, depressed, curious, and so on. Many people are limited to these single word expressions, and suffer from impoverished emotional vocabularies. They have a hard time describing more than a few basic feelings, such as "good" or "bad," "terrible" or "great."

Another way of expressing feelings verbally is to use descriptive phrases: "I feel all jumbled up," "I'm on top of the world," and so on. As long as such phrases aren't too obscure—for example, "I feel somnolent"—they can effectively describe your emotional state.

It's also possible to express emotions by describing what you'd like to do: "I feel like singing"; "I'd like to cry"; I feel like running away," etc. Often these expressions capture the emotion clearly, but in other cases they can be confusing. For instance, if somebody told you, "Every time I see you I want to laugh," you wouldn't know whether you were an object of enjoyment or ridicule.

The ability to verbally express emotions is crucial to effective communication. For example, notice the difference between

When you kiss me and nibble on my ear, I think you want to make love,

and

When you kiss me and nibble on my ear, I think you want to make love and I feel excited (or disgusted),

or between

Ever since we had our fight, I've been avoiding you,

and

Ever since our fight, I've been avoiding you because I've been so embarrassed (or so angry).

Many people think they're clearly expressing their feelings, when in fact their statements are emotionally counterfeit. For instance, it may sound emotionally revealing to say, "I feel like going to a show," or "I feel we've been seeing too much of each other." But neither of these statements actually exhibit emotional content. In the first sentence, the word "feel" really represents an intention: "I *want* to go to a show." In the second sentence, the "feeling" is really a *thought:* "I think we've been seeing too much of each other." The absence of emotion in each case becomes recognizable when you add a word with genuine feeling to the sentence. For instance, "I'm *bored* and I want to go to a show," or "I think we've been seeing too much of each other and I feel *confined.*"

Emotions in Contemporary Society

Once you can detect these kinds of counterfeit emotional statements, you notice that most people do very little sharing of their feelings. To verify this, try counting the number of genuine emotional expressions you hear over a two- or three-day period. You'll probably discover that emotional expressions are quite rare. People are generally comfortable making statements of fact and often delight in expressing their opinion, but they rarely disclose how they feel.

Why do people fail to express their feelings? There are several reasons.

Modeling and instructions Our society discourages the expression of most feelings. From the time children are old enough to understand language, they learn that the range of acceptable emotions is limited. Do these admonitions sound familiar to you?

"Don't get angry."
"There's nothing to worry about."
"That isn't funny."
"There's no reason to feel bad."
"Control yourself—don't get excited."
"For God's sake, don't cry!"

Notice how each of these messages denies its recipient the right to experience a certain feeling. Anger isn't legitimate, and neither is fear. There's something wrong with finding certain situations humorous. Feeling bad is considered silly. Excitement isn't desirable, so keep your emotions under control. And finally, don't make a scene by crying.

Often such parental admonitions are nothing more than a coded request for some peace and quiet. But when repeated often enough, the underlying instruction comes through loud and clear—only a narrow range of emotions is acceptable to share or experience.

In addition, the actions of most adults create a model suggesting that grownups shouldn't express too many feelings. Expressions of affection are fine within limits: A hug and kiss for Mother is all right, though a young man should shake hands with Dad. Affection toward friends becomes less and less frequent as we grow older, so that even a simple statement such as "I like you" is seldom heard between adults.

Social roles Expression of emotions is further limited by the requirements of many social roles. Salespeople are taught to always smile at customers, no matter how obnoxious. Teachers are portrayed as paragons of rationality, supposedly representing their field of expertise and instructing their stu-

The Thinker

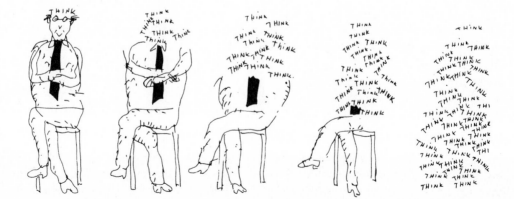

Woody Allen and Janet Margolin in *Take the Money and Run*, 1969. (Culver Pictures)

dents with total impartiality. Students are rewarded for asking "acceptable" questions and otherwise being submissive creatures.

Furthermore, stereotyped sex roles discourage people from freely expressing certain emotions. The stereotype states that men don't cry and are rational creatures. They must be strong, emotionally and physically. Aggressiveness is a virtue ("the Marine Corps builds men"). Women, on the other hand, are often socialized in a manner that allows them to express their emotions by crying. The stereotype states that women should be irrational and intuitive. A certain amount of female determination and assertiveness is appealing, but when faced with a man's resistance they ought to defer.

Inability to recognize emotions The result of all these restrictions is that many of us lose the ability to feel deeply. As a muscle withers away when it is unused, so our capacity to recognize and act on certain emotions reduces. It's hard to cry after spending most of one's life fulfilling the role society expects of a man, even when the tears are in-

197

What other dungeon is so dark as one's own heart! What jailer so inexorable as one's self!

Nathaniel Hawthorne

---

side. After years of denying your anger, the ability to recognize that feeling takes real effort. For someone who has never acknowledged love for one's friends, accepting the emotion can be difficult indeed.

Fear of self-disclosure In a society that discourages the expression of feelings, emotional self-disclosure can be risky. For a parent, boss, or teacher whose life has been built on the presumption of confidence and certainty, it may be frightening to say, "I'm sorry, I was wrong." A person who has made a life's work out of not relying on others has a hard time saying, "I'm lonesome. I want your friendship."

Moreover, one who musters up the courage to share feelings such as these still risks suffering unpleasant consequences. Others might misunderstand: An expression of affection might be construed as a romantic come-on, and a confession of uncertainty might appear to be a sign of weakness. Another risk is that emotional honesty might make others feel uncomfortable. Finally, there's always a chance that emotional candor could be used against you, either out of cruelty or thoughtlessness.

Benefits of Expressing Emotions

Given all the social conditioning and personal risks that discourage us from expressing feelings, it's understandable why so many people are emotionally uncommunicative. This is especially unfortunate when we look at the benefits that can flow from sharing feelings appropriately.

Physical health Sharing emotions is healthy. In fact, keeping your feelings pent up can lead to psychosomatic illnesses. We're not referring to hypochondria, where people believe they are ill but aren't, or malingering, where they pretend to be sick. A psychosomatic disease is real: It does not differ from an organically induced illness. What distinguishes a psychosomatic illness is its psychological basis. Whereas the pain comes from a physical condition, the problem has its origins in some aspect of the person's psychological functioning. Psychosomatic problems can grow out of the chronic stress that results when unexpressive people don't share their feelings. Remember the physiological changes that accompany strong emotions? (Digestion slows; heartbeat increases; adrenaline is secreted; and respiration grows quicker.) Whereas these conditions are short-lived for people who can express their feelings, those who fail to act on these impulses develop a continual state of physiological tension. This tension damages the digestive tract, lungs, circulatory system, muscles, joints, and the body's ability to resist infections. It even hastens the process of aging (McQuade and Aikman, 1974).

Hypertension (high blood pressure) and heart trouble can also have their roots in chronic stress. Over a five-year period Flanders Dunbar (1947) studied a random sample of 1,600 cardiovascular patients at Columbia Presbyterian Medical Center in New York City. She found that four out of five patients shared common emotional characteristics, many of which were representative of either nonassertive or aggressive communicators. In fact, most of the patients were argumentative, had trouble expressing their feelings, and kept people at a distance. McQuade and

Aikman describe other characteristics of cardiovascular sufferers: they are easily upset but unable to handle upsetting situations, anxious to please but longing to rebel, and alternately passive and irritable.

Evidence also suggests that nonassertive people are prone to yet another physical problem. The immunological system, which protects the body against infection, apparently functions less effectively when a person is under stress. The body doesn't always respond quickly enough to infection; and sometimes the body even responds incorrectly, as in the case of allergic reactions. Stress has even been diagnosed as one cause of the common cold. Stress or anxiety alone, however, are not sufficient to cause these disorders; a source of infection must also be present. But as research by Swiss physiologist Hans Selye (1956) suggests, persons subjected to stress have an increased chance of contracting infectious disease. Selye states, "If a microbe is in or around us all the time and yet causes no disease until we are exposed to stress, what is the cause of our illness, the microbe or the stress?"

All this talk about psychosomatic illness is not intended to suggest that nonassertion automatically leads to ulcers and heart trouble, or perhaps worse. Obviously, many shy or aggressive people never suffer from such ailments and many assertive people do. There are also many other sources of stress in our society: financial pressures, the problems of people we care for, pollution, crime, and the nagging threat of war, to name a few. Nonetheless, an increasing amount of evidence suggests that the person who is not fully expressive increases the risk of developing physical disabilities. Just as nonsmokers are less likely to contract lung cancer than their pack-a-day counterparts, skillful communicators have a better chance of living a healthy life.

Increased intimacy Beyond the physiological benefits, another advantage of expressing emotions is the chance of reaching greater intimacy with others. A friend of ours, reflecting on his marriage, affirmed this point.

> For the longest time I held back a lot of feelings from my wife which I thought would hurt her. I did spare her feelings, but by holding back I also felt more and more like a stranger to her. It finally got to the point where I was hiding so much of how I truly felt that instead of an honest, growing marriage, I felt like I was carrying on a charade. Finally I couldn't stand the experience of being isolated from the woman I was committed to spending my life with, and so I began to share the things that were going on inside me—the uncomfortable feelings as well as the pleasant ones. As we began to really talk about who we were again, we uncovered a lot of feelings which we had both been out of touch with. I won't say that this kind of sharing has made our life together easier—it's often hard for one of us to face how the other feels—but I can definitely say that we feel closer now than we have in a long time.*

Conflict resolution Although expressing feeling can sometimes lead to trouble, the consequences of not sharing them can be just as bad. When people don't communicate, boring marriages don't change, friendships continue in hurtful patterns, and job conditions stay unpleasant. How long can such destructive patterns go on? Surely there comes a time when it's necessary either to share emotions or to give up on the relationship. Moreover, research on conflict

*A note of caution: Sharing every emotion you experience at the time is not always wise. When deciding whether to express a feeling that is difficult for you or another person to handle, read the guidelines for self-disclosure in Chapter 7.

resolution conducted by David Johnson (1971) and others suggests that the skillful expression of emotions actually increases the quality of problem solving. After all, unresolved feelings can create obstacles that keep individuals and groups from dealing most effectively with their problems. On the other hand, once the participants in a conflict have expressed their feelings they're in a position to resolve the problems that led to them. Chapter 11 introduces several methods for handling interpersonal conflicts constructively.

Coping with Debilitative Feelings: A Cognitive Approach

At this point you may think that experiencing and expressing emotions is always beneficial. Actually, this position is extreme: Some feelings do little good for anyone. For instance, feeling dejected can sometimes provide a foundation upon which to grow ("I'm so miserable now that I must do something to change"). More often, however, depression prevents people from acting effectively. The same point can be made about rage, terror, and jealousy: Most of the time these emotions do little to promote personal well-being or to improve relationships.

Debilitative vs. facilitative emotions We need to make a distinction, then, between *facilitative* emotions, which contribute to effective functioning, and *debilitative* emotions, which hinder or prevent effective performance. The difference between facilitative and debilitative emotions isn't one of quality so much as degree. For instance, a certain amount of anger or irritation can be constructive, since it often stimulates a person to improve the unsatsfying conditions. Rage, on the other hand, usually makes matters worse, as will fear. A little bit of nervousness before an important athletic contest or job interview might boost you just enough to improve your performance (mellow athletes or actors usually don't do well). But total terror is something else. One big difference, then, between facilitative and debilitative emotions is their *intensity*.

As Gerald Kranzler (1974) points out, intense feelings of fear or rage cause trouble in two ways. First, the strong emotions keep you from thinking clearly. We've seen students in public speaking classes whose fear is so great that they can't even remember their name, let alone the subject of their speech. Second, intense feelings lead to an urge to act, to do *something, anything* to make the problem go away. And because a person who feels so strongly doesn't think clearly, the resulting action might cause more trouble. At one time or another we've all lashed out in anger, saying words we later regretted. A look at almost any newspaper provides a grim illustration of the injury and death that follow from the physical assaults of intensely angry assailants.

A second characteristic of debilitative feelings is their extended *duration*. Feeling depressed for a while after the breakup of a relationship or the loss of a job is natural. But spending the rest of one's life grieving over the loss accomplishes nothing. In the same way, staying angry at someone for a wrong inflicted long ago can be just as punishing to the grudge-holder as to the wrongdoer.

Of all the debilitative emotions, two are common and harmful enough in interpersonal relationships to deserve special mention here. They are anger and jealousy.

Anger While anger may be facilitative, its intensity and duration often make it debilitative. We are taught early in life to hide our

Ronald Colman and Vilma Banky in *The Magic Flame*, 1926. (The Museum of Modern Art/Film Stills Archive)

feelings of anger. The feelings do not go away, however, and they frequently manifest themselves in harmful ways. In some cases the anger builds up until it explodes in a surprising, destructive manner. In other instances the anger smoulders inside, almost literally "eating away at our guts" in the form of psychosomatic illnesses. For instance, S.W. Wolf (1965) found that the mucous lining protecting the inside of the stomach responds minute by minute to both conscious and unconscious emotions. When a person becomes angry, the lining becomes inflamed, producing excessive amounts of acids and gastric juices. In fact, ulcers have been produced experimentally in animals by subjecting them to stress (Sawrey, et al., 1956). People who develop ulcers have stomachs that are almost constantly in a state of agitation, a condition often caused by a failure to appropriately express their feelings.

Millard Bienvenu (1976), in his study of unmarried couples, found that withdrawal was a usual response to feelings of anger. He discovered that effective communicators were distinguished from ineffective ones by the way they handled their anger. We will have more to say about appropriate ways for dealing with anger, both later in this chapter and in Chapter 11.

John Jones and Anthony Banet (1976) discuss a common and destructive "anger cycle." They view anger as a response to the perception of an internal event as threatening one's physical or psychological well-being. The perception of such a threat begins the anger cycle. The second step occurs when the individual analyzes (correctly or incorrectly) the possible danger the threat poses. The third part of the cycle includes an assessment of the individual's power to deal with the threat. The cycle completes itself in one of two ways: If the threat is not very great or the individual feels powerful enough to handle it, a calm or purposeful response follows. If, however, the threat seems great and the individual seems powerless to handle it, anger can emerge as a response. Notice that anger can be a cover-up for other feelings, such as fear or frustration.

Jealousy   Jealousy is actually a combination of many feelings. It includes measures of inadequacy, inferiority, powerlessness, hurt, suspicion, bitterness, and anger. Colleen Kelley (1980) defines jealousy as "the fear of losing to a third party something to which one feels one has a right and which one finds desirable. Thus jealousy involves (1) a valued thing, (2) a perceived threat of loss of this thing to (3) a usurper" (p. 138). Much like anger, jealousy contains a threat against which we feel powerless. The reaction is impulsive: We want to strike out.

Gordon Clanton and Lynn Smith (1976) delineate three possible kinds of loss that determine the strength of one's jealousy. The first is loss of face, or humiliation. Compare, for example, the difference between the slight embarrassment you might feel if a friend beat you in a tennis match and the humiliation you might be likely to feel if your spouse ran off with your best friend. In addition to humiliation, a second type of loss involves the inability to control events. Using our previous example, you would see the person who "belongs" to you slip away, leaving nothing you could do about it. The third type of loss is partnership. The loss of a significant other and all that person represented is extremely serious.

In one study, Ray and Tucker (1980) found that males and females differed in their expression of jealousy. Men reported greater concern with loss of face, while women were more concerned with losing a partner. This finding makes sense, since many men do not want to view themselves as weak or inferior, positions that are associated with loss of face.

Thinking and feeling   Our goal, then, is to find a method for getting rid of debilitative feelings while remaining sensitive to the more facilitative emotions. Fortunately, such a method was developed by cognitive psychologists such as Aaron Beck (1976) and Albert Ellis (1977). This method is based on the idea that the key to changing feelings is to change unproductive thinking. Let's see how it works.

For most people, emotions seem to have a life of their own. People wish they could feel calm when approaching strangers, yet their voices quiver. They try to appear confident when asking for a raise, but their eyes twitch nervously. Many people would say that the strangers or the boss *make* them feel nervous, just as they would say that a bee sting causes them to feel pain. The connection apparent between physical and emotional discomfort becomes clear when considered in the following way:

Activating event	*Causes*	*Consequences*
bee sting	causes	physical pain
meeting strangers	causes	nervous feelings

When looking at emotions in this way, people may believe they have little control over how they feel. The causal relationship between physical pain and emotional discomfort (or pleasure) isn't, however, as great as it seems. Cognitive psychologists and therapists argue that it is not *events*, such as meeting strangers or being jilted by a lover, which cause people to feel poorly, but rather the *beliefs they hold* about these events.

Ellis tells a story that clarifies this point. Imagine yourself walking by a friend's house and seeing your friend stick his or her head out of a window and call you a string of vile names. (You supply the friend and the names.) Under these circumstances, it's likely that you would feel hurt and upset. Now imagine that instead of walking by the house, you were passing a mental institution when the same friend, who was obviously a patient there, shouted the same offensive names at you. In this case, your reaction would probably be quite different; most likely, you'd feel sadness and pity.

In this story the activating event—being called names—was the same in both cases, yet the emotional consequences were very different. The reason for the different feelings has to do with the pattern of thinking in each case. In the first instance you would most likely think that your friend was very angry with you, and imagine you must have done something terrible to deserve such a response. In the second case you would probably assume that your friend had experienced some psychological difficulty and would probably feel sympathetic.

This example illustrates that it is people's *interpretations* of events that determine their feelings. Thus, a more accurate model for emotions would look like this:

The key, then, to understanding and changing feelings lies in the pattern of thought. Consider the part of you that, like a little voice, whispers in your ear. Take a moment now and listen to what the voice is saying.

Did you hear the voice? It was quite possibly saying, "What little voice? I don't hear any voices!" This little voice talks to you almost constantly:

> "Better pick up a loaf of bread on the way home."

> "I wonder when he's going to stop talking."

> "It's sure cold today!"

> "Are there two or four cups in a quart?"

At work or at play, while reading the paper or brushing teeth, we all tend to think. This thinking voice rarely stops. It may fall silent for awhile when you're running, riding a bike, or meditating, but most of the time it rattles on.

Irrational beliefs This process of self-talk is essential to understanding debilitative feelings. Ellis suggests that many debilitative feelings come from accepting a number of irrational beliefs—we'll call them fallacies here—that lead to illogical conclusions, and, in turn, to debilitating feelings.

The fallacy of perfection People who accept this myth believe that a worthwhile communicator should be able to handle any situation with complete confidence and skill. Whereas such a standard of perfection might serve as a target and a source of inspiration (rather like making a hole in one for a golfer), it's totally unrealistic to expect

Activating event	Thought or belief	Consequences
being called names	"I've done something wrong"	hurt, upset
being called names	"My friend must be sick"	concern, sympathy

I never was what you would call a fancy skater—and while I seldom actually fell, it might have been more impressive if I had. A good resounding fall is no disgrace. It is the fantastic writhing to avoid a fall which destroys any illusion of being a gentleman. How like life that is, after all!

Robert Benchley

---

that you can reach or maintain this level of behavior. The truth is, people simply aren't perfect. Perhaps the myth of the perfect communicator comes from believing too strongly in novels, TV, or films. In these media perfect characters are often depicted, such as the perfect mate or child, the totally controlled and gregarious host, and the incredibly competent professional. While these images are certainly appealing, people will inevitably come up short when compared to these fabrications.

Once a person accepts the belief that it's desirable and possible to be a perfect communicator, they come to think that people won't appreciate them if they are imperfect. Admitting one's mistakes, saying "I don't know," or sharing feelings of uncertainty or discomfort thus become social defects. Given the desire to be valued and appreciated, these people are tempted to at least try to *appear* perfect. Thus, many people assemble a variety of social masks, hoping that if they can fool others into thinking that they are perfect, perhaps they'll find acceptance. The costs of such deception are high. If others ever detect that this veneer of confidence is a false one, then the person is considered a phony. Even if the unassertive person's role of confidence does go undetected, the performance consumes a great deal of psychological energy, and diminishes the rewards of approval.

David Burns, in "The Perfectionist's Script

for Self-Defeat" (1980), delineates the costs and benefits of perfectionism. The list of benefits is nonexistent (early successes rarely are maintained); the list of costs is a long one. For example, impaired health, troubled relationships, painful mood swings, anxiety, and decreased productivity (which is ironic since the perfectionist's goal is often higher productivity). The fear of failure, of being less than perfect, often causes the perfectionist to avoid risks, take the safe routes, and engage in the safe relationships. The perfectionist sets high goals (out of fear of being second-rate), fears rejection if he is less than perfect, becomes upset whenever he makes a mistake, and believes that if he pushes himself hard he will do better in the future.

The irony for these people is that their efforts are unnecessary. Research by Eliot Aronson (1972) and others suggests that the people we regard most favorably are those who are competent but not perfect. Why is

ZIGGY

HERE SHE COMES NOW...
...WONDER IF i SHOULD SAY HELLO??
IF i SPEAK FIRST SHE MAY THINK
i'M TOO FORWARD...THEN AGAIN, IF i
WAIT TiLL SHE SPEAKS, MAYBE SHE'LL
THINK i DON'T LIKE HER !!
...AND IF SHE THINKS i DON'T LIKE
HER, THEN SHE MAY NOT SPEAK TO ME
...WORSE YET, SHE MAY NOT LIKE ME..
AND IF i SPEAK TO HER..SHE MAY
TELL ME SO...

???

...i'LL PRETEND
i DON'T SEE HER!

©1974 Universal Press Syndicate

this so? First, many people see the acts of would-be perfectionists as the desperate struggle that they are. It's obviously easier to like someone who is not trying to deceive you than someone who is. Second, most people become uncomfortable around a person regarded as perfect. Knowing they don't measure up to certain standards, most people are tempted to admire this super-human only from a distance.

Not only can subscribing to the myth of perfection keep others from liking you, it also acts as a force to diminish self-esteem. How can you like yourself when you don't measure up to your own standards? You become more liberated each time you comfortably accept the idea that you are not perfect. For example:

1. Like everyone else, you sometimes have a hard time expressing yourself.
2. Like everyone else, you make mistakes from time to time, and there is no reason to hide this.
3. You are honestly doing the best you can to realize your potential, to become the best person you can be.

The fallacy of approval   This mistaken belief is based on the idea that it is vital—not just desirable—to obtain everyone's approval. Communicators who subscribe to this belief go to incredible lengths to seek acceptance from people who are significant to them, even to the extent of sacrificing their own principles and happiness. Adherence to this irrational myth can lead to some ludicrous situations. For example:

1. Feeling nervous because people you really don't like seem to disapprove of you.
2. Feeling apologetic when others are at fault.
3. Feeling embarrassed after behaving unnaturally to gain another's approval.

There is nothing good or bad but thinking makes it so.

Shakespeare
HAMLET

The myth of acceptance is irrational because it implies that some people are more respectable and more likable because they go out of their way to please others. Often this simply isn't true. How respectable are people who have compromised important values simply to gain acceptance? Are people highly thought of who repeatedly deny their own needs as a means of buying approval? Genuine affection and respect are hardly due such characters. In addition, striving for universal acceptance is irrational because it is simply not possible. Sooner or later a conflict of expectations is bound to occur. One person approves of a certain kind of behavior, while another approves only the opposite course of action.

Don't misunderstand: Abandoning the fallacy of approval does not mean living a life of selfishness. It's still important to consider the needs of others and to meet them whenever possible. It's also pleasant—one might even say necessary—to strive for the respect of certain people. The point is that the price is too high when people must abandon their needs and principles in order to gain this acceptance.

The fallacy of shoulds   One huge source of unhappiness is the inability to distinguish between what *is* and what *should be*. For instance, imagine a person who is full of complaints about the world:

"There should be no rain on weekends."
"People ought to live forever."
"Money should grow on trees."
"We should all be able to fly."

205

Beliefs such as these are obviously foolish. However pleasant such wishing may be, insisting that the unchangeable should be altered won't affect reality one bit. And yet many people torture themselves by engaging in this sort of irrational thinking: They confuse "is" with "ought." They say and think:

"That guy should drive better."

"She shouldn't be so inconsiderate."

"They ought to be more friendly."

"You should work harder."

In each of these cases the person *prefers* that people behave differently. Wishing that things were better is perfectly legitimate, and trying to change them is, of course, a good idea; but it is unreasonable for people to *insist* that the world operate just as they want it to. Parents wish their children were always considerate and neat. Teachers wish that their students were totally fascinated with their subjects and willing to study diligently. Consumers wish that inflation wasn't such a problem. But, as the old saying goes, those wishes and a dime (now fifty cents) will get you a cup of coffee.

Becoming obsessed with shoulds yields three bad consequences.

1. This obsession leads to unnecessary unhappiness. People who are constantly dreaming about the ideal are seldom satisfied with what they have. For instance, partners in a marriage who focus on the ways in which their mate could be more considerate, sexy, or intelligent will have a hard time appreciating the strengths that drew them together in the first place.

2. This obsession keeps you from changing unsatisfying conditions. One instructor, for example, constantly complains about the problems at the university: The quality of teaching should be improved; pay ought to be higher; the facilities should be upgraded; and so on. This person could be using the same energy to improve these conditions. Of course, not all problems have solutions. But when they do, complaining is rarely the most productive method of improvement. As one college administrator puts it: "Rather than complain about the cards you are dealt, play the hand well."

3. This obsession tends to build a defensive climate in others. Imagine living around

© 1963 United Feature Syndicate Inc.

someone who insisted that people be more punctual, work harder, or refrain from using certain language. This kind of carping is obviously irritating. It's much easier to be around people who comment without preaching, such as asking, "Could you try to be more punctual?"

The fallacy of overgeneralization   One type of overgeneralization occurs when a person bases a belief on a limited amount of evidence. Consider the following statements:

"I'm so stupid! I can't understand how to do my income tax."

"Some friend I am! I forgot my best friend's birthday."

In these cases people have focused on a limited shortcoming as if it represented everything. Sometimes people forget that, despite their difficulties, they solved tough problems, and that although they can be forgetful, they're often caring and thoughtful.

A second related category of overgeneralization occurs when we exaggerate shortcomings:

"You *never* listen to me."

"You're *always* late."

"I can't think of *anything.*"

Upon closer examination, such absolute statements are almost always false, and usually lead to discouragement or anger. It's better to replace overgeneralizations with more accurate messages:

"You often don't listen to me."

"You've been late three times this week."

"I haven't had any ideas I like today."

The fallacy of causation   People who live their lives in accordance with this myth believe they should do nothing that can hurt or

A man said to the universe:
"Sir, I exist!"
"However," replied the universe,
"The fact has not created in me
A sense of obligation."

Stephen Crane

in any way inconvenience others. This attitude often leads to guilty and resentful feelings, such as:

1. Visiting one's friends or family out of a sense of obligation rather than a genuine desire to see them.
2. Concealing an objection to another person's behavior that is in some way troublesome to you.
3. Pretending to be attentive to a speaker when one is already late for another engagement or is feeling ill.
4. Praising and reassuring others who ask for an opinion, although the honest response is a negative one.

A reluctance to speak out in situations like these often results from assuming that one person can cause another's emotions—that you hurt, confuse, or anger others. Actually, this assumption is seldom correct. A person doesn't *cause* feelings in others; rather, others *respond* to your behavior with feelings of their own. Consider how strange it sounds to suggest that people make others fall in love with them. Such a statement simply doesn't make sense. It would be more correct to say that people first act in one way or another; then others may or may not fall in love as a result of these actions. In the same way, it's incorrect to say that people *make* others angry, upset, even happy. Behavior that upsets or pleases one person might not bring any reaction from another. More accurately,

A man is hurt not so much by what happens as by his opinion of what happens.

Montaigne

---

people's responses are determined as much by their own psychological makeup as by other's behavior.

Restricting communication because of the myth of causation can produce three damaging consequences:

1. People often will fail to meet your needs. There's little likelihood that people will change their behavior unless they know that it affects you in a negative way.

2. You are likely to begin resenting the person whose behavior you fail to complain about. Although this reaction is illogical, as these feelings have never been known, logic doesn't change the fact that burying the problem usually builds up hostility.

3. Once people find out about your deceptive nature, they may find it difficult to determine when you are genuinely upset. Even your most fervent assurances become suspect, as others can never be sure when you are concealing resentments. In many respects, assuming responsibility for others' feelings is not only irrational, it is counterproductive.

The fallacy of helplessness This fallacy suggests that satisfaction in life is determined by forces beyond control. People with this outlook continuously see themselves as victims:

"There's no way a woman can get ahead in this society. It's a man's world, and the best thing I can do is to accept it."

"I was born with a shy personality. I'd like to be more outgoing, but there's nothing I can do about that."

"I can't tell my boss that she is putting too many demands on me. If I did, I might lose my job."

The error in statements such as these becomes apparent once a person realizes that very few paths are completely closed. Most "can't" statements can, in fact, more correctly be rephrased in one of two ways.

The first is to say that you *won't* act in a certain way, that you *choose* not to do so. For instance, you may choose not to stand up for your rights or to follow unwanted requests, but it is usually inaccurate to claim that some outside force keeps you from doing so. The other way to rephrase a "can't" is to say that you *don't know how* to do something. Examples of this sort of situation include not knowing how to complain in a way that reduces defensiveness, or not being aware of how to best conduct a conversation. Many difficulties that a person claims can't be solved do have solutions: The task is to discover those solutions and to work diligently at applying them.

When viewed in this light, it's apparent that many "can'ts" are really rationalizations to justify not wanting to change. Once people persuade themselves that there's no hope, it's easy for them to give up trying. On the other hand, acknowledging that there is a way to change—even though it may be difficult—puts the responsibility for the predicament on your shoulders. Knowing that you can move closer to your goals makes it dfficult to complain about the present situation. You *can* become a better communicator.

The fallacy of catastrophic failure Fearful people who have this belief operate on the assumption that if something bad can happen, it probably will. These statements are typical of such an attitude:

"If I invite them to the party, they probably won't want to come."

"If I speak up in order to try and resolve a conflict, things will probably get worse."

"If I apply for the job I want, I probably won't be hired."

"If I tell them how I really feel, they'll probably laugh at me."

While it's undoubtedly naive to blithely assume that all of your interactions with others will meet with success, it's equally wrong to assume you will fail. One consequence of this attitude is that you'll be less likely to be expressive at important times. To carry the concept to its logical extreme, imagine people who fear *everything*: How can they live their lives? They wouldn't step outside in the morning to see what kind of day it is for fear they'll be struck by lightning or a falling airplane. They wouldn't drive a car for fear of a collision. They wouldn't engage in any exercise for fear the strain might cause a heart attack. Do these examples seem ridiculous? Consider if you have ever withdrawn from communicating because you were afraid of unlikely consequences. A certain amount of prudence is wise, but carrying caution too far can lead to a life of lost opportunities.

Even when one acts in spite of catastrophic fantasies, problems occur. One way to escape from the myth of catastrophic failure is to reassess the consequences that would follow even if you fail in your efforts to communicate. Failing in a given situation usually isn't as bad as it seems. What if people do laugh? Suppose you don't get the job? What if others do get angry at certain remarks? Are these matters really *that* serious?

A rational-emotive approach How can a person overcome irrational thinking? Ellis and Harper (1977) developed a simple yet effective approach that helps people cut down on self-defeating thinking that leads to debilitative emotions.

Monitor your emotional reactions The first step is to recognize debilitative emotions. (Of course, it's also nice to be aware of pleasant feelings when they occur.) As suggested earlier, one way to notice feelings is through proprioceptive stimuli: butterflies in the stomach, racing heart, hot flashes, and so on. While such reactions may call for a trip to the emergency room of the local hospital, more often these feelings reflect strong emotion. You can also recognize certain ways of behaving that suggest a strong emotion, such as stomping instead of normal walking, being unusually quiet, or speaking in a sarcastic tone of voice.

Does it seem strange to suggest that you look for emotions that should be immediately apparent? The fact is, people often suffer from debilitating feelings for some time without noticing them. For example, at the end of a trying day you've probably caught yourself frowning, only to realize that you've been wearing that mask for some time.

Note the activating event Once you're aware of how you're feeling, the next step is to figure out what event activated the response. Sometimes this activating event is obvious. For instance, a common source of anger is being accused unfairly (or fairly) of behaving foolishly, or being rejected by somebody personally important.

Other times there isn't a single activating event, but a series of small incidents which build toward a critical mass, latter triggering a debilitative feeling. This series of incidents may happen when you're trying to work or sleep and are continually interrupted, or when you suffer a string of small disappointments.

The best way to recognize activating events is to notice the circumstances that accompany debilitative feelings. Perhaps they occur when you're around *specific people.* In other cases you might be bothered by certain *types of individuals,* due to their age, role, background, and so forth. Certain *settings* may also stimulate unpleasant emotions: parties, work, or school. In other cases, the *topic* of conversation is the factor that sets you off, whether it be politics, religion, sex, or some other subject.

Record your self-talk Now analyze the thoughts that link the activating event to the feeling. Let's look at a few examples to see how the steps work in practice.

Scott noticed that he became nervous (emotional reaction) whenever he tried to talk with an attractive woman he'd like to date (activating event). After some observation, he discovered that his self-talk included:

1. *"I'm behaving like a fool."*
2. *"I don't know what to say to her."*
3. *"She'd never want to go out with me."*
4. *"I'm no good with women."*

Brenda became infuriated at a friend whom she described as a "leech." This friend would call Brenda frequently, sometimes three or four times a day. She also dropped in for visits at awkward times without being invited. Brenda found that her self-talk focused on the statements:

1. *"After all the hints I've dropped, she should get the idea and leave me alone."*
2. *"She's driving me crazy."*
3. *"I'm a coward for not speaking up and telling her to quit bothering me."*
4. *"If I do tell her, she'll be crushed."*
5. *"There's no solution to this mess. I'm damned if I tell her to leave me alone and damned if I don't."*

Monitoring your self-talk might be difficult at first, but if you persevere, you'll soon be able to identify the thoughts that lead to your debilitative feelings. Once you habitually recognize the internal monologue, you'll identify your thoughts quickly and easily.

Dispute your irrational beliefs This step is the key to success in the rational-emotive approach. Use the list of irrational beliefs on pages 203–209 to discover which of your internal statements are based on mistaken thinking.

You can see how this process works by looking at how Scott disputed his self-talk here instead of accepting his earlier beliefs. He examined each of his statements one at a time to discover which were reasonable.

1. *"This is an exaggeration. I'm certainly not perfect, but I'm not a fool either. A fool would behave much worse than I do. It's more accurate to say that I'm behaving like a nervous guy around a pretty woman, which is exactly the case. There's nothing unusual about that."*
2. *"This is an acurate statement. I'm not sure what to say and so I'm searching for a good topic."*
3. *"This is an irrational, catastrophic belief. She may not want to go out, but on the other hand, she might want to. The only way I'll know is to ask her. In the meantime, it's foolish to expect to worst."*
4. *"This is an exaggeration. Based on my past experience I'd say that I have my strengths and weaknesses when it comes to dealing with women. My drawbacks are that I get nervous and tend to get a crush on lots of nice, beautiful women who I probably wouldn't get along with. On the other hand, I'm honest and kind, and I've had some good times with some fine women."*

Brenda examined her self-talk in the same way.

1. *"If she was perfect, then she would be more sensitive. But since she's an insensitive person, then she's behaving just like I'd expect her to do. I'd sure like her to be more considerate, but there's no rule that says she should be."*

2. *"This is a bit melodramatic. I definitely don't like her interruptions, but there's a big difference between being irritated and going crazy. Besides, even if I was losing my mind, it wouldn't be accurate to say that she was driving me crazy, but rather that I'm letting her get to me. (But it is fun to feel sorry for myself though.)"*

3. *"This is an exaggeration. I am afraid to tell her, but that doesn't make me a coward. It makes me a less than totally self-assured person. This confirms my suspicion that I'm not perfect."*

4. *"There's a chance that she'll be disappointed if she knows that I've found her irritating. But I have to be careful not to catastrophize here. She would probably survive my comments and even appreciate my honesty once she gets over the shock. Besides, I'm not sure that I want to take the responsibility of keeping her happy if it leaves me feeling irritated. She's a big person, and if she has a problem she can learn to deal with it."*

5. *"I'm playing helpless here. There must be a way I can tell her honestly while still being supportive."*

After reading about this method of dealing with unpleasant emotions, some readers have the following objections:

1. The rational-emotive approach sounds like nothing more than trying to talk yourself out of feeling bad. This accusation is totally correct: Cognitive therapists believe that it is possible to convince yourself to feel differently. After all, since we talk ourselves *into* debilitative emotions, what's wrong with talking ourselves *out* of them?

2. This kind of disputing sounds unnatural. "I don't talk to myself in sentences and paragraphs," many people say. There's no need to dispute your irrational beliefs in any particular literary style. You can be as colloquial as you want. The importance here is to clearly understand what thought led you into your debilitative feeling so you can clearly dispute them. When the technique is new for you, write or talk out your thoughts in order to make them clear. After you've had some practice, you will be able to do these steps in a quicker, less formal way.

3. Rational-emotive thinking seems to turn people into calculating, emotionless machines. This is simply not true. There's nothing wrong with having facilitative emotions: They are the stuff that makes life worth living. The goal of this approach is to get rid of the debilitative, harmful emotions that keep us from functioning well. Just as you remove weeds from a garden to let vegetables and flowers grow, so you can use rational thinking to weed out unproductive, harmful feelings to leave room for the productive, positive ones.

4. This technique appears to promise too much. It seems unrealistic to think that you could rid yourself of *all* unpleasant feelings. Rational-emotive thinking probably won't solve emotional problems *totally*, but what it *can* do is reduce the amount, intensity, and duration of debilitative feelings. This method is not the answer to all your problems, but it can make a significant difference, which is not a bad accomplishment.

Sharing Feelings: When and How?

Now that we've talked about how to deal with debilitative emotions, the question remains: How is it possible to best share facilitative feelings with others? It's obvious that indiscriminately sharing every feeling of boredom, fear, affection, irritation, etc. would often cause trouble. On the other hand, we can clearly strike a better balance between denying or downplaying feelings on the one hand and totally cutting loose with them on the other. The suggestions that follow are some guidelines on when and how to express emotions in a way that will give the best chances for improving your relationships.

Recognize your feelings   It's an obvious but important fact that you can best share your feelings when you're aware of what they are. As we've already said, there are a number of ways in which feelings can become evident. Physiological changes can clearly indicate emotions. Monitoring your nonverbal behaviours (facial expression, voice tone, posture, etc.) is another excellent way to keep in touch with your feelings (see Chapter 5). You can also recognize your feelings by monitoring your self-talk as well as the verbal messages you send to others. It's not far from the verbal statement "I hate this!" to the realization "I'm angry (or bored, or nervous, or embarrassed)." Whether you recognize your feelings via any of these ways, the same point applies: It's important to know how you feel in order to tell others about those feelings.

Distinguish between primary and secondary feelings   Many times the feeling we express isn't the only one we're experiencing. Consider the case of Heidi and Mike at a party. The subject of self-defense has come up, and Heidi recounts the time Mike drunkenly picked a fight in a bar, only to receive a sound beating from a rather short, elderly, pudgy customer. Later Mike confronts Heidi angrily, "How could you? That was a rotten thing to say. I'm furious at you." While

Mike's anger may be justified, he failed to share with Heidi the emotion that preceded and in fact was responsible for his anger, namely the embarrassment when a secret he hoped to keep private was exposed to others. If he had shared this primary feeling, Heidi could have better understood his rage, and probably would have responded in a more constructive way. Anger often isn't the primary emotion, although it's the one we may express. In addition to embarrassment, it's often preceded by confusion, disappointment, frustration, or sadness. In each of these cases it's important to share the primary feeling as well as the anger that follows it.

Recognize the difference between feeling and acting   When children are infants, they often go through long spells of late night crying. Most parents experience moments in the wee hours of the morning when they are so tired that they feel like leaving home with all its noise and confusion. Needless to say, they rarely follow through on this impulse.

Of course most of us would like to be the kind of people who are totally patient, accepting, and rational, but we're not. While we don't always want to act on our immediate feelings, we also don't want to ignore them so that they'll build up inside and eventually consume us. For this reason we feel best when we can express what's happening, and then decide whether or not we'll act on it.

For instance, it may be appropriate to acknowledge nervousness in some new situations, even though you might not choose to show it. Likewise, you can acknowledge attraction to certain men or women even though you might not choose to act on these feelings. It's possible to get in touch with the boredom sometimes experienced in meetings and classes, even though you'll most likely resist falling asleep or walking out. In

Dustin Hoffman in *The Graduate,* 1967. (Culver Pictures)

other words, just because you feel a certain way doesn't mean you must always act it out.

This distinction is extremely important, for it can liberate you from the fear that acknowledging and sharing a feeling will commit you to some disastrous course of action. If, for instance, you say to a friend, "I feel so angry that I could punch you in the nose," it becomes possible to explore exactly why you feel so furious and then to resolve the problem that led to the anger. Pretending that nothing is the matter, on the other hand, will do nothing to diminish resentful feelings, which can then go on to contaminate a relationship.

Accept responsibility for your feelings
While you often experience a feeling in response to the behavior of others, it's important to understand that others don't *cause* your feelings. In other words, people don't make you sad, happy, and so on; *you* are responsible for the way you react. Look at it this way: It's obvious that people are more easily upset on some days than on others. Little things that usually don't bother you can suddenly bring on a burst of emotion. Since this is true, it isn't the things or people themselves that determine your reactions, but rather how you feel about them at a given time. If, for example, you're especially harassed due to the press of unfinished

213

work, you may react angrily to a personal joke a friend has made. Was the friend responsible for this upset? No, it's more correct to say that the pressure of work—something within you—set off the anger. The same principle holds true for other emotions: Unrequited love doesn't break our hearts; we allow ourselves to feel hurt, or rather, we simply *are* hurt. A large dose of alcohol doesn't make us sad or happy; those emotions are already within us.

Wayne Dyer (1976), outlining his positive measures for dealing with debilitative emotions and irrational beliefs, includes accepting responsibility. He argues that we need to remind ourselves that it is not what others do that bother us, but our *reactions* to it. "Decide that any and all unhappiness that you choose will never be the result of someone else but rather that it will be the result of you and your own behavior. Remind yourself constantly that any externally caused unhappiness reinforces your own slavery, since it assumes that you have no control over yourself or them, but they have control over you" (p. 171).

It's important to make sure that language reflects the fact of self-responsibility for feelings. Instead of "You're making me angry," say "I'm getting angry." Instead of "You hurt my feelings," say "I feel hurt when you do that." People don't make us like or dislike them, and pretending that they do denies the responsibility each of us has for his or her own emotions.

Choose the best time and place to express your feelings When you do choose to share your feelings with another person, it's important to pick a time and place that's appropriate. Often the first flush of a strong feeling is not the best time to speak out. If you're awakened by the racket caused by a noisy neighbor, by storming over to complain you

might say things you'll regret later. In such a case it's probably wiser to wait until you have carefully thought out how you might express your feelings in a way that would most likely be heard.

Even after you've waited for the first flush of feeling to subside, it's still important to choose the time that's best suited to the message. Being rushed, or tired, or disturbed by some other matter are all good reasons for postponing the sharing of a feeling. Often, dealing with emotions can take a great amount of time and effort, and fatigue or distraction will make it difficult to devote enough energy to follow through on the matter you've started. In the same manner you ought to be sure that the recipient of your message is ready to listen before sharing.

Share your feelings clearly and unambiguously Either out of confusion or discomfort we sometimes express emotions in an unclear way. Sometimes this entails using many words where one will do better. For example, "Uh, I guess what I'm trying to say is that I was pretty upset when I waited for you on the corner where we agreed to meet at 1:30 and you didn't show up until 3:00," would be better stated as, "I was angry when you were an hour and a half late." One key to making emotions clear is to realize that you most often can summarize a feeling in a single word: hurt, glad, confused, excited, resentful, and so on. In the same way, a little thought can probably provide brief reasons for feeling a certain way.

Another way the expression of a feeling may be confused is by discounting or qualifying it: "I'm a *little* unhappy"; "I'm *pretty* excited"; "I'm *sort* of confused." Of course, not all emotions are strong ones—we do experience degrees of sadness and joy—but some communicators have a tendency to discount almost every feeling.

Still another way the expression of an emotion becomes confused is when it is sent in a code. This most often happens when the sender is uncomfortable about sharing the feeling in question. Some codes are verbal ones, as when the sender hints more or less subtly at the message. For example, an indirect way to say, "I'm lonesome" might be, "I guess there isn't much happening this weekend, so if you're not busy why don't you drop by?" This indirect code does have its advantages: It allows the sender to avoid the self-disclosure of expressing an unhappy feeling, and it also serves as a safeguard against the chance of being rejected outright. On the other hand, such a message is so indirect that the chances of the real feeling being recognized are reduced. For this reason people who send coded messages stand less of a chance of having their emotions understood and their needs met.

Finally, you can express yourself clearly by making sure that you and your partner understand that your feeling is centered on a specific set of circumstances, rather than being indicative of the whole relationship. Instead of saying, "I resent you," say, "I resent you when you don't keep your promises." Rather than, "I'm bored with you," say, "I'm bored when you talk about money." Be aware that, in the course of knowing anyone, you're bound to feel positive at some times and negative at others. By limiting comments to the specific situation, you can express a feeling directly without feeling that the relationship is jeopardized.

Readings

Adler, Ronald B. *Confidence in Communication: A Guide to Assertive and Social Skills.* New York; Holt, Rinehart and Winston, 1977.

Aronson, Eliot, *The Social Animal.* New York: Viking Press, 1972.

Beck, Aaron T. *Cognitive Therapy and the Emotional Disorders.* New York: International Universities Press, 1976.

Bienvenu, Millard J., Sr. "Inventory of Anger Communication (IAC)." In *The 1976 Annual Handbook for Group Facilitators,* J. William Pfeiffer and John E. Jones, eds. La Jolla, Calif.: University Associates, Inc., 1976.

Burns, David D. "The Perfectionist's Script for Self-Defeat." *Psychology Today* (November 1980): 34–52.

Buscaglia, Leo F. *Personhood.* Thorofare, N.J.: Charles B. Slack, Inc. 1978.

*Buscaglia, Leo F. *Love.* Thorofare, N.J.: Charles B. Slack, Inc., 1972.

Caraskadon, T.G. "Help Seeking in the College Student: Strength and Weakness." In *Psychological Stress in the Campus Community,* L. Bloom, ed. New York: Behavioral Publications, 1975.

Clanton, Gordon, and Lynn G. Smith. *Jealousy.* Englewood Cliffs, N.J.: Prentice-Hall, 1976.

Coon, Dennis. *Introduction to Psychology: Exploration and Application.* St. Paul, Minn.: West, 1977.

Dunbar, Flanders. *Mind and Body: Psychosomatic Medicine.* New York: Random House, 1947.

Dyer, Wayne W. *Your Erroneous Zones.* New York: Avon Books, 1976.

Egan, Gerard. *You and Me: The Skills of Communicating and Relating to Others.* Monterey, Calif.: Brooks/Cole, 1977.

*Ellis, Albert, and Robert Harper. *A New Guide to Rational Living.* North Hollywood, Calif.: Wilshire Books, 1977.

Gitter, A.G., H. Block, and D. Mostofsky. "Race and Sex in the Perception of Emotion." *Journal of Social Issues* 170 (1972): 63–78.

Jakubowski, Patricia, and Arthur Lange. *The Assertive Option.* Champaign, Ill.: Research Press, 1978.

Johnson, David. "The Effects of Expressing Warmth and Anger upon the Actor and the Listener." *Journal of Counseling Psychology* 18 (1971): 571–578.

Jones, John E., and Anthony G. Banet, Jr. "Dealing With Anger." In *The 1976 Annual Handbook for Group Facilitators,* J. William Pfeiffer

215

and John E. Jones, eds. La Jolla, Calif.: University Associates, Inc., 1976.

Kelley, Colleen. "Jealousy: A Proactive Approach." In *The 1980 Annual Handbook for Group Facilitators*, J. William Pfeiffer and John E. Jones, eds. La Jolla, Calif.: University Associates, Inc., 1980.

Kranzler, Gerald. *You Can Change How You Feel: A Rational-Emotive Approach.* Eugene, Ore.: RETC Press, 1974.

Lazarus, Arnold, and Allen Fay. *I Can If I Want To.* New York: William Morrow, 1975.

McQuade, A., and A. Aikman. *Stress: What It Is and What It Does to You.* New York: E.P. Dutton, 1974.

Phillips, Gerald M. *Help For Shy People.* Englewood Cliffs, N.J.: Prentice-Hall, 1981.

Powell, John. *The Secret of Staying in Love.* Niles, Ill.: Argus, 1974.

Ray, Lisa, and Raymond Tucker. "The Emotional Components of Jealousy: A Multivariate Investigation." Unpublished paper, Bowling Green University, 1980.

Sawrey, W. "An Experimental Investigation of the Role of Psychological Factors in the Production of Gastric Ulcers in Rats." *Journal of Comparative Physiological Psychology* 49 (1956): 457–461.

Schachter, S., and J. Singer. "Cognitive, Social and Physiological Determinants of Emotional State." *Psychological Review* 69 (1962): 379–399.

Selye, Hans. *The Stress of Life.* New York: McGraw-Hill, 1956.

Spielman, Philip. "Envy and Jealousy: An Attempt at Clarification." *Psycho-Analytic Quarterly* 40 (1971): 59–82.

Timmons, F.R. "Research on College Dropouts." In *Psychological Stress in the Campus Community*, L. Bloom, ed. New York: Behavioral Publications, 1975.

Valins, S. "Cognitive Effects of False Heart-Rate Feedback." *Journal of Personality and Social Psychology* 4 (1966): 400–408.

Wolf, S. *The Stomach.* Oxford: Oxford University Press, 1965.

Wood, John T. *How Do You Feel?* Englewood Cliffs, N.J.: Prentice-Hall, 1974.

*Zimbardo, Philip. *Shyness: What It Is, What to Do about It.* Reading, Mass.: Addison-Wesley, 1977.

9

Relationships

■■■■ *After studying the material in this chapter*

You should understand:

1. The four dimensions of interpersonal relationships.

2. The Altman-Taylor model of social penetration.

3. Five reasons why people form relationships.

4. Knapp's stages of relationship formation and dissolution.

5. Eight communication-related characteristics of friendships.

6. The pressures that operate against friendships.

7. Age and sex-related variables influencing friendships.

You should be able to:

1. Identify your relationships according to context, intimacy, love/hate and dominance/submission, and time dimensions.

2. Identify the theory of social attraction that describes the basis of any given relationship in which you are involved.

3. Describe the relational stage of any given relationship in which you are involved.

4. Apply the guidelines on pages 237–238 to improve your relationships.

WANTED: A friend. Need to be considerate, intelligent, outgoing, and a good listener. Must like to watch Sunday football.

AVAILABLE: One older sister. I share my toys, keep the room clean, and can help you with your homework. Sometimes I get moody.

It pays to advertise. Sell a car. Buy a Siberian husky. Rent an apartment. Yet, we are a curious sort of people. For all the prominence that our culture gives to business enterprises and to personal relationships, the reaction to placing an ad in the paper "Friend Wanted" is one of suspicion, of thinking, "Hey, this person must be crazy!"

There are exceptions, though. Recently, a young man in New York had a poster made with his picture, a description of himself, and a note indicating his search for a female friend. The notice was placed in prominent locations throughout the city's subway labyrinth, and within a week, he had over 2,000 responses. Last heard, he was happily engaged.

This success story may have led people to place the following newspaper ads:

SINCERE gentleman 40. Meet lady 30–40 for companionship. Would like long-term relationship if compatible. Call . . .

WOMAN. Young, intellectual, interested in warm, loving male companionship, also intellectual. Write with phone number to . . .

LOOKING FOR PERSON named Jay, male, black, drives green pickup truck. Reward. Call . . .

These advertisements and posters show that personal relationships *are* important. Although you may not have placed an ad for a particular relationship, you probably do have certain expectations and requirements of yourself and others if the relationship is to be successful.

In this chapter, we will look at the different *types* of relationships we share, the reasons for *why* we form them, and the *stages* in developing and ending relationships. After this survey we will take an in-depth look at one particular relationship: friendship.

Types of Relationships

Consider a typical day. With whom do you live, work, study, eat, sleep, party, play? Sometimes there is one person with whom you do all these things. But more commonly we have different relationships for each of our different activities. Let's take a look at three ways of categorizing these relationships.

Context The most obvious way of classifying relationships is to look at the contexts in which they occur. It's very likely that your various relationships take place in several different settings. For example, relationships can form at one's work site. (These usually take up a large amount of time.) Within any given job, there are many relationships existing in a variety of subcontexts. Some involve superiors, some are with subordinates, and still others occur with colleagues of equal status. In certain jobs interaction even takes place with people outside of the organization, as in sales or service positions in which there is continual contact with the public. Then there is the context of family. Here, of course, many relationships exist: between parents and children, between siblings, etc. Family relationships are the earliest type of interpersonal contact and often remain important into later life.

The social context is another that offers several kinds of relationships. Hopefully you're lucky enough to have a few very

Paul Muni in *I Am a Fugitive from a Chain Gang,* 1932. (Culver Pictures, Inc.)

good, important friends. You certainly think of these people differently than more casual friends, whom you may see quite often but value in a different way. Included in the social context are new acquaintances, people you might meet in passing at a party or those you briefly chat with, such as neighbors.

In addition to the work, family, and social categories there are other contexts in which types of relationships can occur: therapeutic, for instance, such as with physicians or counselors; academic, such as are experienced at schools; religious, political, or recreational; random, such as relationships with total strangers—people whom you might chat with while waiting in a line, or those you approach while asking for direc-

tions or some other kind of assistance. Contextual categories are numerous.

Intimacy Important as they may be, contexts don't tell us everything about relationships. You can understand this point by trying a simple experiment. Make a list of all the contexts in which your relationships occur and then list all the people in each of these areas. Now review your list and place a star next to the name of each person with whom you feel close, and a circle next to those to whom you feel distant. It's likely that the context doesn't always determine closeness. You might, for example, feel much closer to one or two co-workers than you do some family members.

This difference brings us to the dimension of intimacy, which is the second way of looking at relationships. There are several kinds of intimacy: intellectual, emotional, and physical. It's possible to be intimate with someone in one of these ways and not in others. You may, for example, share a relationship in which you're not physically close with another person, but are highly intimate on an emotional or intellectual level.

One of the most prominent theories about how intimacy develops in relationships has been described by Irwin Altman and Dalmas Taylor in their book *Social Penetration: The Development of Interpersonal Relationships* (1973). These authors suggest that relationships develop in increments, moving from superficial to more personal levels. As two people learn more about each other, primarily through the process of self-disclosure, the relationship gains importance. Depending on the *breadth* of the information shared (for example, the number of topics you discuss) and the *depth* of that information, a relation-

ship can be defined as casual or intimate. In the case of a casual relationship, the breadth may be high, but not the depth. A more intimate relationship is likely to have high breadth and high depth. Altman and Taylor visualize these two factors as an image of concentric circles (see Figure 9–1). Depth increases as you disclose information that is central to the relationship, information not available unless you provide it; for example, your personal goals, fears, and self-images. Altman and Taylor see relationship development as a progression from the periphery to the center of the circle, a process that typically occurs over time.

Based on this theory of *social penetration*, you can visualize a diagram in which a husband's relationship with his wife has high breadth and high depth, his relationship with his friend has low breadth and high depth, and his relationship with his boss is one of low breadth–low depth. Imagine what your own relationship with various people would look like.

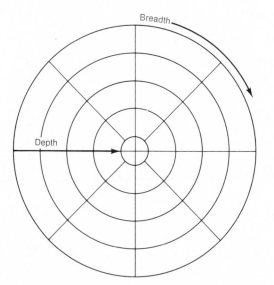

Figure 9–1 The Altman-Taylor Model of Social Penetration

In the local movie theatre, you can buy mint-flavored lozenges with the words: "Will you marry me?" "Do you love me?" written on them, together with the replies: "This evening," "A lot," etc. You pass them to the girl next to you, who replies in the same way. Lives become linked together by an exchange of mint lozenges.

Albert Camus

The Altman-Taylor model can be used to predict a variety of relationships. According to the theory, relationships proceeding rapidly to the central areas can be quite fragile. For example, an experience such as a "one-night stand" of sexual intimacy often lacks the accompanying transactions that build trust and understanding. When interpersonal conflict erupts, the relationship crumbles.

The model also explains the occurrence of situations known as the "stranger on the plane" phenomenon: You board a plane, ready to sleep or read a long-awaited novel, and within five minutes after take-off the person seated next to you begins a story of plight and personal feelings (high depth, and depending how many topics you cover, high breadth). As you will probably never see this person again, you are presumed to be a "safe stranger." Because the relationship is temporary, it can withstand the high-depth disclosures. If this becomes an ongoing relationship, it is likely to experience tensions.

Although Altman and Taylor do not deal extensively with relationship deterioration, the model would indicate that the depenetration process is similar, but in the reverse direction. Interactions experiencing depenetration move from the center to the periphery and decrease in breadth and depth.

There are fewer topics of conversation, and each is more superficial than before. The relationship is being redefined as less intimate.

Love/hate and dominance/submission An intimate relationship isn't always friendly or equal. Robert Carson (1969) argues that relationships may be described along two dimensions. One of these dimensions measures a range of behaviors from dominance or control on one hand to unassertive, following behaviors on the other. This bipolar dimension is called "dominance/submission." The other dimension ranges from accepting, friendly, loving behavior at one extreme to hostile, punishing actions at the other end of the spectrum. This bipolar spectrum is termed "love/hate." Any dyadic (two-person) relationship, the argument goes, may be described along these two dimensions.

The most thorough treatment of this approach was done by Timothy Leary (1955, 1957). He found that the two-dimensional structure can be used to characterize various communication styles. For example, a cold and unfeeling person can be described as dominant/hostile; a person who is distrustful is hostile/submissive; a trusting or gullible person is submissive/loving; and someone who smothers others with kindness can be characterized as loving/dominant.

Some of these combinations may seem odd at first glance. For instance, it's hard to conceive of someone being both dominant and loving or submissive and hostile. These sorts of combinations do exist, however. A typical parent role, for example, is often dominant and genuinely loving. To take a different example, hostile/submissive individuals abound in society. Consider, for example, hostile employees and students who submit to their bosses or instructors while feeling resentful. You can probably think of examples that illustrate all possible combinations of these two relational dimensions.

William Wilmot (1979) describes several types of relationships that can occur along each bipolar dimension. Dominance/submission relationships may be *complementary,* *symmetrical,* or *parallel.* Complementary relationships occur when partners behave differently from one another, but fulfill each other's needs. Relationships in which one partner is talkative and the other quiet or in which one person is aggressive and the other unassertive are complementary ones. Symmetrical relationships are those in which the partners behave equally. Parallel relationships are those in which both complementary and symmetrical behaviors exist. For example, in most relationships there are defined areas in which one partner is dominant and the other submissive, and other areas where equal status is shared.

Wilmot describes the relationships possible along the love/hate dimension as predominately hostile or predominately affectionate. In dyads where nagging, scolding, threatening, and abuse are frequent, the hostility may be the thread that holds the two people together. Martha and George in Edward Albee's *Who's Afraid of Virginia Woolf?* appear to have such a relationship. Destructive as their fighting appears, it is a sign of caring and an attempt to deal with their relational problems.

Time As our "stranger on the plane" and "one-night stand" examples suggested, time is another important way of looking at relationships. We've already seen that intimate relationships have a better chance of lasting if they develop slowly, but looking at the element of time can reveal other factors as well. For example, the amount of time a relation-

Greta Garbo in *Mata Hari.* (Culver Pictures, Inc.)

ship has lasted can be one indicator of its importance. Everyone has heard the line "our friendship goes back a long way," and usually considers such statements as indicating how strong and valuable the relationship is. (Incidentally, the same principle holds true for enemies. The length of time a dispute lasts is one indicator of its importance.)

Of course some relationships can last for years and remain relatively unimportant (as, for example, neighbors who politely but superficially chat every once in a great while). Even in cases such as these, time can be an indicator of the relationship's strength or weakness. In such instances the amount of time we *choose* to spend with someone else indicates commitment to that relationship. You might work or even party with certain people out of duty, avoiding them whenever possible while seeking out other friends voluntarily. Think about the relational implications of the following statements: "I really hate to go. Let's get together soon." versus "Gee, I really don't have the time."

Now, as you might guess, the intimacy, context, and time dimensions of a relationship can form a lovely and complex (typically human) configuration, such that we come out with varied relationships; ones that are short-lived and highly intimate, and others that are long-term, casual acquaintances. If you think of a person with whom you share a special relationship, and a person whom you consider as a casual acquaintance, the differences become evident.

Why We Form Relationships

As the newspaper ads at the beginning of this chapter indicate, some people have extremely clear intentions when they look for relationships. What reasons do you have for interacting with others? You can find out by making a list of your relationships and then seeing which of the following explanations best fits each one:

1. "The other person and I are alike in many ways."
2. "I need things from the other person: guidance, support, information, money, status."
3. "The relationship is a good arrangement for both of us; I get what I'm looking for, and so does the other person."
4. "I care deeply for the other person; because of this caring, I feel glad when he or she is happy and I'm sad when he or she is troubled."
5. "The relationship just happened; we were thrown together and we're still together."

Each of these statements reflects a theory about why people form relationships. Let's take a look at each of these theories, and see which ones seem to best explain why you associate with the important people in your life.

1. "The other person and I are alike in many ways." Just what do you have in common with this person—similar attitudes, hobbies, what? Do you attend the same church? Eat at the same greasy spoon restaurants?

It's comforting to know someone who likes the things we like, who has similar values, and who may even be of the same race, economic class, or educational standing. This basis for the relationship is commonly and most appropriately known as the *similarity thesis.* There are at least two possible hypotheses to study in the dynamics of similarity and interpersonal attraction: (1) people with similar attitudes are attracted to each other; and (2) people who are attracted to each other perceive themselves as similar, whether or not that's actually the case. Both of these ideas have been tested experimentally, and support for each has been demonstrated.

We like people who like what we like, and who dislike what we dislike. Several logical reasons exist for feeling this way. First of all, the other person serves as an external indication—a social validation—that we are not alone in our thinking, that we're not too "weird." Someone else *did* like the same controversial book as you. Thus, this other person offers good support for you, reinforcing your own sense of what is right.

Second, when someone is similar to you, you can make fairly accurate predictions about that person—whether he or she will want to eat at the Mexican restaurant or see the concert you're so excited about. This ability to make confident predictions re-

224

duces much uncertainty and anxiety that might otherwise exist.

There's a third explanation for the similarity thesis. It may be that when we learn that other people are similar to us, we assume they'll probably like us, and so, we in turn like them. The self-fulfilling prophecy creeps into the picture again.

These outcomes have been verified in a number of studies, most notably by Donn Byrne and his associates (Byrne, 1969; Byrne and Blaylock, 1963). These researchers told subjects they would be participating in a group discussion, and that some of the other participants (strangers) would have similar opinions to theirs, while others would not. As expected, students expressed more liking for people who supposedly had views similar to their own, and judged these strangers to be more intelligent, better informed, more moral, and better adjusted than those assumed to have dissimilar attitudes.

Research studies also support the second attraction-similarity relationship: When we like a person, we perceive that similarities exist with that individual. Studies by Byrne and Blaylock (1963) as well as by Levinger and Breedlove (1966) have found that the actual amount of similarity between husbands and wives is significantly less than the amount *assumed* to exist. In discussion of these findings, Ellen Berscheid and Elaine Walster (1978) speculate that couples deemphasize their disagreements in the interest of maintaining a harmonious relationship.

For either direction observed in this attraction-similarity relationship, the research indicates that specific aspects of similarity must be considered. For example, does it matter that the person is similar to you in attitudes, but not in personality (or the converse)? The answer is "Yes." *Attitude similarity* carries more weight than *personality*

■ *A proposal of marriage in our society tends to be a way in which a man sums up his social attributes and suggests to a woman that hers are not so much better as to preclude a merger or partnership in these matters.*

Erving Goffman

---

similarity. Does it matter that you and the other person are similar on a small number of issues of greater importance to you both, than on a large number of other issues of lesser significance? Again, "Yes." Finally, are there any limitations to the degree of similarity and attraction between two people? "Yes." A relationship can become *too* predictable, *too* patterned. This is the "I'm bored!" test of the relationship. It has also been found that people who are less anxious about whether or not others like them, will associate with people having different appearances, experiences, and attitudes.

2. "I need things from the other person . . . "
In Chapter 1 we talked about how communication can satisfy human needs. We discussed Maslow's hierarchy of needs: physiological, safety, social, self-esteem, and self-actualization. We also looked at Schutz' theory of humans seeking inclusion, control, and affection. These theories reflect the need-fulfillment thesis: The idea that people seek out each other and establish certain types of relationships because of the needs they want fulfilled at that time in their lives.

This thesis of complementary need-fulfillment helps explain the times when you have looked at a couple and mumbled to yourself, "I don't know how they get along—they're so different." But think about it—often it's easier for a person who is very aggressive to live with someone more submissive, than for both to be so dominant. In such cases the partners probably serve important functions for each other. The competition of two perfectionists or the doldrum of two introverts can be dysfunctional to the relationship. Consider *The Odd Couple* characters sharing an apartment: Felix Unger compulsively neat and Oscar Madison compulsively sloppy. Although the two are constantly bickering, you get the idea that Felix enjoys taking care of Oscar, and Oscar likes to be the object of Felix's attention.

Need-fulfillment doesn't only work for opposites. It also explains how people with similar temperaments can serve valuable functions for each other. The mutual support might come in having a partner for playing tennis, discussing politics, sharing personal problems, or making love. In all these cases and many more, our relationships are based on having others do things for us that we can't do alone.

3. The relationship is a good arrangement for both of us . . . " This statement reflects one of the more developed theories about interpersonal relationships. The variations on this theory are known as *social exchange theory* and *reward-cost theory,* and its major proponents are psychologists John Thibaut and Harold Kelley (1959) and sociologist George Homans (1961).

These theorists suggest that we seek relationships from which we get *out* as much or more than what we put in. The rewards we get from a relationship (whether tangible or intangible) must outweigh the costs (again, tangible or intangible). Tangible outcomes might be money, property, and other material possessions. Intangibles include fame, status, respect, and support. In addition to costs and rewards, Thibaut and Kelley have identified each person as having a comparison level (CL), the minimum level set as necessary for positive outcomes. The CL is generally composed of *previous* relationships a person has experienced. A comparison

level for alternatives (CL_{alt}) is the person's criterion for deciding whether to continue a relationship. The CL_{alt} is composed of other *possible* relationships. These comparison levels allow for four predictions about relationships:

a. **Stable-satisfactory relationship:** The reward in the current relationship is higher than the general comparison level and the comparison level for alternatives. For example, you perceive that the person you are dating is "better" than your previous dates (the CL) and is better than other possible dates you could have (the CL_{alt}).

b. **Unstable-satisfying relationship:** The reward in the current relationship is higher than the general comparison level, but lower than the comparison level for alternatives. For example, you perceive that the person you are dating is better than your previous dates (the CL), but is not better than other possible dates (the CL_{alt}).

c. **Stable-unsatisfactory relationship:** The reward in the current relationship is lower than the general comparison level, and higher than the comparison level for alternatives. For example, you perceive that the person you are dating is not better than your previous dates (the CL), but is better than your other possible choice (the CL_{alt}).

d. **Unstable-unsatisfactory relationship:** The reward in the current relationship is lower than the general comparison level and lower than the comparison level for alternatives. For example, you perceive that the person you are dating is not better than other previous dates (the CL) and is not better than other possible choices (the CL_{alt}).

Now, to give this theory some intrigue, keep in mind that the comparison levels change over *time* (with age and experience, for example), and can change as a *situation* changes and as the *people* available for comparison change. This is certainly true in the dating practices of many people, whose unstable-satisfying relationships only last until a better, more desirable partner comes along. The same principle also holds true in the business world, where both employers and employees will only maintain a relationship as long as it's rewarding to both of them.

4. "I care deeply for the other person . . . "
In an article on friendship, Paul Wright (1978) takes issue with the reward-cost, grab-the-best-bargain, economic approach of social exchange theories. He suggests that they do not describe the depth, personal involvement, or continuity of many interpersonal relationships, and that a more appropriate concept would be an *investment thesis*. This thesis suggests that a person does more than calculate the rewards of particular relationships. The person also makes an investment of self—of interest, time, energy, and personal resources—to the other person and the relationship shared.

Unlike the social exchange theories, the investment thesis holds that the person looks for more than immediate or tangible rewards. The return on the investment of your self (Wright calls this the dividends) usually takes less concrete and observable forms: enhancement of your sense of individuality, confirmation of your self as a person, increased self-evaluation and self-growth. In Wright's view, a relationship forms and grows to the extent that the person makes a *commitment of self* to the other person and to the relationship.

This investment of self in a relationship is such that when the other person is satisfied or sad, you share in those feelings. A concept closely related to Wright's view of self-investment is that of interpersonal empathy:

the ability to feel as another person does, to see what they see, to perceive and understand what they feel. If you have shared another person's joy as *he or she knows it*, or have felt the pain of that person's troubles *as he or she does*, you have experienced empathy with that person, and have made a self-investment in that relationship.

5. "The relationship just happened . . . "
Some people see spontaneity and circumstance as the reason for certain relationships they share. There is no conscious design to develop a relationship—it just happens. Such events illustrate relationships based on the *proximity thesis:* The less physical distance there is between two people, the more likely it is that they will be attracted to each other. Consider people who are in close proximity to you: classmates, neighbors, office workers. Given your frequent interaction, it's likely that your relationships are stronger with many of these people than with more

"Actually, I'm seeking a meaningless relationship."

Drawing by Richter; © 1970 The New Yorker Magazine, Inc.

distant ones. The influence of proximity is strengthened by the fact that closeness is a kind of similarity, which adds to the attraction explained by that thesis.

The research studies supporting this proximity explanation include studies of integrated housing efforts, and even the arrangement of apartment dwellings. Each study indicates that physical location is important in the *initial* stages of an interaction, but that it is not a sufficient explanation for the *maintenance* of the relationship. So that choice of apartment or favorite seat in class may function to set up the initial phases of a relationship by providing the opportunity for introductory interactions, but it is no guarantee of the development you may seek in the relationship or its subsequent outcomes.

Before moving on to discuss the stages of relationship development, it is interesting to note why people do *not* form relationships. Besides reasons that may be related to avoidance of self-disclosure (see Chapter 7), Maxine Schnall (1981) describes a "social disease" she labels *commitmentphobia*. She describes commitmentphobia as the fear of entering into or sustaining an "exclusive, permanent relationship with a member of the opposite sex." Male commitmentphobes, Schnall suggests, often view commitment and entrapment as synonymous. Commitment to a woman means giving up traditional defenses, including control of others and emotional aloofness. One symptom of the commitmentphobic man is promiscuity. Another is the choice to remain alone, while a third is the apparent but insincere search for the "perfect wife."

The female commitmentphobe often views commitment as a dependency trap in which she will be forced to be subservient to her husband. Independence, bought with money and status, is one way to cope with commitmentphobia. Schnall argues that the problems of the commitmentphobic woman are greater than those of her male counterpart. For example, a single man fits into a stereotypic, acceptable role, while a single woman—even in the relatively enlightened 1980s—often is considered unusual.

Commitmentphobia is not limited to single people. Schnall concludes her article by discussing married commitmentphobes, people who complain incessantly about their marriages but never leave. She closes with the following advice:

> We need to reduce the fear of commitment by dispelling the notion that commitment is synonymous with the loss of identity. We must reassure ourselves and each other that it is possible to be both autonomous and deeply committed to one another. . . . a deep commitment to one person and the experiences of a life lived together, far from being antithetical to personal fulfillment, are often prerequisites for it.

The Stages of a Relationship

Although relationships come in many types and "sizes," social scientists have found that they all grow and dissolve by passing through similar phases. These phases can be broken into as few as three parts (initiation, maintenance, and dissolution), or as many as ten, which we'll now examine. These ten stages are outlined by Mark Knapp in his book *Social Intercourse: From Greeting to Goodbye* (1978).

1. Initiation. This stage involves the initial making of contact with another person. Knapp restricts this stage to first impressions and conversation openers. A scene on a recent TV series illustrates this initial stage. Four male radio station workers are at a local bar, where each tries his opening lines on Jennifer, the vivacious secretary:

Johnny Fever (the afternoon DJ who leaves his nursing home listeners in shock): "You're a Scorpio, aren't you?" (No-go, Johnny.)

Venus Flytrap (the nightime Mr. Cool DJ): "Hey beautiful, can I buy you a drink?" (Sorry, Venus.)

Andy (the country-boy-made-good program manager): "Didn't I see you at Maxie's last Friday?" (Not a chance, Andy.)

Les (the middle-aged, ultra-conservative bumpkin news announcer): "Hi, I'm wealthy."

(In case you're wondering, money won out here!)

While an initial encounter *is* necessary to the succeeding interaction, its importance is overemphasized in books advising how to pick up men and women. These books suggest fail-proof openers ranging from, "Excuse me, I'm from out of town and I was wondering what people do around here at night?" to "How long do you cook a leg of lamb?" Whatever your preference for opening remarks, this stage is important because you are formulating your first impressions and presenting yourself as interested in the other person.

2. Experimenting. In this stage, the conversation develops as the people get acquainted by making "small talk." We ask: "Where are you from?"; "What do you do?"; "Do you know Josephine Mendoza? She lives in San Francisco too."

While small talk might seem meaningless, Knapp points out that it serves four purposes:

a. It is a useful process for uncovering integrating topics and openings for more penetrating conversation.

b. It can be an audition for a future friendship or a way of increasing the scope of a current relationship.

c. It provides a safe procedure for indicating who we are and how another can

come to know us better (reduction of uncertainty).

d. It allows us to maintain a sense of community with our fellow human beings.

The relationship during this stage is generally pleasant and uncritical, and the commitments are minimal. Experimenting may last ten minutes or ten years.

3. Intensifying. In this phase (Knapp thinks most of our relationships don't get beyond experimenting) the relationship develops a character of its own indicated by a common identity: "*We* like to dance." You come to know the other person and develop accuracy in predicting the other's wants and whims. You are more accessible to that person and may use less formal terms, including nicknames and special terms of endearment. A truly *interpersonal* relationship, as we defined it in Chapter 1, begins on this level.

4. Integrating. At this point, the sense of union of the two people is heightened further—the interpersonal synchrony is high. You become identified by others as "a pair," "an item." This oneness may be accented by similar clothing styles, the similar phrasing of terms, and the designation of common property—for example, *our* song, *our* meeting time, or *our* project.

5. Bonding. When the relationship reaches this stage, it achieves some formal social recognition. This can take the form of a contract to be business partners, or a license to be married. During this stage, more regulations for the interaction are established, and the participants may experience some disorientation and uneasiness until they adjust to the social formality and institutionalization of their relationship. Newlyweds, for example, may feel a need to rebel once the ceremony sanctions their relationship—the husband might take up car maintenance and spend all his free time in the garage, and the wife might work late.

6. Differentiating. Now that the two people have formed commonality, they need to reestablish individual identities. How are we different? How am I unique? Former identifications as "we" now emphasize "I." Differentiation often first occurs when a relationship begins to experience the first, inevitable stress. Whereas a happy employee might refer to "our company," the description might change to "their company" when a raise or some other request isn't forthcoming. We see this kind of differentiation when parents argue over the misbehavior of a child: "Did you see what *your* son just did?"

Differentiation can be positive too, for people need to be individuals as well as part of a relationship. The key to successful differentiation is the need to maintain commitment to a relationship while creating the space for members to be individuals as well.

7. Circumscribing. So far we have been looking at the growth of relationships. While some reach a plateau of development, going on successfully for as long as a lifetime, others pass through several stages of decline and dissolution. In the circumscribing stage, communication between members decreases in quantity and quality. Restrictions and restraints characterize this stage, and dynamic communication becomes static. Rather than discuss a disagreement (which requires some degree of energy on both parts), members opt for withdrawal: Either mental (silence or daydreaming and fantasizing) or physical, where people spend less time together. Circumscribing doesn't involve total avoidance, which comes later. Rather, it entails a certain shrinking of interest and commitment.

8. Stagnation. If circumscribing continues, the relationship begins to stagnate. Members behave toward each other in old, familiar ways without much feeling. No growth occurs. The relationship is a hollow shell of its former self. We see stagnation in many workers who have lost enthusiasm for their job, yet who continue to go through the motions for years. The same sad event occurs for some couples who unenthusiastically have the same conversations, see the same people, and follow the same routines without any sense of joy or novelty.

9. Avoiding. When stagnation becomes too unpleasant, people in a relationship begin to create distance between each other. Sometimes this is done under the guise of excuses ("I've been sick lately and can't see you") and sometimes it is done directly ("Please don't call me. I don't want to see you now"). In either case, by this point the handwriting about the relationship's future is clearly on the wall.

10. Termination. Characteristics of this final stage include summary dialogues of where the relationship has gone, and the desire to disassociate. The relationship may end with a cordial dinner, a note left on the kitchen table, a phone call, or a legal document stating the dissolution. Depending on each person's feelings, this stage can be quite short, or it may be drawn out over time, with bitter jabs at one another. In either case, termination doesn't have to be totally negative. Understanding one another's investments in the relationship and needs for personal growth may dilute the hard feelings.

Relational turnover is one of the most common yet least acknowledged experiences of contemporary living. We act toward our most intimate friends and lovers as if they will be with us always, yet there is a good chance they will not. We are taught in our early years how to make social ties, but the process of dissolving them is shrouded in mystery, hurt, and misunderstanding. In a study of friendmaking and breaking, Jeff Bell and Ava Hadas (1977) found that first and third-graders knew how to make friends, but were at a loss about ending friendships. Common responses were that breaking a friendship was out of the child's control—it just happened. Two specific solutions voiced were to "wait until the end of school," or to "just punch him out." Unfortunately, as the years progress, the adult may see similar options as viable. Many marriages end with bitter recriminations, some jobs are terminated with bad feelings, and unhappy friends often drift apart without knowing how to end their relationships in a better way.

After outlining these ten steps, Knapp discusses several assumptions about his model. First, movement through the stages is generally sequential and systematic. We proceed at a steady pace and don't usually skip steps in the development. Second, movement can be forward or backward and there is movement within stages. A relationship, for example, may experience a setback—a lessening of intimacy, a redefining of the relationship. Two people may repeat certain stages, and although the stages are the same, each cycle is a new experience. It may also be the case that certain relationships will stabilize at a particular stage. Many relationships stabilize at the experimenting stage (friend and work relationships), some stabilize at the intensifying stage, and a few stabilize at the bonding stage. With these assumptions in mind, we can use Knapp's model as a set of developmental guidelines for movement within and between the stages of initiation and dissolution.

In a recent study which focused exclusively on children's perceptions of friendship, Robert and Anne Selman (1979) identified five overlapping stages through which children aged three to adolescence progress.

1. Momentary playmate (stage 0, ages 3 through 7). During this stage friends are val- ued for their material and physical offerings. A friend is identified as the person with the trampoline or the chocolate-chip cookie. At this stage, the child does not distinguish between her own viewpoint and that held by others.

2. One-way assistance (stage 1, ages 4 through 9). While the child still does not differentiate her own perspective from that held by others, and the "give and take" of friendship is not yet understood, a friend is identified as the person who does what the child wants.

3. Two-way fair weather cooperation (stage 2, ages 6 through 12). At this stage reciprocity enters into the relationship, so friendship includes a concern for what each person thinks about the other. However, a friend is still someone who serves *self*-interests.

4. Intimate, mutually shared relationship (stage 3, ages 9 through 15). This stage is marked by a significant change in perspective: Friendship is now defined as a collaboration with others for mutual and common interests (as opposed to self-interests). A friend is someone with whom to share secrets.

5. Autonomous interdependent friendship (stage 4, ages 12 and older). During this final stage there is a growing awareness that people have many needs and that relationships are complex. Friends are people who give emotional and psychological support to each other, *and* who allow each other to develop independent relationships. Support, trust, and the ability to "let go" of the other are distinguishing features of this stage.

Friendship: A Special Relationship

What makes a friend? You probably have a variety of friends. If you're lucky you have a few people whom you can count as special friends. It doesn't take any analysis to know that these people matter a great deal to you, and that your life is better for knowing them. But exactly what is it about these people that makes them special? Muriel James and Louis Savary (1976) attempted to answer this question by suggesting eight characteristics that most people commonly expect from this kind of relationship. As you read about these characteristics, see which ones are most important in your friendships.

Availability and *shared activities* are particularly important in the initial stages of a relationship. You expect to see the other person, spend time with him or her, get together to work on the term project, have lunch or dinner, or maybe sit and talk during TV commercials. If these expectations are not met, the relationship may never develop beyond an acquaintanceship. In most cases, being available presumes face-to-face interactions, but there are also times when availability happens through written letters or telephone calls, and you can use these techniques to reach others. When you're feeling down and depressed, you may surprise yourself by what you do. Sometimes, you may call someone you haven't spoken to in months, someone who may not even be a "close" friend, and other times you might write to someone who presumes you died or ran off for a tour of the world. No matter, the person is still available, and that's what is important.

Expectations common to the intermediate phases of relationships include *caring, honesty, confidentiality,* and *loyalty.* You expect these from the other person, and also expect to provide them yourself if the relationship is to be reciprocal. Sometimes, we forget that others expect the same treatment from us!

Although the degree of caring will vary with the type of relationship, James and Savary offer the following definition as a guide:

Caring is not the same as using the other person to satisfy one's own needs. Neither is it to be confused with such things as well-wishing, or simply having an interest in what happens to another. Caring is a process of helping others grow and actualize themselves. It is a transforming experience.

In like manner, honesty, confidentiality, and loyalty are expected in all types of relationships. Honesty in a relationship does not mean that you need to tell everything to the other person, but that you are honest about matters relevant to that relationship, while maintaining a respect for the other person's sense of privacy. Confidentiality and loyalty are two agreements made in relationships, at times in unstated and assumed ways, and sometimes in a quite formal (written) legal manner.

Understanding and *empathy* are the "bonuses" of a relationship. Many relationships can maintain themselves based on the other characteristics, but those that are particularly strong have a mutually high degree of understanding and empathy. Sue and Mary understand how each other work and think, and they can empathize with each other's feelings. It's not that they are so predictable as to be boring, but they do know each other's ways of thinking and feeling almost as well as they know their own. Usually, these features of a relationship take time to develop, and they require clear communication between the two people involved. Each must be willing to express needs, feelings, and wishes as accurately as possible, and also must practice the skills of active listening for the other person.

These expectations for relationships have been noted in different ways by other psychologists, communication researchers, and even young children. In their ongoing research of children's imaginary playmates,

John Caldeira, Jerome Singer, and Dorothy Singer (summarized in Pines, 1978) found consistent evidence that children create playmates who are *always available, steadfast*, and *loyal*. These companions (usually male) talk with the child, and listen even more—the child perceives that they *care. The playmates give unfailing support*, and fill empty spaces in a child's life—times when the child is alone or perhaps without any playmates of the same age. Children who develop imaginary playmates have been found to be highly intelligent, less aggressive, and more cooperative than children without imaginary playmates. They smile more, show a greater ability to concentrate, are seldom bored, watch less TV, and have more advanced language skills. If these playmates do not become a crutch to the child, researchers view the invisible friends as providing an invaluable tool to the child. This tool allows children to rehearse themselves in different roles, to cope with problems that might otherwise produce overwhelming anxiety, and to test ways of mastering these problems.

Pressures on friendships Many times strong friendships wither away. Sad as this may be, it's not surprising, for there are both external and internal pressures on such friendships. The *external* pressures include physical circumstances, such as moving away from friends or changing jobs, and the existence of other competing people and relationships. Two people who have been friends throughout their school years, for example, may experience new tensions when one marries, or when other friends compete for one person's time and attentions. Friends usually come in pairs, and there's a good reason why that's so. In three-person interactions it is almost impossible for one partic-

ipant to extend attention to both of the other two simultaneously. Unless each person is quite secure in the relationship and with self, most triadic arrangements cannot survive the tensions.

Internal factors can also pressure a friendship. One common internal pressure occurs when partners grow at different rates. For instance, a relationship that was born out of one person's dependency on the other loses its main reason for existing if the weaker partner becomes more self-reliant. Similarly, a friendship once based on agreement to avoid discussing any conflicts will be threatened if one person suddenly becomes willing to tackle disputes directly. When such changes occur, the maintenance of the friendship depends on the ability of both persons to adapt to the new conditions. Thus, friendships lasting for long periods are often quite different now than they were at earlier times. The partners were wise enough to adapt to their personal changes rather than clinging to the old ways of relating which may have been comfortable and enjoyable, but are now gone.

Not all friendships can survive these pressures. It's important to realize that the end of a friendship does not always mean that the people have failed. Rather, it may simply reflect the fact that one or both partners has changed and now seeks a different (though not necessarily better) type of interaction. Of course, this kind of ending is easier to accept if both people have other relationships that can support their needs.

One way to avoid the brutal attacks on self (which can follow a separation) is to see the friendship not as a *fraction* of you, but as what James and Savary call an additional "third self." There's you, me, and *us*. And if the friendship changes or dissolves, the separate entities of you and me still exist intact and completely, and a new friendship will bring with it another third self.

Friendships for all ages In comparison to both job relationships and husband and wife relationships, a friendship has distinct advantages: There's no age limit on them. You don't have to wait until you're sixteen to get a license to acquire a friend. You had friends when you were two years old, and probably anticipate having friends for every day you are alive. Let's examine how a person's choice of friends and the qualities preferred in friends might change during a typical lifespan.

Observations of two-year-olds indicate that these youngsters engage in what is known as *parallel play* (Selman and Selman, 1979; Singer, 1973). A child may be in the same room with other children, but each is involved in his or her own activity. They do not interact *with* each other. It is not until the ages of three and four that a child develops a sense of cooperative play involving other children in such activities as playing school, playing house, or jumping rope.

If you have ever watched play between four- and eight-year-olds, you might have noticed a certain ease with which they establish relationships with strangers of similar ages. The range of behavior they find acceptable is extensive. As long as children of this age group do not get hit or have sand thrown in their faces, their relationships with other children are satisfactory. Racial background, social class, and level of intelligence generally do not matter in selecting a playmate. Of course, not all children make friends with ease. In a review of childhood friendships, James and Savary (1976) speculate on a strong relationship between childrearing behaviors and the child's companions. Children who are "unbefriended" at home may

stand around at a playground or at school feeling awkward and excluded, not knowing what to do or say, or how to meet other children. On the other hand, youngsters whose parents spend more time with them are likely to learn how to form friendships and relate to others.

The time between eight and twelve years of age is known as the "chum" period. During these years, children typically select friends of the same sex, and enjoy a variety of activities: playing ball, riding bikes, learning games, and constructing various objects. Psychiatrist Harry Stack Sullivan's (1953) studies of children in this age range indicate that if the chum experience is missing, the child may not develop strong heterosexual attachments later.

At puberty, friendship patterns show other changes. For the first time, the emphasis is on opposite-sex friends. This period of adolescence intensifies pressures on the young adults for achievement (a concern of parents and teachers) and for acceptance (the child's concern). The pressures for acceptance in the social group are great, and often the demands for achievement take second place to the need to have friends. You probably can easily recall the parental arguing required to get you to come in the house and do your homework, and not stay out any longer with friends. James and Savary report this account of a fifteen-year-old boy:

> You had to have a lot of friends. That was more important than anything else. My mother would say, "Are you going out to play now?" and I'd say, "No, I don't play. I want to be with my friends."

This emphasis on acceptance and friends is further intensified for adolescents who are somewhat shy. The fear of being rejected and not having friends can stay with them throughout adult life. And although pressure

Shirley Temple and Bill Robinson in *The Little Colonel.* (Culver Pictures, Inc.)

to form relationships exists, there is little explanation of what to do when a relationship does not succeed. So, the shy adolescents are further intimidated when their first attempt doesn't work.

One of the least-studied periods of friendship are those that occur during the senior years of life. Just as in earlier years, friends are still important and serve a useful function to the aged. In a study of people over seventy years old, Zena Blau (in Brenton,

1974) found that those belonging to friendship cliques were more apt to consider themselves as "middle-aged" than were those without such companions. Research indicates that elderly persons with confidants are better able to cope with the death of a spouse, are more apt to have good morale, and are less vulnerable to mental dysfunctions, such as senility and depression, than those without confidants.

From his observations of members of a

235

senior citizen's center in Washington, D.C., Myron Brenton (1974) found that:

> . . . some talk to no one, participate in no song-fests, no card games, no activities with others. Yet day after day they show up and sit, . . . surrounded by people. They are like young children, who have not yet learned how to relate to other children; they do things by themselves, crocheting, perhaps, or playing solitaire—they are engaged in parallel play. At the Model Cities center a lady of about 75 comes in and follows the same routine everyday: She arrives sometime in midmorning, smiles at everyone, then sits by herself and refuses to say anything to anyone for the rest of the day. About the same time each day, an elderly gentleman shows up, sits down next to her, and talks to her by the hour. She seems not to hear; he seems not to realize that she does not hear. Something, somehow is going on between them.

Brenton speculates that one reason why people are drawn to retirement communities is the fact that there are always new friends when old friends pass away: "The death of friends does not eliminate the need for friends." Reaching out to another person is a lifelong process.

Sex and friendship Several studies have looked at friends selected by men and by women. Do men and women differ in their perceptions of friendship and choices of friends? In a survey of college students, Myron Brenton found that men place more value on friends who provide intellectual stimulation than do women. Traits such as honesty, trust, and acceptance were important to both men and women, but were more important to women. He observed that men and women use different techniques for meeting with friends of the same sex. Traditionally, men get together with their male friends to go fishing, play ball or poker, and

to have a few drinks. Women get together with their female friends at volunteer organizations, book clubs, craftwork sessions and bridge games. For women, there has been a distinct absence of sports-based social activities. Caldwell and Peplau (1977) found that women see friendship as a means for sharing feelings, whereas men determine friends according to similar interests in physical activities.

In 1976, Gerald Phillips and Nancy Metzger published the results of an extensive investigation of friendship. College students completed a lengthy questionnaire called "The Friendship Protocol" which included questions about the subject's closest friend of the same sex, opinions about male-female relationships, and comments about friendship in general. Responses to the questionnaire provided the following differences.

Men tended to agree with these statements:

1. It is easy to make friends.
2. It is possible to size up a friend to see what the friend might provide.
3. Commitment to a friend should be made only when mutuality is proved.
4. If someone hurts you, it is all right to hurt back.
5. Commitment to friends should not interfere with commitment to yourself.

Women tended to agree with these statements:

1. Friendship should be spontaneous.
2. People should talk about the nature of their friendship.
3. Friend-making is a skill that can be learned.
4. I want to understand people.
5. It is possible to be friends with employees or students.

Based on responses to the inventory, Phillips and Metzger concluded that men are more approving of a planned and calculating relationship, whereas women are more concerned with the emotional aspects of the relationship and its spontaneity. Such differences may be the product of the socialization process for men and women. Messages to boys and girls about friends and friendship vary in subtle ways, such as in folktales and children's literature.

Then what a wonderful feast they had! All the boys did Indian dances and learned wild Indian chants, and Peter Pan was made a chief! Only Wendy had no fun at all, for she had to help the squaws carry firewood.

The Prince took Rapunzel to his kingdom where he was received with joy, and they lived long and happily together.

The importance of friendship for men and women, and the value of same-sex friendships is just being realized. Although few studies have gone beyond a philosophical analysis, a nationwide survey of opinions about friendship was recently reported in *Psychology Today* (Parlee et al., 1979). A number of interesting findings were listed:

1. The qualities most valued in friendship are loyalty, warmth, and the ability to keep confidences. Qualities of less importance are age, income, and occupation.
2. One of the most important reasons for ending a friendship is feeling betrayed by the other person.
3. In a crisis situation, 51 percent of the sample indicated that they would seek the help of a friend before seeking the help of a family member.
4. A third of the respondents (male and female) indicated that they had had sexual relations with a friend during the past month.

5. About 29 percent of the sample indicated that they share a close friendship with a person who is homosexual.
6. About 38 percent indicated that they shared a close friendship with a person from a racial background different from their own.
7. A majority of male and female respondents (67 percent of each) indicated that they were lonely "sometimes" or "often".
8. Reports of what friends do together were remarkably similar for both male and female subjects. "Intimate talks" and "doing favors" were at the top of the list of each sex group, with "eating together in a restaurant," "asking favors," and "going out together"—to a movie, drinking, shopping—also ranking high.

Research by Letitia Peplau (1981) indicates that many of the conclusions drawn from research on heterosexual couples applies to male and female homosexual couples as well. For example, regardless of sexual preference, most people want an intimate and loving relationship with one "special" person. All couples agreed that "being able to talk about my most intimate feelings," "laughing easily with each other," "having an egalitarian relationship," and "having a supportive group of friends" were all high priorities.

Making friendships work In a study called "Happily Ever After and Other Relationship Styles: Advance on Interpersonal Relations in Popular Magazines, 1951–1973," Virginia Kidd (1975) described two media views of relationships. First, there is a static vision: "Relationships don't change and people live happily ever after." Second, there is a more realistic vision that emphasizes the dynamic nature of communication. Individuals are constantly changing, and so too are the rela-

Caring is a process of helping others grow and actualize themselves. It is a transforming experience.

Muriel James and Louis M. Savary
THE HEART OF FRIENDSHIP

tionships they share. This second vision implies that we can improve our relationship effectiveness if we understand the transactional nature of the communication process and practice such communication skills as active listening, conflict management, and self-disclosure.

In accordance with Kidd's categories of relationships, William Wilmot (1979) discusses four aspects of his own relationship philosophy and vision. Rather than identify these aspects as "visions," they may be discussed in terms of *social realities*.

1. Relationships do change. Change is inevitable and relationships are no exception to the rule. Unfortunately, sometimes we do get stuck in our relationships. We stifle ourselves and others with expectations that each of us remain the same. We impose the restrictions, and often fight to keep relationships from being redefined. An extreme case of this can be observed in a parent who continues to treat a forty-six-year-old son as the baby, not as an adult and friend. Consider your own relationships. Do you accept the fact that your relationships will change?

2. Relationships require attention. As Wilmot notes, "Participants have to *keep working on their relationships until the day they die.*" He makes another comment: "If we all worked on our relationships as much as we did our jobs, we would have a richer emotional life." Work takes at least forty hours a week of your time. How much time do you devote to developing your close relationships?

3. Good relationships meet the expectations of the participants. Your satisfaction with a relationship is a function of how well that relationship meets *your* goals. For example, people get married for a variety of reasons: companionship, status, love, a good sex life, a name, money. So long as the two people sharing that relationship fulfill their expectations, the relationship is satisfying for them. The conflicts arise when the expectations differ and cannot be met with that relationship. What expectations do you have? What do you want from your relationships?

4. Relationships can be improved by dealing directly with relational issues. The nature of the relationship and its functions are defined by the people, not by some mystical outside force. Knowing how a relationship forms and how it can change should increase the quality of that relationship. Rather than hoping problems won't occur and avoiding them when they do arise, do you use your best communication skills to prevent and confront your interpersonal problems?

Write a few newspaper ads of your own. And then, ask yourself a tough question: Are you the kind of person you would choose for a friend? a lover? a boss? a parent?

WANTED: A good friend. Interested in meeting someone who is patient and loyal, who will keep my secrets and respect my privacy, as I will do for you. Should share many of my interests, especially dancing, occasionally acting foolish, and watching Bogart films. No guarantees, but seeking lasting relationship.

AVAILABLE: A parent who listens. Not a phony. You'll find me to be honest, even when it may hurt, and usually dependable. Right now, I'm practicing my ability to not be threatening and to allow others their separateness. Mixed references, but sincere desire to learn from past mistakes.

WANTED: Teacher who remembers what it was like to be a student: confused, tired, silly, sad, bored, determined. It will help if you take the time to answer our questions, even the ''stupid'' ones, and to let us explain what we think and how we feel. And, if *you're* tired or angry, or just not ready to work with us, let us know. Give us the chance to understand.

Readings

*Altman, Irwin, and Dalmas Taylor. *Social Penetration: The Development of Interpersonal Relationships*. New York: Holt, Rinehart and Winston, 1973.

Bell, Jeff, and Aza Hadas. "On Friendship." Paper presented to the WYOTANA Conference, University of Montana, June 1977.

*Berscheid, E., and E. H. Walster. *Interpersonal Attraction*, 2nd Ed. Reading, Mass.: Addison-Wesley, 1978.

Brenton, Myron. *Friendship*. New York: Stein and Day, 1974.

Buley, Jerry L. *Relationships and Communication*. Dubuque: Kendall/Hunt, 1977.

Byrne, Donn. "Attitudes and Attraction." In *Advances in Experimental Social Psychology* 4. L. Berkowitz, ed., New York: Academic Press, 1969.

Byrne, Donn, and Barbara Blaylock. "Similarity and Assumed Similarity of Attitudes between Husbands and Wives." *Journal of Abnormal and Social Psychology* 67 (1963): 636–640.

Caldwell, Mayta Ann, and Letitia A. Peplau. "Sex Differences in Friendship." Paper presented to the Western Psychological Association Convention, Seattle, Washington, April 1977.

Carson, Robert C. *Interaction Concepts of Personality*. Chicago: Aldine, 1969.

Gillies, Jerry. *Friends: The Power and Potential of the Company You Keep*. New York: Coward, McCann and Geoghegan, Inc., 1976.

Homans, George C. *Social Behavior: Its Elementary Form*. New York: Harcourt, Brace, 1961.

James, Muriel, and Louis M. Savary. *The Heart of Friendship*. New York: Harper and Row, 1976.

Johnson, David W. *Reaching Out: Interpersonal Effectiveness and Self-Actualization*. Englewood Cliffs, N.J.: Prentice-Hall, 1972.

Kelley, Harold H. *Personal Relationships: Their Structure and Processes*. Hillsdale, N.J.: Lawrence Erlbaum Associates, 1979.

Kidd, Virginia. "Happily Ever After and Other Relationship Styles: Advice on Interpersonal Relations in Popular Magazines, 1951–1973." *Quarterly Journal of Speech* 61 (1975): 31–39.

*Knapp, Mark L. *Social Intercourse: From Greeting to Goodbye*. Boston: Allyn and Bacon, 1978.

Leary, Timothy. "The Theory and Measurement Methodology of Interpersonal Communication." *Psychiatry* 18 (1955): 147–161.

Leary, Timothy. *Interpersonal Diagnosis of Personality*. New York: Ronald, 1957.

Levinger, George, and James Breedlove. "Interpersonal Attraction and Agreement." *Journal of Personality and Social Psychology* 3 (1966): 367–372.

Parlee, Mary Brown, and the editors of *Psychology Today*. "The Friendship Bond: PT's Survey Report on Friendship in America." *Psychology Today* 13 (October, 1979): 43–45, 49–50, 53–54, 113.

Peplau, Letitia Anne. "What Homosexuals Want." *Psychology Today* 15 (March 1981): 28–38.

*Phillips, Gerald M., and Nancy J. Metzger. *Intimate Communication*. Boston: Allyn and Bacon, 1976.

Pines, Maya. "Invisible Playmates," *Psychology Today* 12, 38 (1978): 41–42, 106.

Rogers, Carl. "The Characteristics of a Helping Relationship." In C. Rogers, *On Becoming a Person*. Boston: Houghton, Mifflin, 1961.

*Rubin, Zick. *Liking and Loving*. New York: Holt, Rinehart and Winston, 1973.

Schnall, Maxine. "Commitmentphobia." *Savvy* 2 (1981): 37–41.

Selman, Robert L., and Anne P. Selman. "Children's Ideas about Friendship: A New Theory." *Psychology Today* 13 (October 1979): 71–72, 74, 79–80, 114.

Singer, Jerome L. *The Child's World of Make Believe: Experimental Studies of Imaginative Play.* New York: Academic Press, 1973.

Sullivan, Harry Stack. *The Interpersonal Theory of Psychiatry.* New York: Norton, 1953.

Swenson, Clifford H. *Introduction to Interpersonal Relations.* Glenview, Ill.: Scott, Foresman and Co., 1973.

Thibaut, John W., and Harold H. Kelley. *The Social Psychology of Groups.* New York: Wiley, 1959.

Villard, Kenneth L., and Leland J. Whipple. *Beginnings in Relational Communication.* New York: Wiley, 1976.

Wilmot, William W. *Dyadic Communication,* 2nd Ed. Reading, Mass.: Addison-Wesley, 1979.

Wright, Paul H. "Toward a Theory of Friendship Based on a Conception of Self." *Human Communication Research* 4 (1978): 196–207.

10

Communication Climate

■■■■ *After studying the material in this chapter*

You should understand:

1. The definition of communication climate.

2. Characteristics of confirming and disconfirming communication.

3. The categories of defensive and supportive communication.

4. The several types of defense mechanisms and their function.

You should be able to:

1. Describe the communication climates in your various relationships.

2. Identify the behaviors that have created positive and negative climates in your relationships.

3. Identify the defense-arousing and supportive behaviors you use.

4. Identify any defense mechanisms you use and the parts of your self-concept you are defending by using them.

5. Respond to others' criticism in a non-defensive manner.

Just as physical locations have their own weather patterns, interpersonal relationships have unique climates too. You can't measure the interpersonal climate by looking at a thermometer or glancing at the sky, but it's there nonetheless. Think about a relationship in which you're presently involved. How would you describe the climate between you and the other person or people? Fair and warm? Stormy? Cold? Hot? Almost everybody who tries this simple exercise immediately recognizes that their relationships *do* have a feeling, a pervasive mood that colors the goings-on of the participants. And it's this feeling we call a *communication climate.*

What Is Communication Climate?

Social scientists define communication climates as the social/psychological context in which a relationship functions. The key word in this definition is *context.* A climate doesn't refer so much to specific activities as to the emotional backdrop against which those activities are carried out. For example, as professors we've taught courses in interpersonal communication for several years. During this time, some of our classes have been exciting, friendly ones, while others (thankfully not too many) have been dull, uncomfortable experiences. In other words, the content of the course has remained basically the same, but the climates have varied.

What creates a positive or negative climate? There are two answers to this question. One concerns the sending behavior of the people involved. As you'll read later in this chapter, there are a number of behaviors likely to create positive, supportive climates and others almost certain to stimulate negative, defensive feelings. You'll see that criticism, secrecy, and indifference, for ex-

ample, are almost certain to pollute the emotional climate of a relationship.

But climates aren't created solely by senders. Receivers play a strong role by interpreting messages in ways that leave them feeling better or worse about the communication environment. Imagine, for instance, that your boss mentions that he or she wants to see you first thing Monday morning. As you read in Chapter 8, this kind of activating event can lead to at least two interpretations. You might think, "Here comes trouble. I must have done something wrong. I know I've made a few mistakes lately, but I've also worked especially hard. It's not fair!" Needless to say, this self-talk leads to feelings of apprehension and defensiveness, which would probably affect your personal and working behavior and would show up in your meeting. On the other hand, you could interpret the request for a meeting in an entirely different way, thinking, "The boss mentioned last week that some people around here were working much harder than others—probably wants to give me some praise for putting out so much. It's nice to be appreciated!" Again, this interpretation would obviously affect your behavior, in the meeting with your boss as well as with others.

Because communication is a process, the thoughts and actions of senders and receivers affect each other, so that a shared climate begins to evolve. Such situations develop at home when one person becomes quiet. The other might interpret the silence as anger and react by either retreating or becoming defensive. This response in turn is likely to cause the first person to ask, "What's the matter with *you?*" By this time it's easy to imagine how an uncomfortable climate can evolve from a simple, innocuous event. Of course, positive climates also develop from the interaction of two or more persons. Warmth and supportiveness beget the same behavior in others, and a reciprocal spiral of positive feelings begins to grow as the participants build on each other's behavior.

Characteristics of Positive and Negative Climates

What makes some climates positive and others negative? A short but accurate answer is that *communication climate is determined by the degree to which people see themselves as valued.* Communicators who perceive others in a relationship as being concerned about their welfare feel positive, while those who feel unimportant or abused bring negative attitudes to the relationship.

Confirming and disconfirming responses
Evelyn Sieburg and Carl Larson (1971; Sieburg, 1974, 1976) outline one set of behaviors that express an uncaring attitude called *disconfirming responses.* A disconfirming response is one in which the sender indicates lack of regard for the receiver, usually by ignoring some important part of the receiver's message. This is, of course, a severe blow to the other person's self-esteem. To be told that an aspect of yourself is "wrong" at least leaves some room for argument. You can acknowledge the attack and talk about it. But a disconfirming response does not attack an aspect of your self-concept: It denies the importance and even the existence of that element . . . and of you.

A *confirming response*, on the other hand, is one in which the speaker acknowledges the other person as important. Unlike disconfirming responses, which cause the other person to feel ignored, confirming responses cause the other person to feel valued: The

other person's existence is acknowledged and his or her importance is confirmed.

Martin Buber (1957), the philosopher, and R. D. Laing (1961), the psychologist, both discuss the importance of confirmation. For Buber, confirmation is something for which everyone strives. For Laing, based on his experiences working with children and families, recognition and acknowledgment—confirmation—is necessary for healthy mental development. Without them, Laing found, a child could become schizophrenic.

Studies by Sieburg (1969), Mix (1972), and others suggest that the most important single factor affecting outcomes in both family and organizational settings is communication that implies acceptance or rejection, confirmation or disconfirmation. For example, Clarke (1973) found that perceived confirmation was a better predictor of marital satisfaction and attraction than self-disclosure, and Cissna (1979), who also studied married couples, found that husbands and wives whose spouses communicated with them in a direct and empathic way were likely to feel confirmed by their partners.

Confirmation and disconfirmation also has been studied in the educational setting. Sundell (1972) studied the behavior of teachers and students in junior high schools and found that confirming teachers were confirmed by their students, and disconfirming teachers were disconfirmed by their students. Jacobs (1973) found that reactions to interviews between professors and students were determined to a large extent by the professors' confirming behavior. Students who were deliberately disconfirmed by their professors during the interview were more dissatisfied with the interview experience and their own performance than those who were deliberately confirmed.

Finally, a recent study by Heineken (1980) focused on the therapeutic setting in an at-

Stan Laurel and Oliver Hardy in *The Further Perils of Laurel and Hardy*.

Once upon a time there was a world with no conflicts.

The leaders of each nation recognized the need for cooperation and met regularly to solve any potential problems before they could grow. They never disagreed on areas needing attention or on ways to handle these areas, and so there were never any international tensions, and of course there was no war.

Within each nation things ran just as smoothly. The citizens always agreed on who their leaders should be, so elections were always unanimous. There was no social friction between various groups. Age, race, and educational differences did exist, but each group respected the others and all got along harmoniously.

Personal relationships were always perfect. Strangers were always kind and friendly to each other. Neighbors were considerate of each other's needs. Friendships were always mutual, and no disagreements ever spoiled people's enjoyment of one other. Once people fell in love—and everyone did—they stayed happy. Partners liked everything about each other and were able to satisfy each other's needs fully. Children and parents agreed on every aspect of family life, and never were critical or hostile toward each other. Each day was better than the one before.

Of course, everybody lived happily ever after.

This story is obviously a fairy tale. Regardless of what we may wish for or dream about, a conflict-free world just doesn't exist. Even the best communicators, the luckiest people, are bound to wind up in situations when their needs don't match the needs of others. Money, time, power, sex, humor, aesthetic taste, as well as a thousand other issues arise, and keep us from living in a state of perpetual agreement.

For many people the inevitability of con-flict is a depressing fact. They think that the existence of ongoing conflict means that there's little chance for happy relationships with others. Effective communicators know differently. They realize that while it's impossible to *eliminate* conflict, there are ways to *manage* it effectively. And those effective communicators know the subject of this chapter—that managing conflict skillfully can open the door to healthier, stronger, and more satisfying relationships.

What Is Conflict?

Stop reading and make a list of as many different conflicts as you can recall. Include both conflicts you've experienced personally and ones that only involve others.

This list will probably show you that conflict takes many forms. Sometimes there's angry shouting, as when parents yell at their children. In other cases, conflicts involve polite discussion, as in labor-management negotiations or legal trials. Sometimes conflicts are carried on through hostile silence, as angry couples act when conducting an unspoken feud. And finally, conflicts may wind up in physical fighting between friends, enemies, or even total strangers.

Whatever forms they may take, all interpersonal conflicts share certain similarities. Joyce Frost and William Wilmot (1978) provide a thorough definition of conflict. They state that conflict is *an expressed struggle between at least two interdependent parties who perceive incompatible goals, scarce rewards, and interference from the other parties in achieving their goals.* Let's look at the various parts of this definition so as to develop a clearer idea of conflicts in people's lives.

Expressed struggle Another way to describe this idea is to say that both parties in a

Wild Bill Hickock. The Museum of Modern Art/Film Stills Archive)

conflict know that some disagreement exists. For instance, you may be upset for months because a neighbor's loud stereo keeps you from getting to sleep at night, but no conflict exists between the two of you until the neighbor learns about your problem. Of course, the expressed struggle doesn't have to be verbal. You can show your displeasure with somebody without saying a word. A dirty look, the silent treatment, or avoiding the other person are all ways of expressing yourself. But one way or another, both parties must know that a problem exists before they're in conflict.

Perceived incompatible goals All conflicts look as if one party's gain will be another's loss. For instance, consider the neighbor whose stereo keeps you awake at night. Does somebody have to lose? If the neighbor turns down the noise, then he loses the enjoyment of hearing the music at full volume; but if the neighbor keeps the volume up, then you're still awake and unhappy.

But the goals in this situation really aren't completely incompatible—solutions do exist that allow both parties to get what they want. For instance, you could achieve peace and quiet by closing your windows or getting the neighbor to close his. You might use a pair of earplugs. Or perhaps the neighbor could get a set of earphones, allowing the music to play at full volume without bothering anyone. If any of these solutions prove workable, then the conflict disappears.

Unfortunately, people often fail to see mutually satisfying answers to their problems. And as long as they *perceive* their goals to be mutually exclusive, then, although the conflict is unnecessary, it is still very real.

Perceived scarce rewards Conflicts also exist when people believe there isn't enough of something to go around. The most obvious example of a scarce resource is money—a cause of many conflicts. If a person asks for a raise in pay and the boss would rather keep the money or use it to expand the business, then the two parties are in conflict.

Time is another scarce commodity. As authors and family men, all three of us are constantly in the middle of struggles about how to use the limited time we have to spend. Should we work on this book? Visit with our wives? Play with our children? Enjoy the luxury of being alone? With only twenty-four hours in a day, we're bound to wind up in conflicts with our families, editors, students, and friends—all of whom want more of our time than we have available to give.

Interdependence However antagonistic they might feel toward each other, the parties in a conflict are usually dependent upon each other. The welfare and satisfaction of one depends on the actions of another. If this weren't true, then even in the face of scarce resources and incompatible goals there would be no need for conflict. Interdependence exists between conflicting nations, social groups, organizations, friends, and lovers. In each case, if the two parties didn't need each other to solve the problem,

they would go separate ways. In fact, many conflicts go unresolved because the parties fail to understand their interdependence. One of the first steps toward resolving a conflict is to take the attitude that "we're all in this together."

Conflict Is Natural and Inevitable

Frost and Wilmot's definition asserts that conflicts are bound to occur, even to the most happy, successful, lucky people. It's vitally important to recognize the inevitability of conflict, for failing to do so can lead to a lot of unnecessary grief. Expecting life to be free of conflict is like expecting the weather to be perfect every day. If you maintain this kind of hope, you're bound to be disappointed. On the other hand, having a more realistic attitude about the weather can help you get through (and even take advantage of) stormy days.

Even after we recognize the inevitability of conflict, most people tend to view it as an unpleasant though necessary activity, similar to figuring out income taxes or visiting the dentist. A quick look at our culture reveals several reasons for this bad image. The first relates to unrealistic teaching. From the time children can understand speech, most of them are raised on a diet of fairy tales that paint the ideal world as free of conflicts. The storybook ending of living "happily ever after" implies that if people are truly good they live harmonious lives that are free of any friction. Many TV shows perpetuate this image. While TV characters do have problems, they're inevitably simple enough to be cleared up before the final commercial, hardly a reflection of real life.

While TV and newspapers show that conflicts exist in the real world, most of the struggles these media describe cannot be

called constructive. Soldiers and innocent civilians die in wars, angry demonstrators riot, and social groups shout angrily at each other. This sort of hostility and violence is hardly a testimonial to the benefits of conflict.

In addition, many families present conflict as dangerous and undesirable. Some parents are verbally or physically abusive to each other and their children. Because people learn from models, their children may grow up to be the same kind of fighters as were their parents. This is why so many adults who are child-beaters were, as children, victims of abuse themselves. In other cases, the horror of viewing destructive aggression may lead children to avoid conflicts when they grow up.

At the other end of the spectrum, families in which conflicts are not acknowledged create the idea that confrontations are to be avoided. Many parents never acknowledge the conflicts that they feel with each other, even to themselves. When disagreements do come up, they're handled privately—"Not in front of the children." Many parents feel compelled to keep up a "couple front," making it look to the children as if adults agree on everything. Parental advice and commands repeatedly suggest that conflict is bad:

"Now don't get angry. . . . "

"Don't talk back."

"There's nothing to fight about."

"If you can't say something nice, don't say anything."

Moreover, adults without noticeable conflicts are presented as models:

"She doesn't have an angry bone in her body."

"He's such a nice person."

"They're always so friendly."

A quarrel between friends, when made up, adds a new tie to friendship, as experience shows that the callosity formed round a broken bone makes it stronger than before.

St. Francis De Sales

Teachings such as these are confusing to children who *know* that they experience conflict. What's a youngster to do when a brother or sister won't share, when parents are critical, when friends are uncooperative or cruel? Surely turning the other cheek isn't *always* the answer.

While children hear so much preaching about being nice, they're also being presented with messages that praise aggressiveness. Sports heroes frequently wind up in fights, often to the noisy approval of fans. Sarcasm and humor are often used as effective putdowns by the same adults who talk so much about kindness. Grownups who preach about pleasantness threaten ominously, "If you don't stop fighting you'll be sorry!"

Why is it that overt disagreement seems to be such a taboo in our society? What forces so many people to express their conflicts indirectly in such destructive, crazy ways? The answer lies in what Herbert Simons (1972) has termed a "system view" of conflict. Communicators that hold this view believe (usually not consciously) that maintaining the status quo is an extremely important goal, and that people should avoid rocking the boat in any way—even when the present system is clearly unsatisfactory.

The tendency to keep an unsatisfying system running smoothly occurs in many settings. Both managers and employees continue plugging away at old ways of doing business rather than face the challenge of developing better methods. Teachers and students often look with hostility at each

Well-washed and well-combed domestic pets grow dull; they miss the stimulus of fleas.

Francis Galton

---

other across a gap of mutual mistrust and fear. Many families suffer through what Thoreau called lives of "quiet desperation," rather than speaking up and trying to change their lives.

Yet many people support the status quo only because they don't acknowledge that conflicts can be positive, and because they don't possess the skills to manage their disagreements constructively. This chapter should help people develop a more powerful awareness of the skills involved in managing conflicts.

So far, we've discussed beliefs about conflict that apply equally to both sexes. In addition, most of us have been exposed to the idea that men and women "ought" to deal with disagreements in different ways. Probably the biggest difference has to do with emotions. The cultural stereotype of female behavior holds that women have a great capacity for expressing emotions, while men are generally expected to be more "logical" and issue-oriented. Thus, for many people of both sexes, it's more appropriate to hear a woman say she's disappointed or confused than it does to hear a man send the same messages. The same holds true for nonverbal expressions. While most people wouldn't be surprised to see a woman cry, the same behavior coming from a man is usually more of a shock.

Just as many people are used to perceiving women as extremely emotional, so they also find it easier to accept assertiveness when it comes from a man. Even in these relatively more liberated times, many people find the widely circulated guide "How to Tell a Businessman from a Businesswoman" amusing:

> A businessman is aggressive; a businesswoman is pushy.
>
> He loses his temper because he's so involved in his job; she's bitchy.
>
> He follows through; she doesn't know when to quit.
>
> He's firm; she's stubborn.
>
> He isn't afraid to say what he thinks; she's opinionated.

In the last decade, there has been increasing recognition that such stereotypes have more to do with cultural conditioning than with biology. Yet even the most ardent liberationists will admit that many people—both men and women—still accept and live by these attitudes.

Styles of Conflict

People have their individual styles of handling conflict—characteristic approaches they take when their needs appear incompatible with what others want. Sometimes a style is helpful and sometimes not. In either case people should recognize their own styles so they can make the styles work for them.

Individual styles What's your style of handling conflict? Let's find out by inventing two hypothetical characters—Sally and Ralph—and see how they manage a problem that you might find familiar.

Sally and Ralph have been friends for several years, ever since they moved into the same apartment building. While they had always exchanged favors in a neighborly way, lately Ralph has been depending more and more on

Sally. He asks her to care for his cat and houseplants almost every other weekend while he travels, borrows food and cash without returning it, and drops in to talk about his unhappy love life at least once a week. Until lately, Sally hasn't minded much, but now she's getting tired of Ralph's behavior.

Take a look at the six alternatives below and rank them in the order you'd choose. Mark your most likely response as number 1, your next most likely as number 2, and so on.

1. Steer clear of Ralph as much as possible. Pretend not to be home when he drops by. Make excuses for why you can't help him with his problems.
2. Do the favors for Ralph, hoping that he'll stop imposing soon. After all, nobody's perfect and it isn't worth making an issue over this.
3. Do the favors for Ralph, but casually hint about the inconvenience involved.
4. Tell Ralph about the inconveniences that resulted from helping him, but state that you're willing to do a few favors for him as a friend, even though they're something of a nuisance. After all, friends ought to help each other out, even if it causes some trouble. You just want him to meet you halfway.
5. Tell Ralph that you're fed up with his demands, that you don't mind helping once in awhile, but that his continued imposition will jeopardize your friendship.
6. Tell Ralph how his requests make you feel and ask him to work with you to find a way to solve his problems that's less of a strain for you.

Make sure you've ranked your responses before going on. Each one of the choices above represents a different orientation to the conflict between Sally and Ralph. A close examination will show the different ways that people handle their own conflicts, and give you an idea of the styles that you use most often.

1. Avoidance/withdrawal. People who avoid conflicts usually believe that it's easier to put up with the status quo than to face the problem head on and try to solve it. This attitude usually doesn't make sense, for the costs of avoiding an issue are high. Avoiding the issue uses up a great deal of energy without resolving the aggravating situation. In addition, avoiders usually lose a chunk of their self-respect since they so clearly downplay their own concerns in favor of the other person's. Finally, failing to deal with a problem can often result in spoiling an entire relationship.

Every time Sally hides from Ralph or changes the subject so he won't ask her for a favor, she becomes uncomfortable and probably leaves Ralph feeling the same way. After this goes on for awhile, it's likely that whatever enjoyment Sally and Ralph had found together will be eclipsed by their new way of relating and the friendship will degenerate into an awkward, polite shell.

This kind of avoidance is particularly sad since the immediate fears of dealing with an issue are usually way out of proportion to what is likely to happen. This isn't to blame avoiders, who may not know any better way to act. We simply want to point out the typically unsatisfactory results of such a conflict style.

In a few cases, however, avoidance may be the best course. If a conflict is short-lived, it might not be worth resolving. For example, you might let a friend's annoying grumpiness pass, knowing that the friend has been sick lately but will soon feel better. If the issue is genuinely a minor one, you might decide not to confront a person with it. You may have a neighbor, for instance, whose

People always say they are not themselves when tempted by anger into betraying what they really are.

Edgar Watson Howe

---

lawn sprinklers occasionally hit your newly washed car. In your opinion, this may not even be worth mentioning. Or you might reasonably choose to keep quiet if the conflict occurs in an unimportant relationship, such as an acquaintance whose language you find offensive but whom you don't see often enough to make it an important issue.

2. Accommodation. Accommodators deal with conflict by giving in, putting the other's needs ahead of their own. Certainly, accommodation is sometimes appropriate, such as when the other person's needs really are more important than yours. For instance, if a friend wants to have a serious talk and you feel playful, you'd most likely honor the friend's request, particularly if the person was facing some kind of crisis and wanted your help. In most cases, however, accommodators fail to assert themselves either because they don't value themselves sufficiently, or because they don't know how to ask for what *they* want.

There are also aggressors who use accommodation as a tactic. Guiltmakers accommodate others but try to extract payment by punishing the other person. We've all seen guiltmakers in action. "Go on," they say, "go ahead and use the car. I didn't really need to do those errands and buy food today anyhow . . . " Or, "No really, I'll be happy to help. I'm feeling a little sick, but it will pass."

Pseudoaccommodating is another style of crazymaking. In this stratagem, the communicator disguises aggression by pretending to give in. People with this style make agreements for the sake of peace but then don't keep them. In the short run this style gets the people two results: peace and quiet, and the chance to do what they want. Of course, in the long run this behavior can damage relationships.

3. Smoothing over. In terms of assertiveness, people who smooth conflicts over are more bold than withdrawers or accommodators. They may let you know what they want, but in a way that doesn't reflect how strongly they feel. The goal here is to preserve an image that "everything is OK" above all else. Sometimes people who smooth over get what they want and sometimes they don't, but in either case they fail to communicate the full extent of their message.

Just as withdrawal and accommodation are useful orientations in certain situations, so is the smoothing over approach. If the other person is liable to react defensively to the statement about conflict and if the relationship really is more important than the concerns of either party, then smoothing the matter over may be an adequate response. The danger from such a style, however, is that it doesn't usually resolve the problem or prevent it from reccurring.

Smoothing over is sometimes a form of aggression. Subject changing is one type of aggressive smoothing over. Subject changers briefly mention the issue that's concerning them ("I sure wish it were a little quieter around here sometimes so I could get my work done"), and then drop the subject when the other person responds. It's easy to see how this style of hinting can get annoying.

"Crisis ticklers," on the other hand, bring up what's bothering them without ever mentioning it explicitly. For instance, instead of expressing concern about spending too much, a crisis tickler might say, "Gee, things are sure getting expensive lately." But the crisis tickler would back off if the partner asked if anything was wrong.

Joking can be an extremely aggressive though subtle smoothing over behavior. Jokers use humor to smooth over conflicts by kidding about a subject that is actually quite serious, or by making jokes when a partner wants to deal with a conflict. The joker can handle any protests about such kidding by saying, "Gee, I was just trying to lighten things up a little." Jokers can also disguise their own aggressive feelings by joking about them. While the jokes might earn a few laughs, this kind of humor often diminishes the issue, thus keeping jokers from getting what they want.

4. Compromising. Unlike the three previous orientations, compromisers bring their concerns into the open and try to satisfy both their own needs and those of others. The only problem with compromising is that by definition nobody is totally satisfied with the outcome.

While compromising may be preferable to avoidance or power plays, it does have its problems. First, if the people involved see a compromise coming they might inflate their demands, still attempting to get everything they want. This situation occurs in labor negotiations, where both parties begin discussions with exaggerated claims. While this strategy may appeal to gameplayers, it minimizes trust. More commonly, compromises are unsatisfying because they often leave one or both parties unhappy. For example, if Sally grudgingly agrees to help Ralph occasionally, she will still resent his behavior and he won't be getting enough assistance. The best to be said for compromises is that they're more attractive than some of the previous alternatives for handling conflicts.

5. Competition. We're so familiar with competition as a style of conflict that it doesn't need much explanation. The main element

The Chinese have a story based on three or four thousand years of civilization. Two Chinese coolies were arguing heatedly in the midst of a crowd. A stranger expressed surprise that no blows were being struck. His Chinese friend replied, "The man who strikes first admits that his ideas have given out."

Franklin Delano Roosevelt

in competition is power: Whoever has the most clout wins. The kindest thing to be said about this orientation is that it's honest. It may also be a satisfactory style in those rare cases when there clearly are "good guys" and "bad guys," but such instances are not common.

The biggest problem with power is that in a competitive situation both parties often lose. International politics offers an obvious example: If World War III ever starts, who will win? The same kind of total loss all too often occurs in interpersonal conflicts. For example, in many contested divorces who besides the lawyers really win when the contesting couple spend thousands of dollars, experience intense pain and bitterness, and in many cases confuse and sadden the lives of their children?

6. Integration. Communicators who handle their conflicts in an integrated way are concerned about their own needs as well as those of the other person. But unlike compromisers, they won't settle for only a partially satisfying solution. Let's imagine that Sally cares about herself and also about Ralph, and that the relationship is also important to Ralph who isn't just interested in exploiting Sally. They may be able to talk matters out and find a way of being friends, which gives both of them the things they want.

■■■■ *Better an honest slap, than a false kiss.*

Jewish proverb

While integration sounds as if it is the perfect way of handling all conflicts, it does have drawbacks: It takes time and effort to find integrative solutions, and the process can be both frustrating and tiring. The relationship has to be extremely important to both partners for this method to work. And there are times when there simply isn't a totally satisfying solution to a problem, despite the best efforts of everyone. Even though the attempt to work matters through can affirm the goodwill of everyone, it's disappointing to try so hard and come up short.

We'll have more to say about integrative styles of handling conflicts later in this chapter.

The preceding six approaches are often classified in four categories. The first is *non-assertiveness*. Nonassertive communicators either ignore their own needs or acknowledge those needs but accept an unsatisfying situation. Avoidance, withdrawal, accomodation, smoothing over, and compromising are often (but not always) nonassertive behaviors.

A second method of coping with conflicts is with *indirect aggression*. Indirectly aggressive people express their hostile feelings in a disguised manner. Psychologist George Bach (1968) describes indirect aggression as "crazymaking." He uses this term because of the effect such behavior usually has on its target. Making one's partner feel guilty, changing the subject when conflict arises, joking about a partner's sensitive areas, gossiping about the partner to others, and withholding affection are all crazymakers. Notice that several of the conflict styles mentioned

at the end of the preceding paragraph can, under different circumstances, also be indirect means of expressing aggression.

A third approach to conflict is *direct aggression*. The competitive style described earlier is directly aggressive. While such aggression is sometimes appropriate, it can also be a form of overreaction. Common consequences of direct aggression are anger and defensiveness on one hand, or hurt and humiliation on the other. In either case, aggressive communicators build themselves up at the expense of others.

A final type of communication is *assertion*. This term is virtually synonymous with the integrative style we have already defined. Assertive communicators express their needs, thoughts, and feelings clearly and directly, but without judging others or dictating to them. They have the attitude that most of the time it is possible to resolve problems to everyone's satisfaction. Possessing this attitude and the skills to bring it about doesn't guarantee that assertive communicators will always get what they want, but it often increases their chances of success. An additional benefit of such an approach is that it maintains the self-respect of both asserters and those with whom they interact. As a result, people who manage their conflicts assertively usually feel better about themselves and each other afterward—not often the case with other styles.

Which style to use? A look at your own behavior and that of others will show you that very few people use the same conflict style all the time. For instance, take someone whose coworkers may describe as a power-oriented competitor. This person uses his position and knowledge as weapons to get what he wants from others with whom he works. But while he is a fighter on the job, his behavior is completely different with his friends away from work. With them he's a collaborator, interested in discovering their needs and working to solve them as well as his own.

His style fits still another pattern with his children. Rather than deal with problems involving them, he'll avoid the issue in any way possible: making jokes, pretending to "forget" about his promises to discuss a problem, or retreating into his work. Many of us are like this man, changing our behaviors to suit various circumstances.

The person in this example changes conflict styles depending on whom he's dealing with; but this isn't the only determinant of which style to use. Sometimes people switch styles depending on the issue involved. For instance, you might be inclined to compromise on an issue that isn't vitally important to you, while you'd be more likely to confront others when the problem is a critical one.

Another factor governing our choice of conflict style is the mood we happen to be in. On some days you're probably most inclined to be an accommodator, giving in to the demands or desires of others. But at other times you might be feeling more angry or grouchy, and be inclined to compete, even on unimportant issues.

Many communicators use one or two styles exclusively because these ways of relating are the only ones they know. We've already seen that patterns of thinking and acting are formed early in life, and during these first critical years (and often beyond) many people see only avoiding, smoothing over, and competition. Not knowing that there are other alternatives which might be more effective, they use these styles throughout their lives to handle their own conflicts. This lack of awareness about effective communication styles explains why so many educators see a need for training parents in com-

munication skills, so that children will grow from the start learning ways of relating that will help them throughout adulthood.

Even when aware of different conflict styles, some communicators rely heavily on only one or two. These behaviors are usually ones that worked well in the past, and so the tendency is to continue relying on them, even though their usefulness may be gone. Frost and Wilmot cite the example of the man who is "stuck" in the style of a 1960s protestor, seeing every issue as a fight against the establishment. This man identifies reflexively with the underdog, without considering whether the underdog is correct. He sees those in power as always evil and wrong, and tries to use any power at his disposal to defeat those "enemies." This man finds enemies where none exist, and creates problems unnecessarily.

Another common example of relying on longstanding but obsolete behavior is the student who accommodates and withdraws from those in authority because standing up to such people in the past met with punishment. It may make sense to give in to a harsh parent or authoritarian teacher when you're small and powerless, but such behavior isn't necessary as an adult, especially when others are willing and interested in dealing constructively with problems.

It should now be clear that there's no single "best" style of dealing with conflict. What's appropriate behavior for communicating with a police officer you believe has unfairly given you a speeding ticket might not be the best way to act with a neighbor whose dog is digging up your garden. And the right way to talk to your neighbor might not work at all when discussing the way you've drifted apart with an old friend. The key to success, then, is to develop a *repertoire* of conflict styles so that when issues come up you'll be able to choose the way of communicating that works best for the given situation. Before introducing a new style of communicating to add to that repertoire, we next want to offer some guidelines to tell whether the styles of communication you're presently using are helping or hindering your present conflicts.

Functional and Dysfunctional Conflict

Some bacteria are "good," aiding digestion and cleaning up waste, while others are "bad," causing infection. There are helpful forest fires which clean out dangerous accumulations of underbrush and harmful ones which threaten lives and property. In the same way, some conflicts can be beneficial. They provide a way for relationships to grow by solving the problem at hand and often improving other areas of interaction as well. Other conflicts can be harmful, causing pain and leaving a relationship weaker. Communication scholars usually describe harmful conflicts as *dysfunctional* and beneficial ones as *functional*.

What makes some conflicts functional and others dysfunctional? Usually the difference doesn't rest in the subject of the conflict, for it's possible to have good or poor results on almost any issue. Sometimes certain individual styles of communication are more productive than others, as you've just learned. In other cases the success or failure of a conflict will depend on the method of resolution the parties choose. We'll talk more about types of conflict resolution later in this chapter. We want now to describe several symptoms that distinguish functional and dysfunctional conflicts.

Polarization In a dysfunctional conflict biases are rampant. Participants see themselves as "good" and the other person as "bad"; their actions as "protective" and the other's as "aggressive"; their behavior as "open and trustworthy" and the other's as "sneaky and deceitful." Researchers Robert Blake and Jane Mouton (1964) found that people engaged in this kind of polarization underestimate the commonalities shared with the other person, and so miss areas of agreement and goodwill.

By contrast, participants in a functional conflict realize that the other person's needs may be legitimate too. A person who is allergic to cigarette smoke recognizes that smokers aren't necessarily evil people who delight in tormenting him or her, while the smoker sympathizes with the other's need for cleaner air. In issues such as this functional conflict is marked by mutual respect.

Unwillingness to cooperate Participants in a dysfunctional conflict see each other as opponents and view the other's gain as their loss: "If you win, I lose" is the attitude. This belief keeps partners from looking for ways to agree or find solutions that can satisfy them both. People rarely try to redefine the situation in more constructive ways, and seldom give in, even on noncritical issues.

A more functional approach recognizes that by cooperating it may be possible to find an answer that leaves everyone happy. Even nations basically hostile to each other often recognize the functional benefits of cooperating. For example, the United States and the Soviet Union have clear-cut differences in certain areas, yet work together in fields such as disease control, halting air piracy, and disarmament. This same kind of cooperation is possible in interpersonal conflicts. We will have a great deal to say about

Harold Lloyd in *The Freshman*, 1925. (Culver Pictures)

cooperative problem solving later in this chapter.

Coercion In destructive conflicts the participants rely heavily on power to get what they want. "Do it my way, or else" is a threat commonly stated or implied in dsyfunctional conflicts. Money, favors, friendliness, sex, and sometimes even physical coercion become tools for forcing the other person to give in. Needless to say, victories won with these kind of power plays don't do much for a relationship.

More enlightened communicators realize that power plays frequently are a bad idea, not only on ethical grounds but because they often have a way of backfiring. Since it's rare that a party in a relationship is totally powerless, it's possible to win a battle only to lose a war. One classic case of the dysfunctional consequences of using power to resolve conflicts occurs in families where authoritarian parents make their children's requests into "unreasonable demands." It's easy enough to send a five-year-old out of a room for some real or imagined misbehavior, but

■■■■ *The test of a man or woman's breeding is how they behave in a quarrel.*

George Bernard Shaw

---

when that child grows into a teen-ager he or she has many ways of striking back.

Escalation In destructive conflicts the problems seem to grow larger instead of smaller. As you read in Chapter 10, defensiveness is reciprocal: If you attack me, the tendency is for me to strike back even harder. We've all had the experience of seeing a small incident get out of hand and cause damage out of proportion to its importance.

One clear sign of functional conflict is that in the long run the behavior of the participants solves more problems than it creates. We say "long run" because facing up to an issue instead of avoiding it frequently makes life more difficult for a while. In this respect handling conflicts functionally is rather like going to the dentist: You may find it a little (or even a lot!) painful for a while, but you're only making matters worse by not facing the problem.

Losing sight of the original issue In dysfunctional conflicts the partners often bring in issues having little or nothing to do with the original problem. Take for example a couple who originally are having trouble deciding whether to spend the holidays at his or her parents' home. As they begin to grow frustrated at their inability to solve the dilemma, one of them—let's say the man—angrily remarks, "Your mother is always trying to latch onto us!" to which the woman replies, "If you want to talk about latching on, what about *your* folks? Ever since they loaned us that money they've been asking about every dime we spend." "Well," the man retorts, "if you could ever finish with school and hold down a decent job, we wouldn't have to worry about money so much. You're always talking about wanting to be an equal partner, but I'm the one paying all the bills around here."

You can imagine how the conversation would go from here. Notice how the original issue became lost as the conflict expanded. It's obvious that this kind of open-ended hostility is unlikely to solve any of the problems it brings up, not to mention the potential for creating problems not even existing before.

Shortsightedness Shortsightedness can produce dysfunctional conflicts even when partners do not lose sight of the original issue. One common type of shortsightedness occurs when disputants try to win a "battle" and wind up losing the "war." Friends might argue about who started a fight; but if one person succeeds in proving that he was "right" at the cost of the friendship, then the victory is a hollow one. Another type of shortsightedness happens when partners are so interested in defending their own solution to a problem that they overlook a different solution that would satisfy both their goals. A final type of shortsightedness occurs when one or both partners jump into a conflict without planning the necessary steps. We will have more to say about preventing these last two types of shortsightedness in a few pages.

One characteristic of communicators who handle conflict well is their ability to keep focused on one subject at a time. Unlike those dysfunctional battlers whom Bach calls "kitchen sink fighters," skillful communicators might say, "I'm willing to talk about how my parents have been acting since they made us that loan, but first let's settle the business of where to spend the holidays." In other words, for functional problem solving, the rule is "one problem at a time."

So far we've looked at the differences between the *processes* of functional and dysfunctional conflicts. Now let's compare the *results* of these different styles.

Dysfunctional conflict typically has three consequences. First, none of the parties are likely to get what they were originally seeking. In the short run it may look as if one person might win in a dispute while the other loses, but most often both parties suffer in some way. For instance, an instructor might win by forcing his unpopular grading system on students who clearly would lose out if they received grades lower than the ones they believed they deserved. But in situations such as this, instructors also fail to get what they want, for instead of trying to truly understand and master the material, the students will most likely become preoccupied with beating the system by simply memorizing facts, trying to "psych out" the forthcoming exams, or even cheating. Obviously this behavior prevents good learning, which means that the instructor has failed just as much as the students have lost the fairness and the interesting instruction they sought. In the long run, everyone has lost.

A second consequence of dysfunctional conflicts is that they threaten the future of the relationship. Let's return to that feuding couple. It's easy to imagine how the resentments of both partners would affect their behavior. For example, it's unlikely that either would feel affectionate after such an exchange, and so we might expect their home life to deteriorate: As their disappointment grows, they would probably be less willing to help each other in their usual ways. The wife might be less cooperative about doing her share of cooking and cleaning, while the hus-

band wouldn't offer advice on how to complete school assignments. Thus, if this couple can't solve their original problems, it's likely that dissatisfaction with each other will grow like a cancer until it has poisoned most every part of their relationship. This effect of individual conflicts on an overall relationship explains why it's important to deal successfully with seemingly inconsequential matters such as arriving on time for appointments or who takes out the trash, for every time partners don't resolve a small conflict they weaken their entire relationship.

Failure to resolve interpersonal problems is also personally destructive to each participant. We discussed the range of emotions in Chapter 8. Take a moment now and think about the feelings you've experienced when you were engaged in an unresolved conflict. It's likely that you felt (and still may feel) inadequate, foolish, unworthy, unlikeable, or unloveable. Poorly managed conflicts have a strong effect on our self-esteem and can bring about effects that can linger on for years, threatening both our peace of mind and our future relationships with others.

In contrast to these dismal outcomes, functional conflicts have positive results. One benefit to skillfully handling issues is that interpersonal involvement increases. When we engage in a conflict productively, we get excited, motivated to act. In contrast to an apathetic person, the functional communicator is determined to do something to make the relationship better.

Skillfully handled conflict also promotes growth in a relationship. Along with restoring harmony, dealing with a conflict teaches people things about each other they didn't know before. They learn more about each other's needs and how such needs can be satisfied. Feelings are clarified. Backgrounds are shared. Of course growth can occur in nonconflict situations too; the point here is

▰▰▰ Conflict Basic as Hunger?

Psychologists often find themselves in the position of proving scientifically what people have always known implicitly.

So it is with new data on the value of conflict.

Conflict, a Canadian psychologist reported in Scientific American, *215:82, 1966, may be the same sort of driving force as hunger, thirst, sexual appetite, and pain. If so, it can be placed among the ranks of those conditions which are most efficient in producing learning, with important implications for education.*

All of the basic drives have in common the fact that they arouse the individual physically, sharpen his faculties, motivate him to act, and enhance his learning capacity. . . .

SCIENCE NEWS

---

that dealing with problems can be an opportunity for getting to know each other better. Moreover, conflicts provide the opportunity for new kinds of sharing. We often fail to know where another person stands on an issue until that issue is confronted.

Constructive conflict also provides a safe outlet for the feelings of frustration and aggression that are bound to occur in any relationship. When people accept the inevitable fact that they'll occasionally disagree with each other, they can be willing to let their partners express that disagreement, and in so doing defuse a great deal of it. One characteristic of good interpersonal communicators is that they allow each other to blow off steam without taking offense.

Finally, functional conflicts allow each person involved to establish his or her personal identity within the relationship. To see

how important this individual identity is, think back to the early stages of your relationships. (Try to recall a wide variety: romantic, friendship, business, academic.) In many cases the earliest stages of relationships are marked by such a desire to promote harmony that the members behave unnaturally: They're so polite, so concerned with each other's happiness that they ignore their own needs and wants. In this effort to keep everything smooth, the parties give up a bit of themselves. But when conflicts finally do surface, each gives the other a chance to show where he or she stands, to say, "I understand what you want, but let me tell you what's important to *me*." When this and later conflicts are handled skillfully, they allow the relationship to grow while at the same time letting each person remain an individual.

Resolving Interpersonal Conflicts

After reading the last section you can see that "functional" is the key word when dealing with interpersonal conflicts. You need to find effective ways of communicating *during* a conflict, and of course you want to create an *outcome* satisfying for everyone concerned. In the next few pages we'll look at three styles of resolving conflict. While each has its advantages and drawbacks, you'll see that some ways of managing disputes are more functional than others.

Win-lose Win-lose conflicts are ones in which one party gets what he or she wants while the other comes up short. People resort to this method of resolving disputes when they perceive a situation as being an "either-or" one: Either I get my way or you get your way. The most clear-cut examples of win-lose situations are certain games such as baseball or poker in which the rules require a winner and a loser. Some interpersonal issues seem to fit into this win-lose framework: two coworkers seeking a promotion to the same job, say, or a couple arguing over how to spend their limited money.

Power is the distinguishing characteristic in win-lose problem solving, for it's necessary to defeat an opponent to get what you want. The most obvious kind of power is physical. Some parents threaten their children with warnings such as "Stop misbehaving or I'll send you to your room." Adults who use physical power to deal with each other usually aren't so blunt, but the threat often exists nonetheless. For instance, behind the legal system is the implied threat, "Follow the rules or we'll lock you up."

Real or implied force isn't the only kind of power used in conflicts. People who rely on authority of many types engage in win-lose methods without ever threatening physical coercion. In most jobs supervisors have the potential to use authority in the assignment of working hours, job promotions, desirable or undesirable tasks, and of course in the power to fire an unsatisfactory employee. Teachers can use the power of grades to coerce students to act in desired ways.

Intellectual or mental power can also be a tool for conquering an opponent. Everyone is familiar with stories of how a seemingly weak hero defeats a stronger enemy through cleverness, showing that brains can triumph over brawn. In a less admirable way, crazymakers can defeat their partners in effective, if destructive ways: by inducing guilt, avoiding issues, withholding desired behaviors, pseudoaccommodating, and so on.

Even the usually admired democratic principle of majority rule is a win-lose method of resolving conflicts. However fair

Lone Hand Saunders. (The Museum of Modern Art/Film Stills Archive)

it may be, this system results in one group getting its way and another being unsatisfied.

There are some circumstances in which the win-lose method may be necessary, as when there are truly scarce resources, and where only one party can achieve satisfaction. For instance, if two suitors want to marry the same person, only one can succeed. And to return to an earlier example, it's often true that only one applicant can be hired for a job. But don't be too willing to assume that your conflicts are necessarily win-lose. Many situations seeming to require a loser can be resolved to everyone's satisfaction.

There is a second kind of situation wherein win-lose is the best method of conflict. Even when cooperation is possible, if the other person insists on defeating you, then the most logical response might be to defend yourself by fighting back. "It takes two to tango," the old cliché goes, and it also often takes two to cooperate.

A final and much less frequent justification for trying to defeat another person occurs when the other party is clearly behaving in a wrongful manner, and where defeating that person is the only way to stop the wrongful behavior. Few people would deny the importance of restraining a person who is deliberately harming others, even if the belligerent person's freedom is sacrificed in the process. It seems justifiable to coerce others into behaving as we think they should only in the most extreme circumstances.

Lose-lose In lose-lose methods of problem solving neither side is satisfied with the outcome. While the name of this approach is so discouraging that it's hard to imagine how anyone could willingly use the method, in truth lose-lose is a fairly common approach to handling conflicts.

Compromise is the most respectable form of lose-lose conflict resolution. In compromising, all the parties are willing to settle for less than they want because they believe that partial satisfaction is the best result they can hope for. In *Interpersonal Conflict Resolution*, Albert Filley (1975) makes an interesting observation about our attitudes toward this method. Why is it, he asks, that if someone says, "I will compromise my values," we view the action unfavorably; yet we talk admiringly about parties in a conflict who compromise to reach a solution? While compromises may be the best obtainable re-

sult in some conflicts, it's important to realize that both people in a dispute can often work together to find much better solutions. In such cases "compromise" is often a negative concept.

Most of us are surrounded by the results of bad compromises. Consider a common example, namely the conflict between one person's desire to smoke cigarettes and another's need for clean air. The win-lose outcomes on this issue are obvious: Either the smoker abstains or the nonsmoker get polluted lungs—neither solution is very satisfying. But a compromise whereby the smoker only gets to enjoy a rare cigarette or must retreat outdoors to smoke, and the non-smoker still must inhale some fumes or feel like an ogre is hardly better. Both sides still have lost considerable comfort and goodwill.

The costs involved in still other compromises are even greater. For example, if a divorced couple compromise on childcare by haggling over custody and then finally grudgingly split the time with their youngsters, it's hard to say that anybody has won.

Compromises aren't the only lose-lose solutions, or even the worst ones. There are many instances in which the parties both strive to be winners, but as a result of the struggle both wind up losers. On the international scene, many wars illustrate this sad point. A nation that gains military victory at the cost of thousands of lives, large amounts of resources, and a damaged national consciousness hasn't truly won much. On the interpersonal level the same principle holds true. Most of us have seen battles of pride in which both parties strike out and both suffer. It seems as if there should be a better alternative, and fortunately there often is.

No-lose In this type of problem solving the goal is to find a solution satisfying the needs of everyone involved. Not only do the partners avoid trying to win at each other's expense, but there's a belief that by working together it's possible to find a solution in which everybody reaches his or her goals without needing to compromise.

One way to understand how no-lose problem solving works is to look at a few examples.

A boss and her employees get into a conflict over scheduling. The employees often want to shift the hours they're scheduled to work in order to accommodate personal needs, while the boss needs to be sure that the operation is fully staffed at all times. After some discussion they arrive at a solution that satisfies everyone: The boss works up a monthly master schedule indicating the hours during which each employee is responsible for being on the job. Employees are free to trade hours among themselves, as long as the operation is fully staffed at all times.

A conflict about testing arises in a college class. Due to sickness or other reasons a certain number of students need to take exams on a makeup basis. The instructor doesn't want to give these students any advantage over their peers, and doesn't want to go through the task of making up a brand new test for just a few people. After working on the problem together, instructor and students arrive at a no-lose solution. The instructor will hand out a list of twenty possible exam questions in advance of the test day. At examination time five of these questions are randomly drawn for the class to answer. Students who take makeups will draw from the same pool of questions at the time of their test. In this way, makeup students are taking a fresh test without the instructor having to create a new exam.

A newly married husband and wife found themselves arguing frequently over their

I will not play at tug o' war.
I'd rather play at hug o' war,
Where everyone hugs
Instead of tugs,
Where everyone giggles
And rolls on the rug,
Where everyone kisses,
And everyone grins,
And everyone cuddles,
And everyone wins.

Shel Silverstein

budget. The husband enjoyed buying impractical and enjoyable items for himself and the house, while the wife feared that such purchases would ruin their carefully constructed budget. Their solution was to set aside a small amount of money each month for purchases. The amount was small enough to be affordable, yet gave the husband a chance to escape from their spartan lifestyle. Additionally, the wife was satisfied with the arrangement since the luxury money was now a budget category by itself, which got rid of the "out of control" feeling that came when her husband made unexpected purchases. The plan worked so well that the couple continued to use it even after their income rose, by increasing the amount devoted to luxuries.

While solutions like these might seem obvious when you read them here, a moment's reflection will show you that such cooperative problem solving is all too rare. People faced with these types of conflicts often resort to such dysfunctional styles of communicating as withdrawing, avoiding, or competing, and wind up handling the issues in a manner resulting in either a win-lose or lose-lose outcome. As we said earlier, it's a shame to see one or both parties in a conflict come

Bing Crosby in *Going My Way*, 1944. (Culver Pictures)

away unsatisfied when they could both get what they're seeking by communicating in a no-lose manner.

In order for no-lose problem solving to work, a seven-step approach suggested by Deborah Weider-Hatfield (1981) seems helpful.

1. Define the conflict intrapersonally. The place to begin is by deciding what it is you want or need. What are the causes of the conflict for *you?* Before communicating with the other person you need to determine what it is that is bothering you. Sometimes the answer is obvious, as in our earlier example of the neighbor whose loud stereo music kept others awake. In other instances,

however, an immediate problem hides the real need. For example, a couple we know had the following problem: After dating for a few months, Beverly started to call Jim after they parted for the evening—a "goodnight call." While this was fine with Jim at the beginning, it became a habit that kept them talking on the phone for at least an hour.

When Jim first thought about this problem, he said that his need was to have Beverly not call him after he got home from their date. After thinking about it for awhile, he realized that he didn't care if she called once in a while, or for a short period of time. What he really wanted was to spend his time after he went home undisturbed before turning in. While this newly defined need doesn't sound too different from his first statement, you'll soon see that the difference is a significant one.

Because one's needs aren't always immediately clear, it's necessary to think about a problem alone, before approaching the other person involved. Thinking about the problem alone requires certain skills, such as the ability to describe your own feelings and recognize that you "own" them, that is, that they are *your* feelings and not necessarily shared by anyone else or caused by anyone else. Describing the other person's behavior in a nonevaluative way is another necessary skill, as is being able to empathize with the other person—seeing the conflict from her point of view.

At the end of this first stage both you and the other person understand the conflict from an intrapersonal perspective. You understand your own behavior and feelings, as well as your perceptions of the other person's behavior and feelings. And the other person has the same understanding of her own behavior, feelings, and perceptions.

You are now ready to talk to each other.

2. Define the conflict interpersonally. Once your own wants and needs are clear it's time to find out what the other person wants and needs. (This is when the listening skills described in Chapter 6 and the supportive behaviors described in Chapter 10 become most important.) When Jim began to talk to Beverly about her telephoning, he learned some interesting things. In his haste to hang up the phone the first few times she called he had given her the impression that he didn't care about her once their date was over. Feeling insecure about his love, she called as a way of getting his attention and expressions of love.

Once Jim realized this fact, it became clear that he needed to find a solution that would leave Beverly feeling secure and at the same

The first fight is a ritual, a test of the relationship. Very often it will be provoked deliberately, usually over a false issue (I know a couple who fell out forever, after a very promising start, over whether the Marx Brothers were greater than W. C. Fields), just to see what happens. Do they really care? How do they both feel? How deeply? Of course, all it really proves is that they can survive until the next fight.

Jane O'Reilly

time allow him to be uninterrupted when he got home. Individual perceptions of the conflict were shared and a mutual definition of the problem was recognized.

Arriving at a mutual or shared definition of the problem requires skills associated with creating a supportive and confirming climate. The ability to be nonjudgmental, descriptive, and empathic are important support-producing behaviors. Both Jim and Beverly needed to engage in active listening to discover all the details of the conflict.

When they're really communicating effectively, partners can help each other clarify what it is that they're seeking. Truly believing that their happiness depends on the other's satisfaction, they actively try to analyze what obstacles need to be overcome.

3. Identify mutually shared goals. This may well be the most important step in the no-lose or win-win conflict strategy. You and the other person express your individual goals in the hopes that some mutually shared goal can be defined. The honest disclosure of each person's goals serves a variety of purposes. First, each person learns how far apart he is from the other person. If goals are vastly different it may be necessary to alter the relationship dramatically, or even end it. If Jim's goal, for example, was to control Beverly's behavior, and Beverly's goal was to manipulate Jim into a permanent relationship, they might decide that a dramatic change is called for.

Disclosure of each person's goal may also stimulate a reexamination of the causes of the conflict. New information may be helpful in determining the root causes of the conflict if they haven't already been determined.

Finally, disclosure, as we discussed in Chapter 7, has a number of important messages for the other person. For example, the other person is told, in effect, that she is trusted and important. A recent investigation by Michael Fahs (1981) on the effects of self-disclosing communication on the reduction of interpersonal conflict confirms the importance of disclosure in win-win conflict. In Fahs' study, college students were instructed to play a conflict game which, if they played cooperatively, resulted in the best outcome. One student in each pair was a confederate, someone trained to be disclosive or non-disclosive. The disclosure—"Hey, look, I'm sorry if I'm out of it today, but I've been taking some pills to control my weight. So if I start to make you uncomfortable, try to understand, ok"—made the confederate vulnerable by being fairly intimate. Cooperation in the pairs where disclosure took place was four times as great as in those where there was no disclosure. The act of disclosing was an important way to tell the other person, "I trust you."

Once mutually shared goals are identified—based on each person's understanding of his own and the other's needs, desires, and individual goals—solutions may be sought.

4. Generate possible solutions. In this step the partners try to think of as many ways to satisfy both their needs as possible. They can best do so by "brainstorming"—inventing as many potential solutions as they can. The key to success in brainstorming is to seek quantity without worrying about quality. The rule is to prohibit criticism of all ideas, no matter how outlandish they may sound. An idea seeming farfetched can sometimes lead to a more workable one. Another rule of brainstorming is that ideas aren't personal property. If one person makes a suggestion, the other should feel free to suggest another solution that builds upon or modifies the original one. The original solution and its offshoots are all solutions that will be considered later. Once partners get over their possessiveness about ideas, the level of defensiveness drops and both people can work together to find the best solution without worrying about whose idea it is.

All of the supportive and confirming behaviors discussed in Chapter 10 are important during this step. Two, however, stand out as crucial: the ability to communicate provisionalism rather than certainty, and the ability to refrain from premature evaluations of any solution. The aim of this step is to generate *all* the possible solutions—whether immediately reasonable or not. By behaving provisionally and avoiding any evaluation until all the solutions are generated, creative and spontaneous behavior is encouraged. The final result is a long list of solutions which most likely contains the best solution, one which might not have been expressed if the communication climate were defensive.

Jim and Beverly used brainstorming to generate solutions to their telephone problem. Their list consisted of: continuing the calling but limiting the time spent on the phone; limiting the calls to a "once in a while" basis; Beverly's keeping a journal that could serve as a substitute for calling; Jim's calling Beverly on a "once in a while" basis; cutting out all calling; moving in together to eliminate the necessity for calling; getting married; and breaking up. While some of these were clearly unacceptable to both of them, they listed all the ideas they could think of, preparing themselves for the next step in no-lose problem solving.

5. Evaluate the possible solutions and choose the best one. The time to evaluate the solutions is after they have all been generated, after the partners feel they have exhausted all the possibilities. In this step, the possible solutions generated during the previous step are evaluated for their ability to satisfy the mutually shared goal. How does each solution stand up against the individual and mutual goals? Which solution satisfies the most goals? Partners need to work cooperatively in examining each solution and in finally selecting the best one.

It is important during this step to react spontaneously rather than in a strategic fashion. Selecting a particular solution because the other person finds it satisfactory, while seemingly a "nice" thing to do, is as manipulative a strategy as getting the other person to accept a solution you think is satisfactory that he or she may find less than suitable. Respond as you feel as solutions are evaluated, and encourage your partner to do the same. Any solution agreed upon as "best" has little chance of satisfying both partners' needs if it was strategically manipulated to the top of the list.

The solution Beverly and Jim selected as satisfying her need to feel secure, his need to be undisturbed before turning in, and their mutual goal of maintaining their relationship at a highly intimate level, was to limit both the frequency and length of the calls. Also, Jim agreed to share in the calling.

6. Implement the solution. Now the time comes to try out the idea selected to see if it does, indeed, satisfy everyone's needs. The key questions to answer are *who* does *what* to *whom*, and *when?*

Before Jim and Beverly tried out their solution, they went over the agreement to make sure it was clear. This step proved to be important, for a potential misunderstanding existed. When will the solution be implemented? Should Beverly wait a few weeks before calling? Should Jim begin the calling? They agreed that Jim would call after their next date.

Another problem concerned their different definitions of length. How long is too long? They decided that more than a few minutes would be too long.

The solution was implemented after they discussed the solution and came to mutual agreement about its particulars. While this may seem awkward and time consuming, both Beverly and Jim decided that without a clear understanding of the solution, they were opening the door to future conflicts.

Interestingly, the discussion concerning their mutual needs and how the solution satisfied them was an important part of their relationship development. Jim learned that Beverly felt insecure about his love (sometimes); Beverly learned that Jim needed time to himself, and that this did not reflect on his love for her. Soon after implementing the solution they found that the problem ceased to exist. Jim no longer felt the calls were invading his privacy, and Beverly, after talks with Jim, felt more secure about his love.

7. Follow up the solution. To stop after selecting and implementing a particular solution assumes any solution is forever, that time does not change things, that people remain constant, and that events never alter circumstances. Of course this is not the case: As people and circumstances change, a particular solution may lose its effectiveness or,

I'm lonesome; they are all dying; I have hardly a warm personal enemy left.

James McNeill Whistler

---

on the other hand, increase its effectiveness. Regardless, it remains for a follow-up evaluation to take place.

After you've tested your solution for a short time, it's a good idea to *plan* a meeting to talk about how things are going. You may find that you need to make some changes or even rethink the whole problem.

Reviewing the effects of your solution does not mean that something is wrong and must be corrected. Indeed, everything may point to the conclusion that the solution is still working to satisfy the individuals' needs and the mutually shared goal, and that the mutually shared goal is still important to you.

It is important at this stage in the no-lose problem-solving process to be honest with yourself as well as the other person. It may be difficult for you to say, "We need to talk about this again," yet it could be essential if the problem is to remain resolved. Planning a follow-up talk at the same time the solution is first implemented is important.

Beverly and Jim decided to wait one month before discussing the effects of their solution. Their talk was short since both felt the problem no longer existed. Also, their discussions helped their relationship grow: They learned more about each other, felt closer, and developed a way to handle their conflicts constructively.

This no-lose method is especially attractive when you consider the alternatives already discussed. It's easy to see how such a system can work well for solving individual conflict; but just as significantly, communicating in this manner can improve entire relationships.

By asking the following questions, you can see for yourself how well your present styles of managing conflicts affect your relationships, and how well new styles tried might work.

1. How much do we learn about each other? A conflict should help us gain new information, especially in the area of the conflict. We should be more aware of each other's likes and dislikes, needs, wants, and desires. The more we learn about each other, the more beneficial the conflict is to our relationship.

2. How effectively do we influence each other? After a conflict we should be more aware of the power each of us has to influence the other, and we should be more willing, now, to accept that influence. To the extent that we avoid coercion and the use of crazymakers, conflict is beneficial. We are more effective at influencing each other.

3. How much do we fear and trust each other? A constructive conflict should leave us fearing each other less, and trusting each other more.

4. Do we seek revenge? The extent to which we conduct a fair fight, a no-lose or win-win one, determines the extent to which either of us seeks revenge. If we understand each other, engage in conflict sincerely, and work hard to satisfy both our concerns, no one should seek revenge, and the relationship should be more stable and enduring.

5. How good do we feel about ourselves? A constructive conflict should raise our self-worth and increase how good we feel about ourselves.

6. How good do we feel about our relationship? Just as a constructive conflict increases our feelings of self-worth, it should increase the positive feelings we have for our relationship. We should feel closer to each other, and look at our relationship as more important than it was before the conflict.

Of course, some conflicts are going to be better than others in terms of the ultimate effects on our relationship. But every conflict has the potential to help our relationship grow and become more meaningful.

Readings

Bach, George R., and Ronald M. Deutsch. *Pairing*. New York: Avon, 1970.

*Bach, George R., and Peter Wyden. *The Intimate Enemy*. New York: Avon, 1968.

Blake, Robert R., and Jane S. Mouton. *The Managerial Grid*. Houston: Gulf Publishing Co., 1964.

Ellis, Donald G., and B. Aubrey Fisher. "Phases of Conflict in Small Group Development." *Human Communication Research* 1 (1975): 195–212.

Fahs, Michael L. "The Effects of Self-Disclosing Communication and Attitude Similarity on the Reduction of Interpersonal Conflict." *Western Journal of Speech Communication* 45 (1981): 38–50.

Filley, Alan C. *Interpersonal Conflict Resolution*. Glenview, Ill.: Scott, Foresman, 1975.

Filley, Alan C., Robert J. House, and Steven Kerr. *Managerial Process and Organizational Behavior*, 2nd Ed. Glenview, Ill.: Scott, Foresman, 1976.

*Frost, Joyce Hocker, and William W. Wilmot. *Interpersonal Conflict*. Dubuque, Iowa: Wm. C. Brown, 1978.

Gordon, Thomas. *Parent Effectiveness Training*. New York: Peter H. Wyden, 1970.

Jandt, Fred E. *Conflict Resolution Through Communication*. New York: Harper and Row, 1973.

Myers, Michele Tolela, and Gail E. Myers. *Managing by Communication: An Organizational Approach*. New York: McGraw-Hill, 1981.

Rosenfeld, Lawrence B. *Now That We're All Here . . . Relations in Small Groups*. Columbus, Ohio: Charles E. Merrill, 1976.

Simons, Herbert. "Persuasion in Social Conflicts: A Critique of Prevailing Conceptions and a Framework for Future Research." *Speech Monographs* 39 (1972): 227–247.

*Thomas, Kenneth. "Conflict and Conflict Management." In *Handbook of Industrial and Organizational Psychology*, Marvin D. Dunnette, ed. Chicago: Rand McNally, 1976.

*Weider-Hatfield, Deborah. "A Unit in Conflict Management Skills." *Communication Education* 30 (1981): 265–273.

Name Index

Subject Index

Acknowledgments continued from copyright page.

page 35 Reprinted from *Shyness: What It Is, What to Do About It* by Philip Zimbardo, Copyright © 1977. By permission of Addison-Wesley Publishing Co., Reading, Mass.

page 47 *Garfield* cartoon by Jim Davis. © 1981 United Feature Syndicate, Inc. Used by permission.

page 48 Reprinted with permission from the *Journal of Creative Behavior*, Vol. 14, No. 2, 1980, Published by the Creative Education Foundation, Buffalo, NY; with special thanks to William Higginbotham for recounting the original story.

page 50 *Peanuts* cartoon by Charles Schulz. © 1967 United Feature Syndicate, Inc. Reprinted by permission.

page 61 Herman cartoon by Jim Unger. © 1981, Universal Press Syndicate. Reprinted with permission. All rights reserved.

page 63 From "Strictly Personal" by Sydney J. Harris. Copyright Field Enterprises, Inc. Courtesy of Field Newspaper Syndicate.

page 65 Reproduced by permission from *Introduction to Psychology* by Dennis Coon. Copyright © 1977 West Publishing Company. All rights reserved.

page 67 © 1979 by permission of *Redbook Magazine* and Jerry Marcus.

page 71 "Coming and Going" from *Speaking Poems* by Ric Masten. Published by Sunflower Ink, Palo Colorado, Carmel, CA 93923.

page 83 Reprinted from *Word Play: What Happens When People Talk* by Peter Farb. © 1974 by Alfred A. Knopf, Inc. Used by permission.

page 95 Hagar cartoon by Dik Browne. © 1981 King Features Syndicate, Inc. Used by permission.

page 96 Excerpt from pp. xvi–xvii in *Working: People Talk About What They Do All Day and How They Feel About What They Do* by Studs Terkel. © Pantheon Books, a Division of Random House, Inc. Reprinted by permission.

page 97 Used courtesy of author, Edward Sherman.

page 102 "Tumbleweeds" by Tom K. Ryan. © 1979 United Feature Syndicate. Courtesy of Field Newspaper Syndicate.

page 104 From *I and Thou: Here and Now: Contributions of Gestalt Therapy.* Reprinted courtesy of the author, Claudio Naranjo.

page 114 Excerpt from *Zorba the Greek* by Nikos Kazantzakis. Copyright © 1953, 1981 by Simon & Schuster, Inc. Reprinted by permission of Simon & Schuster, a Division of Gulf & Western Corporation.

page 118 "Nothing" from *Love Poems for the Very Married* by Lois Wyse (World Publishing Co.). Copyright © 1967 by Lois Wyse. By permission of Harper & Row, Publishers, Inc.

page 121 Copyright © 1943 James Thurber. Copyright © 1971 Helen W. Thurber and Rosemary Thurber Sauers. From *Men, Women, and Dogs*, published by Harcourt Brace Jovanovich. Copyright © Collection James Thurber, Hamish Hamilton, London.

page 135 Cartoon by Richter; © 1968 The New Yorker Magazine, Inc. Used by permission.

page 147 "Peanuts" cartoon by Charles Schulz. © 1977 United Feature Syndicate, Inc.

page 148 From *The Best of Sydney J. Harris* by Sydney J. Harris. Copyright © 1957 by Sydney J. Harris. Reprinted by permission of Houghton Mifflin Company.

page 149 Reprinted courtesy of the *San Francisco Examiner.*

page 151 "Momma" by Mell Lazarus. Courtesy of Mell Lazarus and Field Newspaper Syndicate.

page 155 Reprinted by permission of the poet, Lenni Shender Goldstein.

page 163 "Peanuts" cartoon by Charles Schulz. © 1978 United Feature Syndicate, Inc.

page 169 From *Group Processes: An Introduction to Group Dynamics* by Joseph Luft. Used by permission of Mayfield Publishing Company. Copyright © 1963, 1970 by Joseph Luft.

page 175 From *The Best of Sydney J. Harris* by Sydney J. Harris. Copyright © 1957 by Sydney J. Harris. Reprinted by permission of Houghton Mifflin Company.

page 176 From "Mending Wall" from *The Poetry of Robert Frost*, edited by Edward Connery Lathem. Copyright 1930, 1939, © 1969 by Holt, Rinehart and Winston. Copyright © 1967 by Lesley Frost Ballantine. Reprinted by permission of Holt, Rinehart and Winston, Publishers, and by Jonathan Cape, Ltd.

page 179 "Hands #1" from *Voice of the Hive* by Ric Masten. Published by Sunflower Ink, Palo Colorado, Carmel, CA 93923.

page 183 Used by permission of Charles Scribner's Sons from *Look Homeward, Angel* by Thomas Wolfe. Copyright 1929 Charles Scribner's Sons; renewal copyright © 1957 Edward C. Aswell, Administrator, C.T.A. and/or Fred W. Wolfe. And by permission of William Heinemann, Ltd., Publishers.

page 184 "Peanuts" cartoon by Charles Schulz. © 1961 United Feature Syndicate, Inc.

page 185 From *The Velveteen Rabbit* by Margery Williams. Published by Doubleday & Company, Inc. Used with permission of William Heinemann, Ltd., Publishers.

page 186 "Miss Peach" by Mell Lazarus. Courtesy of Mell Lazarus and Field Newspaper Syndicate.

page 191 Drawing by Weber. Used by permission. © 1981 The New Yorker Magazine, Inc.

page 196 Cartoon by Richard Stine. Reprinted by permission of Carolyn Bean Associates, Publishing. © 1974 Richard Stine. Drawing from *Smile in a Mad Dog's i* by Richard Stine.

page 204 "Ziggy" cartoon by Tom Wilson. © 1974, Universal Press Syndicate. Reprinted with permission. All rights reserved.

page 204 Excerpt from p. 127 in *Benchley Beside Himself* by Robert Benchley. Copyright 1930 by Robert C. Benchley. Reprinted by permission of Harper & Row, Publishers, Inc.

page 206 "Peanuts" cartoon by Charles Schulz. © 1963 United Feature Syndicate, Inc.

page 227 Cartoon by Richter; © 1970 The New Yorker Magazine, Inc. Used by permission.

page 256 "Peanuts" cartoon by Charles Schulz. © 1965 United Feature Syndicate, Inc.